FRONTIERS OF ACCESS TO LIBRARY MATERIALS
No. 3

FRONTIERS OF ACCESS TO LIBRARY MATERIALS

Sheila S. Intner, Series Editor

No. 1 Barbra Buckner Higginbotham and Sally Bowdoin. *Access versus Assets: A Comprehensive Guide to Resource Sharing for Academic Librarians*

No. 2 Murray S. Martin. *Collection Development and Finance: A Guide to Strategic Library-Materials Budgeting*

No. 3 Chiou-sen Dora Chen. *Serials Management: A Practical Guide*

SERIALS MANAGEMENT: A PRACTICAL GUIDE

CHIOU-SEN DORA CHEN

American Library Association
Chicago and London
1995

Project Editor: Joan A. Grygel

Index prepared by Carol Kelm

Cover design: Tessing Design

Composition by Publishing Services, Inc., in Caslon
on Xyvision/Linotype L330

Printed on 50-pound Publishers Smooth, a pH-neutral stock, and bound
in 10-point C1S cover stock by McNaughton & Gunn, Inc.

The paper used in this publication meets the minimum requirements of
American National Standard for Information Sciences—Permanence of
Paper for Printed Library Materials, ANSI Z39.48-1992∞

Library of Congress Cataloging-in-Publication Data

Chiou-sen, Dora Chen.
Serials management : a practical guide / Chiou-sen Dora Chen.
p. cm. — (Frontiers of access to library materials ; no. 3)
Includes bibliographical references (p.) and index.
ISBN 0-8389-0658-3 (alk. paper)
1. Serials control systems. I. Title. II. Series.
Z692.S5C49 1995
025.3′432—dc20 95-17986

Printed in the United States of America.

99 98 97 96 95 5 4 3 2 1

Contents

Figures

Preface

The intended audiences for this book are serials librarians, nonprofessional serials supervisors, and library school students who are interested in serials management. Serials publishers, agents, and users can also use this book to gain an understanding of the library serials operation and promote cooperation among serials community members for mutual benefit.

This book places major emphasis on serial acquisitions because that is the unique function in serials management. Collection development and public services are discussed from the perspective of how the acquisitions function supports them. The principles and techniques of collection development and public services are not taught here. Cataloging is excluded from this book for two reasons: (1) there is no lack of learning resources for this subject: it is well taught in library schools, and there are books and journals devoted to it; (2) devoting one chapter of the book to serials cataloging is not sufficient to explain this complex function. Readers who wish to be serials catalogers should learn the subject from other sources.

To set the stage for serials management discussions, chapters 1 and 2 explain the definition and characters of serials and the organization of serials management. Chapter 3 discusses working relationships between collection development and serial acquisitions functions. Chapters 4, 5, and 6 explain acquisition techniques in detail: serial vendors, acquisition methods, and acquisitions processing. Serial preservation and bindery issues are discussed in chapter 7. Chapter 8 analyzes serial records and their control. A basic list of information sources about serials cataloging is also provided. Types of public services that may be provided by the serials department are explored in chapter 9. Serials automation, covered in chapter 10, places emphasis on general concepts and issues but not on the technical details of system selection and implementation. The last chapter describes current topics being discussed by serials librarians and suggests ways to follow trends and inquiries into future challenges. The bibliography represents a core group of titles consulted by the author that readers may also wish to consult. The appendix directs readers to sources that can help them keep up with serials management literature after reading this guide.

There is some bias toward the operations typically found in academic libraries. I gained my working experience from a large research library and believe converting the knowledge of managing a large and complex serials operation to a smaller operation is easier than the other way around. However, differences in the serials management requirements and methods between large academic libraries and small public or school libraries are recognized and emphasized in the book, and readers are constantly reminded to consider the local environment and needs.

This book is designed to teach practical knowledge and skills required by a working serials manager. Therefore, it does not treat the subject of serials management as a scholarly research topic but rather as a vital function that needs to be carried out efficiently to sustain library operations. It avoids emphasis on historical factors, philosophical theories, and statistics but concentrates on plain explanations and instructions. It also presents serials management as a changing function with flexible, even controversial, choices in some areas to provoke readers to think and open the door for future reading and research. I hope that this book will serve not only as a foundation for readers entering the serials management field but will lead them to pursue further development in the field through working experience, reading, research, and professional activities to become serials experts and scholars.

I wish to thank Ryoko Toyama for helping to launch this project, Beryl Smith and Jane Bishop for reading and revising the first draft, Gracemary Smulewitz for her help in the preparation of illustrations, and Book Industry Study Group, Inc., and Innovative Interfaces, Inc., for granting the permission to use their materials as illustrations. A special thanks goes to Dr. Sheila Intner, the editor, for her advice and encouragement.

Chapter 1

Definition and Character of Serials

Serial is a common term on the library scene. It appears frequently in the library literature and is used constantly by librarians in their daily work. Yet there seems to be a great deal of confusion about how this term is being defined and used. If you were to ask librarians what they refer to when they say "serial," you would likely receive a variety of answers. One librarian would be talking about periodicals only; a second librarian about yearbooks, periodicals, and newspapers; and a third librarian about all continuously received publications. So what exactly is a serial?

Defining a serial is no easy task, not only because there are several types of serials but because some serials have dual personalities that behave both as a serial and a book, such as monographic series and loose-leaf services. When serials experts tried to define serials in the past, almost all of them voiced the difficulty of providing a short and precise definition. As Donald Davinson said: "It would be pleasant to be able to supply a short, neat, all-embracing definition that is unquestioningly accepted universally. It is not possible to do so."[1] In Andrew Osborn's book, *Serials Publications: Their Place and Treatment in Libraries,* the section "Definition of a Serial" is twenty-one pages long.[2] Marcia Tuttle gives two pages to "Definition of Serials" in her book, *Introduction to Serials Management.*[3] When *Anglo-American Cataloguing Rules,* second edition (AACR2), was published in 1978, a definition for the serial was provided in the glossary. This definition stays unchanged in the 1988 revision of AACR2 (AACR2R). Since AACR2 has been adopted as the cataloging standard for English-language materials, its serial definition has also been accepted by librarians as the standard definition of the term.

AACR2 Definition

AACR2 defines a serial as "a publication in any medium issued in successive parts bearing numeric or chronological designations and intended to continue indefinitely. Serials include periodicals; newspapers; annuals (reports, yearbooks, etc.); the journals, memoirs, proceedings, transactions, etc., of societies; and numbered monographic series."[4] This definition, beginning with the statement that a serial is a publication in any medium, leaves an open door for future developments and changes in serial publications. In libraries, the word *format* is often used in place of *medium*. Familiar media or formats are paper, audio and video for sound recordings, tapes and films, microform for microfilm and microfiche, and electronic transmission techniques used for computer files. The definition then points out main characteristics of serials. First, serials are published successively, one issue after another; each issue bears a sequence designation that can be in numeric order, such as volume 1, number 1, or in chronological order, such as 1993, 1994. Many serials give both numeric and chronological designations, such as volume 20, number 1, January 1994. Second, serials are continuous publications; when a publisher launches a serial, the intention is to publish it indefinitely. Although many serials do cease publication after a time, and some short-lived serials meet their death after only one or two issues, that nonetheless was not the publishers' original intention.

Following the definition, different types of serials are listed to provide a further clarification of the term. Careful reading reveals two "etc."s in the listing, leaving the door open for types of serials not included in the list. This was done purposely, because the changeable character of serials makes it impossible to know with certainty the multiple faces and personalities of these publications. The safe way to deal with serials is always to leave room for change.

Types of Serials

There are five major categories of serials. Most libraries will offer most, if not all, types.

Periodicals and Newspapers

Periodicals are the most popular type of serials. A collection of articles written by various authors makes up the contents of periodicals. The word *periodical* often has been used loosely as a synonym for the word *serial*. In addition to the general serial characteristics described in the AACR2 definition, a periodical is further qualified by its frequency. A periodical is a serial published more than once a year with regular frequency, such as daily, weekly, monthly, quarterly, semiannually, etc. In most cases a periodical issue bears a double-tier numeric designation to indicate its publication sequence, such as volume 1, number 1. Some publishers prefer to use months or seasons in combination with the year to indicate a chronological sequence, such as January 1993 or Spring 1994. The use of seasons is common with quarterly periodicals.

All journals and magazines are periodicals. In earlier times, journals were periodicals published by learned societies and scholarly associations for the purpose of communicating research and scholarship among fellow researchers and scholars, such as *Journal of the American Chemical Society.* Magazines were periodicals published by commercial publishers to satisfy popular interests and provide general information, such as *Time* and *Newsweek.* Today many scholarly journals are published by profit-making commercial publishers, and the fine line between journals and magazines has become fuzzy.

Technically speaking, newspapers are also periodicals because their publication pattern fits the description of periodicals. In libraries newspapers often are treated as a special serials group because they need more staff attention than periodicals in general. Their high publication frequency keeps librarians busy in timely receiving and claiming; their information content is devoted to current events that creates an urgency in readers' access; their oversize loose leaves pose a challenge in maintaining pages in good order; and their poor-quality paper cannot endure the long retention period required by many libraries. Managing newspapers is not only labor intensive but also nerve-racking.

Because periodicals usually are the major publication type in a library's serials collection, it is fair to call them the mainstream publications in serials. In managing serials, libraries often divide them into two groups, periodicals and nonperiodical serials. All serials that are not defined as periodicals are lumped in the latter group. The management of periodicals is quite different from the management of other types of serials. Library staff spend more energy and time in managing periodicals due to higher publication frequency and users' demands. There also are differences in acquisition methods. Periodicals received as subscriptions require prepayment to the publishers. Nonperiodicals usually are paid for as they are received by the library and are acquired on so-called standing orders.

Continuations

The nonperiodical serials often are referred to as continuations. The main player in continuations is annuals, i.e., once-a-year publications, such as annual reports and yearbooks. A few continuations are published regularly but less frequently than annuals, such as biennials, triennials, etc. Irregular serials have unpredictable publication frequencies, and the interval between issues is irregular. If a general publication pattern is more frequent than once a year, such materials may be handled as periodicals; otherwise, they are handled as continuations. By the same rule of thumb, a society's memoirs, proceedings, and transactions can be treated as a periodical or as a continuation, according to its publication frequency. Frequency is a key factor in categorizing types of serials.

Monographic Series

Now it is time to turn to those publications with dual or changeable personalities. They can act as a monograph or as a serial. *Monograph* is a term used by librarians to indicate nonserial publications. AACR2R defines monograph as "a nonserial item (i.e., an item either complete in one part or complete, or intended to be completed, in a finite number of separate parts)."[5] As with the serial, a monograph can be a publication in any medium. When its medium is paper, *monograph* is used as a synonym for *book.*

The main player in the group with dual personalities is the monographic series. According to the AACR2R glossary, monographic series are "a group of separate items related to one another by the fact that each item bears, in addition to its own title proper, a collective title applying to the group as a whole. The individual items may or may not be numbered."[6] For example, *Foundations in Library and Information Science* is the collective title of a monographic series. Within this series there are many individual monographs written by different authors or edited by different editors. *A Practical Approach to Serials Cataloging,* written by Lynn S. Smith, was published as volume 2 of this series, and *Introduction to Serials Management,* written by Marcia Tuttle, was published as volume 11. Both volumes are monographs, if we ignore the fact that they bear a series volume number. Each monograph has an author, a title, a publishing date, and, most important of all, an ISBN number. However, if we look at the series title *Foundations in Library and Information Science,* it is a serial because it contains successive parts bearing numeric designations (each monograph published within the series is a successive part and bears a volume number), and as far as we know it is intended to be continued indefinitely. Therefore, the series is a serial, but volumes within the series are monographs.

According to AACR2, a numbered monographic series is a serial. *Foundations in Library and Information Science* is a numbered series because each monograph in this series bears a numeric volume number. If no monographic volume in a series bears a numeric or chronological number, the series is an unnumbered monographic series, and the series is then not a serial. Generally speaking, numbered monographic series are irregular serials. Very few monographic series are published at regular intervals. Some publishers may set a certain number of volumes to be published in each year, but the regularity is never as rigid as with periodicals. Although more than one monographic number in a series may be published in a year, the series is never categorized as a periodical; monographic series belong to continuations.

Supplements and Special Issues

Supplements and special issues are not mentioned in the AACR2 definition, but they are definitely related to serials. These may be published for a variety of reasons, such as to celebrate a special occasion, to highlight an important current event, or to serve as an extra issue devoted to a special feature. They are also published to accommodate the overflow of manuscripts from regular issues. Supplements and special issues may be sent free of charge to serial subscribers, or there may be an extra cost in addition to the regular subscription fee. When an extra cost is involved, it is often a publisher's sales technique for promoting new publications. For example, a publisher may launch a new monographic series as the supplement to an existing journal and join the journal and the series into a combined subscription with a higher fee than the original journal subscription cost. This sales technique uses journal subscribers as the captive audience for newly launched monographic series. Using the same technique, a monograph may be published as a special issue of a periodical, with an extra charge, to promote the sale of a newly published monograph. Since supplements and special issues are used to accommodate irregularities, there are no set publication patterns and rules. In order to gain a better picture of what they are, they can be divided into a serials group and a monographs group, then subdivided into regular and irregular publications.

In the serials group, special issues and supplements are published as serial issues. Regularly published special issues usually are extra feature issues included in the subscription cost but not fitted into the numbering sequence. For instance, a monthly periodical may publish thirteen issues each year instead of twelve. The extra issue may be devoted to a special topic, and its publication pattern may be repeated each year. A good example is *Fortune 500* published as a regular special issue to *Fortune*. Regularly published supplements may be used to update a serial, for instance, when quarterly supplements temporarily bridge the gap in information content between annuals. Such quarterly supplements become obsolete and are discarded when the new annual is published. Regular supplements can also be used to update a monograph until a new edition is published, such as annuals or yearbooks that supplement encyclopedias. Irregular serial supplements and special issues are unpredictable publications. Some issues bear numeric or chronological sequences, such as "supplement to volume 5, number 3" and "1994 special issue." Others give no clue as to where they fit. The only certainty about these publications is that they pose a challenge for serials librarians to deal with them properly.

In the monographic group, special issues and supplements are published as monographs. A good example is a monographic series published regularly as a supplement to a periodical. For instance, each year a monograph will be received as a supplement to a periodical. In the meantime, this monograph belongs to a monographic series. Confusing? Yes, very confusing! But some publishers like to do it. Irregular monograph supplements are issued for special occasions, special topics, etc., such as a book about a publishing house in celebration of its one-hundredth anniversary. Once I encountered a small publisher who lagged seriously behind a periodical's publication schedule and could not afford to give a refund or credit to subscribers for the unpublished years, so some unsold monograph inventories were dug out and sent to subscribers as substitutes for the unpublished periodical issues. I truly do not know how to categorize this one.

Supplements and special issues are challenges to serials librarians. The policy on handling them varies among libraries. As a general practice, supplements published as serial issues are treated as part of the serial and bound together with regular issues; monographic supplements are cataloged as books and physically separated from serials in the collection.

Monographs Treated as Serials

There is a group of publications belonging to monographs that is treated as serials in the library in regard to both cataloging and acquisition practice. These are books that regularly update the contents of older editions with new editions. In most cases, the new edition supersedes the older one, and the updating is done at regular intervals, such as annually, biennially, quinquennially. Monographs with this publication pattern are often referred to as "pseudoserials." A library may treat them as books by acquiring each edition as a separate book order and cataloging each edition as a separate book, but treating them as serials is more efficient and economical. A serials standing order will secure all the orders for future editions as they are published and eliminate the need for individual orders. One open-entry serial cataloging record can replace all the individual cataloging records for each new edition.

Loose-leaf services offer a challenging publication pattern. The base volume is published as a book in a binder, and updates are published continually to be added to or replace pages in the book binder. The updates usually are intended to be continued indefinitely. It is not a publication with a dual personality as a monographic series is, but it is a combination of a book and a serial. Usually the loose-leaf service initial volume is cataloged as a book, but its updates are handled as serials in acquisitions.

Government Document Serials

Government agencies publish many serials, for example, the United States Government Printing Office publishes major titles such as *Congressional Record* and *Federal Register*. Commonly published government serials are annual reports. Serials published by government agencies are government documents and are often referred to as document serials. There are international, federal, state, municipal, local, and foreign document serials. Some libraries treat document serials as parts of their document collections; others treat them as parts of their serials collections. The difference in such practices may influence the location of document serials in a library, but the same serial definition is applied to the document serials.

Following this discussion of what a serial is, what a mixture of a serial and a monograph is, and what can be treated either as a serial or as a monograph, it should be obvious why there is such confusion about the definition of a serial. To add to the confusion, although the AACR2 definition is accepted by most librarians as a good definition for serials, not every library follows it in practice. Local environment and operating conditions can influence how a library chooses to define serials in its working practice. One library may have a serials department that handles all the publications discussed previously, another may have a serials department that handles only some of them.

Serial Publication Patterns

Serials may be blamed for giving headaches to librarians, but they are also praised as being interesting and stimulating. Most serials librarians agree that managing serials is a very challenging task because they are continuous publications with unpredictable publication patterns. A monograph is a completed work—what you see is what you get—but a serial is an unfinished product. It has a past history, a present status, and an unknown future. The library has to investigate its past, understand its present, and be alert to its future development. Managing serials is not only a long-term project but also a complicated task; the complexity comes mostly from changes. On a serial's long publication path, changes may occur, such as title changes, frequency changes, or price changes. Each time there is a change, serial records have to be altered to reflect that change, the processing method has to be adjusted to accommodate that change, and a managerial decision may be required to deal with that change. For instance, if there is a periodical title change, the old title's cataloging record, acquisitions record, bindery record, holdings record, etc., have to be altered to reflect the change. A whole set of new records has to be created to accommodate the new title, and reading room display shelves and bound periodical stacks need to be adjusted for the change. If there is a major increase in subscription price, or a change in editorial policy, managerial judgment is needed to decide whether the library should continue the subscription. Some of these changes fit into common patterns, and libraries have established standard ways of dealing with them. However, some can only be described as "wacky," and it takes ingenuity to find a solution. Some of the more-common changes related to serial publications are discussed in the next three sections.

Title Changes

When a serial title changes, it requires major changes to all serial records related to this title. Yet title changes are a common phenomenon. Librarians try to make publishers understand that a title change means extra work for the library and unnecessary title changes are not welcome. The Serials Section of American Library Association, Association for Library Collections and Technical Services, has a committee that publicly solicits nominees for an annual Worst Serial Title Change of the Year Award. While publishers are not thrilled by such an award, the hope is that they will think twice before they implement title changes in their publications. Worse than title changes are title splits and title merges. When one title splits into two or more titles it is called "title split." When two or more titles merge into one title it is called "title merge." The worst scenario is created when a publisher cannot make up its mind, so that a title may be split first into two titles, then one split title may be merged into another title, then the merged title may be changed to a new title. Once I had to make a two-page chart to trace the publication history of one periodical.

Frequency Changes

Frequency change is also common and annoying. A monthly can be changed into a quarterly, or vice versa. Some inconsiderate publishers will change frequency in the middle of a volume and then compound the crime by asking for a price increase because the publication frequency has been increased. Because many libraries treat periodicals and nonperiodicals differently—periodicals may be unclassified and shelved alphabetically according to titles in the periodicals stacks, but annuals may be classified and intershelved with monographs—a frequency change from quarterly to annual can cause a major headache in deciding where to shelve the title.

In addition to changing the frequency, a serial can be temporarily suspended. Temporary suspension means a serial stops publication for a period of time. Reasons for suspension could be that the publisher has financial trouble or there are not enough qualified manuscripts, the editor has taken a leave, etc. Usually the publisher does not announce the suspension until pressed by subscribers' claims. How long the suspension will last is a guessing game. If the problem that caused the suspension cannot be solved, a suspension can become a cessation, which means the serial ceases publication completely.

Other Changes

Publication size can be changed. A periodical that was nineteen centimeters tall may suddenly change its size to twenty-eight centimeters. If the change occurs in the middle of the volume, it creates a binding problem with issues in different sizes having to be bound into one physical volume.

Sequence designation changes are not common but can be a nightmare when they happen. If a publisher suddenly abandons the numeric sequence used for 50 volumes and switches to a chronological sequence from volume 51 on, what can be done? What one expects to be volume 51 is now indicated solely as 1993 with no trace of the number 51. Notes have to be made in the cataloging record, the acquisitions record, the bindery record, etc., and then one keeps fingers crossed that library staff and users will not be confused. Another alternative is to relabel the spines of all previous fifty volumes from volume numbers to years. This is a clean-cut method but very labor intensive and, therefore, very costly.

In the volatile publishing world of mergers and acquisitions, publisher changes also happen. This can result in price changes, editor changes, and even content changes.

This section has described a sampling of common changes that may provide a better understanding of the complexity and unpredictability of serials. No matter how many examples of changing patterns are given here, however, they can never cover all that will be encountered when you start to work with serials. Even a seasoned serials librarian encounters changes that have never been dealt with before. This makes managing serials a challenge and ensures that the work is never boring.

Serial Publications in Different Formats

The AACR2R glossary defines the word *format* as "in its widest sense, a particular physical presentation of an item."[7] Serials can be found in any format. The discussion here will be limited to the three popular serials publication formats: paper, microform, and electronic publishing. Paper is the traditional format and the most familiar. Microform and electronic publishing may need some introduction.

Microform

Microform is a generic term used for information borne in microimages. Microimages are texts and graphics reduced to such small size that they can no longer be read without the assistance of equipment known as *readers*. Serials librarians deal with at least two kinds of microforms: microfilm and microfiche. A microfilm is a long strip of film wound onto a reel. A microfiche is a sheet of film. Some libraries may also have micro-opaques in their microforms collection. Micro-opaques are opaque sheets bearing microimages. They are becoming obsolete now, having been replaced by microfilm and microfiche.

Microforms can be produced in either positive or negative. Positive means the reader projects information contents in a dark image over a light background. The negative is the reverse. There are three types of microform, based on the chemical processing compounds, that are available on the market: silver halide, diazo, and vesicular. Silver halide is most suitable for archival purposes due to its longevity; however, it is more expensive than diazo and vesicular and is subject to scratching if not handled properly during repeated use. Diazo is inexpensive but has the shortest shelf life among the three types, making it suitable only for materials with short retention value. Vesicular is quite acceptable for library use because it is durable and less expensive.

Advantages

The original purpose for producing serials in microforms was preservation. Paper, because of the acid in its makeup and processing, turns brittle with time, limiting its life span. This phenomenon is especially true with newspapers, since they tend to be printed on poor-quality paper. Many serials, especially newspapers and periodicals, are published on microfilm or microfiche in addition to the paper format. In most cases, the paper format and microform versions are issued by different publishers. The microform publisher obtains the rights to reproduce serials in microforms from the paper-format publisher. In the United States, University Microfilm International (UMI) is a major microform publisher for serials. Each year it produces a newspaper catalog as well as a serials catalog listing all the titles it has available in microfilm and microfiche, based mainly on the theory that it is a better alternative for the library to acquire serials in microform than to bind the paper format.

Advantages of selecting microforms include saving the cost of binding, saving staff time involved in handling the bindery process, avoiding the necessity of buying replacement issues when issues are missing for binding, having a complete collection without gaps caused by out-of-print or missing issues or mutilation to the bound volumes inflicted by users, and saving shelf space because microforms occupy much less space than bound volumes. However, there also are disadvantages in replacing bound periodicals with microforms. With a microform collection, the library has to acquire microfilm and microfiche readers and provide an appropriately appointed reading area with staff to provide assistance. In addition, patrons almost always prefer to read the paper format. The bottom line for both librarians and library patrons is that there are two choices for accessibility: using the paper format but taking the risk that wanted materials may be missing or damaged, or using microforms, which are less convenient but always available. Since microforms are mostly for controlled in-house use and are easily replaceable, materials rarely are missing, while paper volumes may be out on loan, misshelved (or hidden by selfish users), or have missing pages. With such choices, microforms are appreciated as a welcome addition to library collections.

Acquisition Options

Since serials in microform are reproductions of the paper format, microforms are published much later than the paper edition. For instance, for the weekly periodical *Business Week,* UMI delivers microfilm annually or semiannually and microfiche are delivered quarterly. If a library opts for microforms, it should acquire the microform subscription in addition to a paper subscription. The common practice is to have current issues available to the public in paper format until the microform edition is received. Then the paper edition is discarded, and the microform edition is retained in the library's permanent collection.

Microforms also play a major role with government document serials. With the vast number of documents published by government agencies all over the world, microforms have become an economical and practical method of preserving and distributing documents. The United States Government Printing Office has an extensive depository program that provides free distribution to designated depository libraries of the majority of federal government publications. To save the reproduction and shipping cost, many U.S. documents serials are published and distributed in microforms. Therefore, depository libraries are forced to establish microform collections.

If materials are available in both microfilm and microfiche, librarians have to make a choice. Microfilm has been a dominant form for archival preservation. A reel of microfilm contains much more information than a sheet of microfiche. Microfiche gained popularity in the 1980s when UMI started to produce periodicals in microfiche. The main attraction of microfiche is the increase in delivery frequency. Microfilm subscriptions typically are delivered annually or semiannually, but microfiche subscriptions are delivered quarterly. For libraries that retain paper periodicals until the microform edition is received, the increased frequency of delivery provides faster relief for the congestion on the periodicals reading-room shelves and fewer inquiries about missing issues. There are other advantages of using microfiche over microfilm. Microfiche is easier to handle, the reading machine is cheaper and easier to operate, microfiche sheets take much less shelving space than microfilm reels, and replacing a sheet of microfiche is much cheaper than replacing a reel of microfilm. A big drawback for microfiche is misfiling. It is quite easy to misfile a microfiche sheet in the collection, but the problem can be controlled by limiting the refiling to library staff trained to handle the material.

Electronic Publishing

With the advance of computer technology, publishing and information services have been using powerful computer applications to store and retrieve information, leading to the birth of electronic publishing. An accurate definition of electronic publishing is difficult to give at this time because the field still is developing and changing constantly. Publishers, scholars, and librarians are being challenged every day to contribute to and keep up with what is happening in the field of electronic publishing. Books, journals, and conferences are devoted to the topic. The terminology appears everywhere, but the definitions vary.

When AACR2R was published, it gave librarians a much-needed guideline to define computer-related electronic publishing. To accommodate the new format AACR2R added a chapter on cataloging computer files. In the glossary, AACR2R defined a computer file as "a file (data and/or programs) encoded for manipulation by computer."[8] As a beginner's guide, this discussion will be limited to serials on CD-ROM and electronic journals.

Serials on CD-ROM

CD-ROM is the acronym for compact *d*isc-*r*ead *o*nly *m*emory. The silver colored 4¾″ compact disc looks very much like a music CD, and the information stored on the disc is for reading only. This means the end user can retrieve information but cannot write on, add, or delete information from the disc. To retrieve information stored on the disc a CD-ROM workstation is required, consisting of a computer, a monitor, and a CD drive or player. A printer may also be needed. Libraries do not always choose to provide a printer because the expense of paper can escalate out of control when users overprint; libraries may prefer to sell regular computer floppy disks to users for downloading needed information. The computer also must have installed search-and-retrieval software to use with CD-ROMs. Since a dedicated workstation allows only one user to access the CD-ROM at a time, libraries can set up a local area network (LAN) to allow multiple-user access. Remote dial-in access is also possible. CD-ROM technology is developing and changing very rapidly. LAN and remote access are being improved constantly by the newer and better software and hardware companies.

Advantages. The two most-attractive advantages of using CD-ROM to store and deliver information are its large storage capacity and the versatility of computer searching. With these two attractions, CD-ROM has become the ideal format for publishing bulky reference tools needing constant updating such as indexes and abstracts. In paper format, indexes and abstracts are typically published monthly, then cumulated quarterly, annually, quinquennially, etc. The bulk of paper volumes takes up valuable shelf space, and users must comb through many volumes with limited search keys to find wanted citations. Although microforms can provide continuous cumulative updating due to larger information storage capacity, the search provision is the same as the paper format. Indexes and abstracts on CD-ROM surpass paper and microform versions because of the CD-ROM's storage capacity and the ease and efficiency of executing a computer search. Another advantage of CD-ROM is its transportability. This enables CD-ROM to compete with online search databases provided by information vendors such as Dialog and BRS. Online search databases are off-site, and searches via telecommunication are costly. CD-ROM brings the database to the library as a local database. Although the CD-ROM database is updated only periodically and is not as up-to-date as the online search database, this local database allows patrons to have direct access without telecommunication costs.

Evolution. Major index and abstract publishers, such as H. W. Wilson Company and Information Access Corporation, and CD-ROM publishers, such as SilverPlatter, are pioneers in publishing indexes and abstracts in CD-ROM version. UMI also began CD-ROM publishing in addition to being a major microform publisher. As a step beyond the indexing and abstracting reference service, publishers also started to produce CD-ROM with indexes and abstracts plus the full text of indexed journal articles. For example, UMI's *Business Periodicals Ondisc* is a combination of *ABI/INFORM,* an abstract and index database with access to more than 800 business and management periodicals, plus the full text of articles from more than 350 ABI journals from 1987 forward, and the disc is updated monthly. Besides indexes and abstracts, other bulky reference tools also have started to appear in CD-ROM versions, such as Bowker Electronic Publishing's *Books in Print Plus* and *Ulrich's Plus,* and *CDCS Impact* produced by Auto-Graphics for the U.S. government documents catalog. A CD-ROM publisher may or may not be the information provider or copyright holder of the intellectual property. For example, H. W. Wilson Company is both the CD-ROM publisher and the information provider of Wilson indexes. SilverPlatter also publishes Wilson indexes but is not the information provider of these indexes. SilverPlatter has to negotiate with Wilson to obtain permission to publish Wilson indexes in CD-ROM version.

When CD-ROM was launched in 1985, there were doubts about its longevity. It was labeled as a transition format that would be replaced soon by a technically more-advanced information delivery method. Contrary to this prediction, CD-ROM publication has flourished and is established as an important part of library collections, especially in academic and research libraries where library patrons may wait in lines to use CD-ROM databases.

Standardization. While patrons seem to be happy with the new format, librarians have mixed feelings toward CD-ROM. Librarians are proud to be able to present patrons with a new medium that greatly improves user services; they also are frustrated by the lack of standardization in the industry. With no mutually agreed-upon standards, each publisher's product requires a specific kind of software and hardware not compatible with other publishers' products. Under these circumstances, one index can have CD-ROM versions produced by different publishers with different hardware and software requirements. For example, H. W. Wilson Company is the sole publisher of the *Social Sciences Index* in paper edition, but the CD-ROM version of this index is produced by Wilson, UMI, SilverPlatter, etc. If the library acquired the CD-ROM from SilverPlatter, it has to use the hardware and software specified for the SilverPlatter products, not the hardware and software used by the Wilson CD-ROM products. Furthermore, there is no standardization for search software. This means that to assist patrons, reference librarians have to be familiar with various search methods for the different publishers' products. Therefore, the value of the information contents is not the only consideration in CD-ROM acquisition. Librarians also are required to consider the compatibility and value of the hardware and software. This added complexity may have a negative impact on the decision to acquire a CD-ROM product with desired information contents. To reduce the complexity of the CD-ROM acquisition process, some publishers offer libraries a package deal that includes the initial installation of the hardware and software designed for their CD-ROM products, a free trial period, and training in using the product before the library makes a final acquisition decision. Serials vendors, such as EBSCO and Faxon, also handle subscriptions for serials in CD-ROM and provide assistance to libraries in acquiring the correct hardware and software. The CD-ROM industry is working on standards, and the librarian's hope for the future is that all CD-ROM products will require the same hardware and software.

Acquisition methods. Acquiring serials on CD-ROM is quite different from the acquisition of other library materials. Most publishers only lease their CD-ROM products to the library with a licensing agreement between the publisher and the library. In most cases, when a new disc is shipped to the library, the old disc has to be destroyed or returned to the publisher. If the library cancels the subscription, the latest received disc has to be returned to the publisher, and the library is left with no holdings in its collection. As security for the future, some libraries still maintain their subscriptions in paper or microform in addition to the new CD-ROM subscription. Maintaining dual subscriptions in two formats is a costly practice. Libraries hesitate to leap into CD-ROM acquisitions because they cannot justify the high subscription cost for a CD-ROM version that they do not own. Most publishers also impose limitations or require extra charges for multiple access to the CD-ROM by means of LANs or remote access. To promote sales, some publishers are willing to negotiate with libraries to solve the problems of leasing versus owning and the extra cost of multiple access.

CD-ROM is a promising format. Its storage capacity and the efficiency of computer searching are very valuable for serials. Serials librarians also are thrilled by the full text articles on disc. When full text becomes more popular, there is a hope that libraries will be able to cancel paper and microform subscriptions. This means savings of a tremendous amount of time and work devoted to handling paper periodicals. It could eliminate the receiving of individual journal issues, claiming delinquent issues, display of current issues in the periodical reading room, bindery work, shelving of bound periodicals, replacement orders for missing issues, etc. For public services, there is no need to worry about periodicals missing from shelves, and interlibrary loan requests are also reduced. For libraries with tight periodical shelves, the CD-ROM full text provides a solution to the space problem.

CD-ROM may be qualified as an established format for serials, but it is not fully mature and stable. The CD-ROM industry is working on standards, and publishers are continuing their effort to improve their products with newer technologies. Librarians have to observe the new developments of CD-ROMs closely.

Electronic Journals

Electronic journals are the new focus in serial publications. Their development is being followed closely by scholars, librarians, vendors, and publishers. The definition of electronic journals is vague because the term is used with various meanings. In its broad sense it can include any serials that are published originally in or converted to the electronic format and received either online or off-line. Or it can be limited solely to journals published and received online and delivered through computer networks. Each issue may include a group of articles, just a single article, or an index and abstract list that can be used to request journal articles. Journals may be published regularly or irregularly whenever an article is ready to be delivered to subscribers.

Electronic journals have started a revolution for scholarly communication, bringing excitement and chaos at the same time. The traditional method of gathering, publishing, and distributing information has been challenged by this new method of enabling authors to deliver information directly to readers through shared networks. This new phenomenon has initiated endless discussion and speculation. What is an electronic journal? What are publishers' and libraries' roles in this publication method? What impact will electronic journals have on the future of serial publications? Questions are numerous, and there are no firm answers because this new format is still at an early stage of development. This section explains the status of electronic journals at this writing and is to be used as a base so readers can follow future developments. The field is changing constantly, and new developments are evolving rapidly. As reports, literature, and conferences related to electronic journals flourish, readers should have no difficulty in keeping up with the latest developments.

Evolution. Scholars were the main force behind the birth of electronic journals, through their use of the Internet and BITNET to facilitate publication distribution. Internet and BITNET users started by writing electronic mail to each other; soon, personal communications grew into group discussions, called *listservs*. Next, newsletters and nonrefereed journals began appearing in the network for quick information dissemination; now, there are refereed electronic journals observing the same standards as printed journals. *Psycoloquy,* a refereed electronic journal sponsored by the American Psychological Association and coedited by Stevan Harnad of Princeton University and Perry London of Rutgers University, is an example of a scholarly refereed journal. Scholars' main interest in acting as publishers or editors of electronic journals is to speed up the communication of research ideas and accomplishments among their colleagues. They are not publishing to make a profit; neither authors nor editors require payment. While their institutions bear the cost of connecting to networks, scholars usually have free access to use them for distributing and receiving serials. Therefore, serials available on the Internet and BITNET appear to be free to scholars. For the benefit of readers who have no access to these networks, some journals also distribute paper copies or disks off-line. Subscribers may be required to pay a fee to subsidize the cost of producing and distributing off-line products.

Scholars' enthusiasm stimulated research organizations, scholarly associations, and university presses to venture into publishing electronic journals. Although the purpose is not to make profit but to promote scholarship, they have to meet the standard operational costs of publishing; thus, their publications are not free. This publishing group is working on innovative ways to improve the production and distribution of electronic journals. For instance, the *Online Journal of Current Clinical Trials,* a joint venture of the American Association for the Advancement of Science and Online Computer Library Center (OCLC), is the world's first electronic, full-text-with-graphics, peer-reviewed journal. With the improvement of the access software Guidon, subscribers are now able to access its complete text and graphics through Internet. Besides launching new electronic journals, this group also has begun to add the electronic format to some existing paper journals and to start new journals with both paper and electronic formats to give subscribers a choice. For example, *Electronic Letters,* published by the Institute of Electrical Engineers (IEE), has been available as an online journal since October 1993; Duke University Press has made the new journal *International Mathematics Research Notes* available in both paper and electronic formats.

By comparison, trade publishers have been more conservative and cautious in embracing electronic journals. As profit-making organizations, they have to make sure a journal can sustain its existence by yielding a profit before making the production decision. Since electronic journals were started by scholars whose intention was not to make profit, the publishing history of this format is very short, and the number of publications is small. There are very few facts that can be used to calculate profit. Some major publishers are actively working with libraries on electronic publishing projects to gain experience with production costs, user behavior, distribution methods, etc. Two well-publicized projects are the TULIP Project and Red Sage Project. In the TULIP Project, Elsevier Scientific Publishers offers a group of material science and engineering journals in ASCII and bit-mapped page images to selected higher education institutions. Each institution may choose from different delivery options and processing methods for making these journals available to users and then is responsible for collecting the usage data. The Red Sage Project has three partners: Springer-Verlag New York, AT&T Bell Laboratories, and the University of California at San Francisco (UCSF). With technical assistance from Bell Laboratories, Springer-Verlag provides a group of radiology and molecular biology journals in ASCII and bit-mapped page images to UCSF, which then makes them available to users' terminals by using the RightPages software program. This project explores the idea of a virtual library delivering information electronically to each user's office or home computer and the related technical and behavioral issues associated with such delivery. It has attracted the attention of other publishers, who have expressed their wish to participate. With more publishers joining the project, it may have an important impact on the development of standards for electronic information delivery.

Issues of concern. Scholars are attracted to electronic journals for several reasons. One is the ease and speed of communicating research ideas and results among fellow Internet users. Two, scholars and libraries have free access to the Internet as long as their institutions are bearing the cost of using the network. This free flow of information on the Internet seems to be the perfect answer to the problem created by the escalating serial prices and decreasing library acquisitions budgets. Another attraction is that information comes directly to users' desks. Users can eliminate trips to the library and the frustration of failing to find the journal issue they want because it is being used by someone else or off the shelf for other reasons. Scholars also like the ability to manipulate the information by downloading and printing it or using computer search-and-retrieval capabilities. However, concerns shared by publishers, librarians, and even scholars about this new publication method have slowed down the progress of electronic journals publishing. Answers have been formed for some concerns, but most of them are still waiting for solutions.

A common concern among scholars is the credibility of information communicated in the electronic journals. When anyone can write, edit, or publish on the Internet, who decides what information is needed, and who controls its quality? Publishing without editorial control and peer review may create more junk than valuable information and add more confusion for scholars who must filter out the useful information from the information explosion. In addition, the academic world casts doubts on whether such casual publications will lend weight to authors' research and scholarship accomplishments in the tenure and promotion process. These concerns have gradually moved electronic serials from the realm of newsletters and unrefereed journals to become refereed journals. However, the peer-review process is time-consuming and costly; thus, it has slowed down the speed of publishing and changed the no-cost theory of electronic journals. Production and delivery remain speedy processes. Whenever an article is ready for publication, it can be delivered electronically to subscribers immediately, without waiting for other articles in the issue to be ready for printing and mailing as is the case with paper journal publishing.

Copyright and access control are common concerns among publishers. The Copyright Act of 1976, written mainly to protect intellectual properties regardless of their presentation formats, also applies to electronic publications. However, electronic information can easily be manipulated and copied, which makes it difficult to define and control its "fair use." Most free journals or articles available on the Internet impose no limitation on access, copying, or reproduction if the source and the author's name are cited in doing so. Other publishers have begun to rely on licensing agreements with subscribers to control access. Publishers and subscribers have to negotiate terms and conditions in licensing agreements. They commonly limit who may have access to the journal and where they may obtain it. Site licenses limit the access to particular locations, such as within the library, within the university campus, or within a company building. This type of license contradicts the virtual library idea in which users may access information from their own terminals anywhere. The concurrent-use license, which limits the number of users who may access the journal simultaneously, is favored by librarians and users. Publishers may require password or proprietary software, which is changed periodically, to control access to their journal databases. Subscribers are responsible for safeguarding keys to access to prevent abuse of privileges. Publishers may also adopt software that enforces security checks of computers accessing the database. With the combination of agreement negotiations and technological capabilities, publishers have a variety of methods of controlling access and guaranteeing fair use. However, there are negative impacts on users. Security controls may raise production costs, which have to be passed on to subscribers, and tight security control reduces ease of access.

Constant change in and improvement of electronic information delivery and receiving methods are being followed closely by all parties involved with electronic publishing. The technology is developing at a very rapid rate. Newer and better software keeps popping up. There are file transfer protocols (FTP), Gopher, Network News Transfer Protocol (NNTP), Wide Area Information Service (WAIS), Mosaic, World Wide Web (WWW), etc. Electronic journals may start with text only, then add software for transmitting graphics. Scholars now look forward to multimedia journals that give both video and audio presentations. The future seems to be limitless. While publishers are busy choosing the best software, libraries are getting dizzy trying to accommodate the different choices. It is an expensive practice to constantly review, purchase, and learn to use new products. However, no relief seems to be in sight because computer technology is progressing nonstop, and it is counterproductive to refuse newer and better products.

The Internet is the modern vehicle for scholarly communication, and it provides a superhighway for transmitting electronic journals. However, scholars, publishers, and librarians worry about the future of the Internet. When the number of profit-making electronic journals starts to swell in the Internet, will it still remain free? Will the information superhighway be immobilized by traffic jams created by increasing numbers of users? Will commercial telephone companies take over the control of the information highway? These are some of the speculative questions that arise.

The cost of electronic journals is an interesting issue lacking conclusive answers. Comparing a refereed electronic journal with a paper journal of matching quality, the editorial cost is similar; there are savings in production with the elimination of printing and mailing, but the constant upgrade of delivery software is costly. Currently, delivery on the Internet is not a cost concern, but will it change in the future? Advertisements provide substantial revenue for paper journals, but so far they seem to have no place in electronic journals. Will the number of personal subscribers decrease with the coming of the virtual library? Will selling articles be more profitable than selling issues? There are lots of discussions and questions about costs, but not enough data has been produced by scientific studies to reach any conclusions.

Many discussions are about the library's role in this new publishing method. Some scholars feel libraries have no role to play because authors and readers are in direct contact, the information flow among scholars using the Internet is free, and users can have access to journals from their own terminals without going to the library. When there were only a few free newsletters or nonrefereed journals existing on the Internet, that might have been true. However, as the quantity of electronic journals begins to grow, quality improves, and not all subscriptions are free, libraries will be responsible for preserving and disseminating electronic journal information in the same way they do information in other formats. Otherwise, the privilege of accessing electronic journals may be enjoyed only by an elite group of scholars who are sufficiently knowledgeable about computer technology to find and retrieve electronic journals, have access to computers connected to journal databases, and can afford the subscription costs. It is worrisome to hear some publishers announce they are not responsible for archiving back files or for making back files available. Libraries must assume the responsibility of archiving back files.

Treatment in libraries. Libraries may wish to treat electronic journals in the same way they treat other formats. For example, the same collection-selection criteria and cataloging treatment are applied to all journals in different formats. After all, what is important to users is a journal's contents, not its packaging. However, with computer technology and equipment playing essential roles in electronic information delivery, procedures for receiving and processing electronic journals have to be different from those used with hard copy journals. Basically, there are two main factors that influence the procedure: how the publisher distributes the journal and how the library makes it available to the public. Since various software packages are available for transmitting information electronically and each publisher might make a different choice, each title may require a different receiving procedure. After journals are received, libraries may choose different methods of processing and making them available to the public according to local policies, systems, computer facilities, and software. For example, received journals can be stored in the institution's mainframe computer, merged into the online public access catalog (OPAC), downloaded to a disk, or printed out on paper; or the library can simply provide FTP commands to patrons for direct access from the publisher's database. Patrons may access journals from the campus-wide network system, the OPAC, dedicated workstations, reading the printed copy, or FTP. They may access journals from their desks in the virtual-library model or still have to go to the library due to a site restriction or limitations on computer capabilities. Libraries need to think ahead and keep up with the newest technology to the extent that their budgets, facilities, and staff are able. They should guide users to take advantage of modern information delivery technology. For example, making electronic journals available in printed copies only defeats the advantages provided by the electronic format. With print copies, users cannot enjoy the computerized search and retrieval and the ease of data manipulation, and the library is still burdened with binding and shelving paper copies and worrying about the storage space and the deterioration of paper copies.

At this pioneering stage, some libraries are taking an aggressive and structured approach toward this new challenge by setting up a task force on electronic journals to study ways to archive them and make them available to users and to develop policies and procedures for handling this new type of material. University Libraries of the Virginia Polytechnic Institute and State University, Cornell University, and Massachusetts Institute of Technology are examples of such pioneers.[9] Some libraries are learning by doing. They are dealing with one title at a time by making only a few high-demand titles available in whatever way they can. The best method of handling electronic journals will prevail when libraries gain more experience and publishers establish uniform standards.

Notes

1. Donald Davinson, *The Periodicals Collection,* rev. and enl. ed. (London: Andre Deutsch, 1978), 7.
2. Andrew D. Osborn, *Serials Publications: Their Place and Treatment in Libraries,* 3d ed. (Chicago: American Library Association, 1980), 3–23.
3. Marcia Tuttle, *Introduction to Serials Management* (Greenwich, Conn.: JAI Press, 1983), 5–7.
4. Michael Gorman and Paul Winkler, eds. *Anglo-American Cataloguing Rules,* 2d ed., 1988 rev. (Chicago: American Library Association, 1988), 622.
5. Ibid., 620.
6. Ibid., 622.
7. Ibid., 618.
8. Ibid., 617.
9. Several research libraries' electronic journal task force reports are available in the Association of Research Libraries SPEC Kit 202: *Electronic Journals in ARL Libraries: Issues and Trends* (Washington, D.C.: Association of Research Libraries, 1994). The Association of Research Libraries SPEC Kit 201, *Electronic Journals in ARL Libraries: Policies and Procedures* (Washington, D.C.: Association of Research Libraries, 1994), provides samples of collection development policy and procedure statements, training documents, and sample Gopher and OPAC screens.

Chapter 2

Organization of Serials Management

There are different approaches to organizing library work. One basic approach is by function: collection development, acquisitions, cataloging, reference, circulation, etc. Other approaches may be by subject: science, art, East Asian literature, etc.; by material type: serials, government documents, rare books, etc.; by media: audiovisual materials, electronic publications, etc.; or by user group: graduate library, undergraduate library, etc. A library may mix and match different approaches to organizing its work according to local environment and needs. There is no single perfect organizational model that suits every library. This is also true with the organization of serials management. In *The Good Serials Department,* edited by Peter Gellatly, organization of serials management in various libraries is presented, but it provides no comparison among different types of organizations to indicate which model is most suitable for which type of library.[1] This confirms the thinking that any method of organization is viable as long as it works for the library. Therefore, this chapter does not tell readers what is the best organizational model for serials management but, rather, explains different models readers may encounter at their workplaces.

Defining the Scope

The organization of serials management is tied to how a library defines its scope. A discussion on the scope of serials management is a prerequisite for discussion of its organization. Defining serials management is similar to defining serials. Each librarian may give a different definition, and each library may choose its own interpretation. Broadly speaking, every aspect of library work touching upon serials is within the scope of serials management: deciding collection policy, allocating funds, handling acquisitions, cataloging and classifying, processing, and using serials in providing user services. Thus, every librarian seems to be involved with serials management. If the question "How are serials doing?" is asked, every librarian has some comments. The director is concerned about the increasing serials prices causing a budget problem; the selector is trying to keep up with new developments in the electronic format; the acquisitions librarian is planning serials automation; the cataloger is analyzing a complex title change for a periodical; the reference librarian is introducing the new periodicals index on CD-ROM to users; and the circulation librarian is settling on a different loan period for serials.

Although every function in a library touches serials, there is a degree of difference in the specialization required to deal with serials. In a narrower and more practical sense, only functions requiring the concentration of specialized knowledge in dealing with serials are considered as the main areas of serials management. In both collection development and public services, the concentration of specialization is on the information content of materials, not their format. The purpose of collection development is to build a library collection that suits user needs. Considerations of inclusion or exclusion of materials in the library collection is mainly based on the information content, not whether the materials are monographs or serials. In public services, the essential specialization for a reference function includes knowledge of information sources, ability to interpret user inquiries, and skill to match a user's need with the proper source to locate the wanted material for the user. The role of serials in the reference function is incidental, as serials are information sources. It is not logical for collection development librarians to specialize only in serials selection or for reference librarians to provide information found only in serials. However, in technical services, there is a need for a work force specialized in serials because the format has a major impact on how the acquisition and cataloging functions are performed. Serials require open orders; their acquisition methods and procedures are different from those of monographs. Likewise, cataloging has to accommodate serials' unique publication patterns. This is why AACR2R has a separate chapter dealing with serials.[2] To be a serials cataloger, one has to acquire the knowledge of serials rules in addition to general cataloging rules; thus, many libraries believe serials management falls mainly into technical services.

Even in a narrower interpretation, serials management means serials acquisitions—a function that truly requires unique specialization. Plainly speaking, procedures developed for monograph acquisitions cannot be used for serials acquisitions, and the serials acquisitions staff have to learn a different set of rules and procedures to perform their duties.

Organization of Serial Functions

Serial functions may be divided into collection development, technical services, and public services. In collection development, there are acquisition policies, selection decisions, and fund allocations for serials; in technical services, there are procurement and cataloging for serials; and in public services, there are reference services and circulation for serials plus periodical reading room and stacks management. Organizing serials management means organizing these functions. A library has the choice of (1) establishing a separate serials department to handle all or part of serial functions or (2) having each function handled by a different department, for example, serial selections and fund allocations might be done by the collection development department, procurement by the acquisitions department, cataloging by the cataloging department. The first choice is referred to as a centralized serials organization and the second choice is a decentralized organization. The following sections will discuss the centralization and the decentralization of serial functions and different ways of organizing a centralized serials department.

Centralization versus Decentralization

The first recommendation to organize a separate serials department came from J. Harris Gable in 1935.[3] The first serials department was established in the Library of the New York University in 1939 as "a recognition of the importance of serials and the special problems connected with their administration."[4] Since then, the debate over whether a library should or should not have a separate serials department has been a never-ending controversy. In practice, many libraries have established separate serials departments, others maintain decentralized operations, and still others go through reorganizations between centralized and decentralized serial organizations. Since library work is basically organized according to function, a department organized according to format does complicate the organizational structure. Yet many libraries choose to have a separate serials department for various sound reasons. Five commonly recognized advantages for having a separate serials department follow.

First, being continuous publications with complex characteristics and a changeable nature, serials are very different from monographs. Monographs are steady and clear publications, but serials are unpredictable and vague. The operational routines developed for monographs cannot accommodate all the exceptions caused by title changes, frequency changes, merges, supplements, suspensions, etc. Serials require different workflow procedures that can take care of all their complexities. Such procedures do not exist with monographs.

Second, with their complex characteristics, there is no denying that serials are more difficult to work with than monographs are. Staffs trained to work with monographs are not prepared to handle serials; staffs trained to work with monographs and serials may have a tendency to work with monographs first, then agonize over serials as headaches. But for staffs trained to work with serials, the complexities associated with serials are viewed as normal routines, and their familiarity with serials enables them to perform their work with efficiency and quality. In addition, with serials being so unpredictable, knowledge of how to deal with exceptions is mostly gained through working experience rather than preparatory training; thus, experience becomes especially valuable. There are virtues in training and maintaining a serials team in a department.

Third, serials operations involve a string of interwoven steps, and close coordination of these steps is essential to achieve efficiency. Based on descriptions given by James D. Thomas for types of processing interdependence, Mitsuko Collver labels the relationship among these steps as reciprocal interdependence, meaning "each function requires repeated inputs from and interaction with other functions."[5] She stated:

> In library work, the serials operations of preorder searching, ordering, paying, receiving and checking-in, claiming, updating holdings information, precatalog searching, cataloging, recataloging, production and maintenance of the catalog, binding, and public service of periodicals are reciprocally interdependent. None of the major operations can continue for long without calling at least some of the others into play. . . . For this reason, all serials related activities should be grouped into one unit for the benefit of maximum coordination.[6]

Among interwoven steps, weakness in one can cause extra work for the others and lower the quality of the serials operation. For example, if a preorder searching is not done thoroughly and does not discover that a journal subscription can include supplements at extra cost or exclude the supplements by stating so in the order, the order may be placed without any reference to supplements. When the first supplement arrives with an invoice, the receiving staff is faced with the task of investigating why the supplement appeared. Then the selector must be consulted to decide whether the library wishes to include supplements in the subscription. If the selector's decision is positive, the order staff must alter the order record to reflect the inclusion of supplements; if the decision is negative, the order staff has to negotiate with the publisher or the vendor to exclude them. Then the question is whether the received supplement can be returned. If the answer is no, the invoice has to be paid and the selector has to decide whether to keep or discard the supplement; if the answer is yes, the supplement has to be returned with a request to cancel the invoice. If the publisher neglects to cancel the invoice, statements will haunt the invoice staff until further work is done to clear the problem. In the meantime, the cataloging record needs to be reviewed to ascertain whether there is a note about supplements. In this case, if the involved steps are the responsibility of different managers, it will take more time and effort to coordinate both the investigation and work required to correct the mistake than if they are under one manager. When supervision is centralized, there is more incentive to raise the quality of a weak link to improve the efficiency of the whole operation.

Fourth, serials workers tend to maintain higher morale and efficiency in a centralized department than in a decentralized working environment. Working with temperamental publications such as serials, staff members experience many emotional ups and downs. The joy and pain created by working with serials are hard for nonserials workers to understand and appreciate. When a periodical changes its title every other month, when a ceased publication suddenly rises again amongst all the records created to bury it, when a publisher threatens legal action over an unpaid invoice for a special supplement that the library never ordered or received—these are just a few examples of causes of frustration and stress for serials workers. Although staff members are capable of handling these sticky situations, they do appreciate a pat on the shoulder by a sympathetic and understanding supervisor or colleague to ease their frustration. They also like to share their triumphs with their colleagues. When a periodical issue finally arrives after three claim letters and two telephone calls, when the publisher finally stops sending a title that was canceled a year ago and clears all invoice statements associated with the title, when the notorious anonymous user finally stops ripping out pages from a particular periodical—these are examples of happy occasions. This mutual appreciation of their ability to cope with and conquer serials is very important for wiping out frustrations associated with serials work and boosting morale, and it can only be obtained when serials workers are grouped together. In a decentralized organization, it is hard to expect a nonserials worker to have patience for complicated serials tales or to appreciate the serials worker's changing moods.

Fifth, the role of serials is growing steadily in library collections, especially in academic, research, and large public libraries. Serials absorb a large portion of the materials budget and are used heavily. Such an essential collection in the library needs a person who is responsible for coordinating serial functions, is accountable for serials activities, and serves as a spokesperson on serial concerns. Without a separate serials department, it is difficult to identify such a person in the library.

Since centralization versus decentralization is a never-ending controversy, there are reasons libraries choose not to set up a separate serials department. For example, there may be no need for a small library to have a separate serials department when there are only a couple of thousand current titles and a small staff involved. Other reasons include that

centralization overplays the need for serial specialization and staff can be cross-trained to perform both monograph and serial tasks

combining serial and monograph staff members can create a more flexible and productive work force (when the demand for monograph work is high, serials workers can be shifted to ease the work load and vice versa)

having a separate department may create a negative attitude between the serials staff and the monographs staff that is counterproductive

without a separate serials department, the library can save a manager's position

Scope of the Serials Department

If a library chooses to have a separate serials department, the next step is deciding what functions should be centralized in this department. The scope of the serials department can vary according to each library's preference. It can be as wide as including all functions related to serials or as narrow as only performing serials acquisitions. It is uncommon for a library to assign all serials functions to the serials department, but, rather, it will put the emphasis on functions that require serials specialization. Osborn stated:

> There are three main areas of serial activity in libraries which are large enough to require specialization of functions. Each of them may have one or more staff members who work exclusively with serials. The areas are the acquisition department, which procures serials and commonly has the current checking records under its supervision; the catalog department, where there is usually a serial cataloging section or division; and the current-periodical room, which is sometimes supplemented by a document or a newspaper room.[7]

Technical Services and the Serials Department

Technical services are considered the core of a serials department. When a library organizes its technical services functions, whether to centralize or decentralize the serials operation is a major consideration. Assuming there are four basic components in the technical services organization—monograph acquisitions, serial acquisitions, monograph cataloging, and serial cataloging—Figure 1 shows technical service organization models by juggling these four components to reflect different perspectives. This illustration is biased to the possibilities of organizing serials in their relationship to monographs, but it does not represent all the organizational possibilities or include all the functions that may be considered in a library's technical services organization.

What should be the dividing line between serials and monographs when there is a separate serials department or section? There is no doubt that the procurement of periodicals and newspapers belongs to serials acquisitions. The gray area is nonperiodical serials. Within this group, annuals are likely to be grouped with serials acquisitions because they function as serials; the main controversy surrounds publications with a mixed personality of both serials and monographs, such as monographic series, loose-leaf services, and pseudoserials. Multiple-volume monograph sets in publication can also be a problem because they function as continuations during the publication period. For instance, if the library wishes to order a ten-volume set with only volume 1 published so far and the rest of the set to be published gradually in the future, the library must place a standing order for nine volumes to be published in the future to ensure receiving each volume immediately after its publication instead of placing a separate firm order for each volume after obtaining the information of its publication. This is the same principle as using a serial order to handle a monograph.

The dividing line between serial and monograph acquisitions ranges from one extreme, in which the serials unit handles all subscriptions and standing orders, to the other, in which it handles only subscriptions. The advantages of handling all serial orders are that staff members are trained to handle continuous orders, and acquisition procedures are designed for them. For monograph acquisitions to handle standing orders, extra efforts are needed for staff training and development of new procedures. The disadvantage is the possibility that duplicate orders may increase for monographic series, multiple-volume monograph sets, and pseudoserials because individual titles may be acquired as monographs on firm orders or received in an approval plan by monograph acquisitions, as well as being received on standing order in the serials unit. However, with automation, the risk of duplication can be

FIGURE 1. Technical Service Organization Models

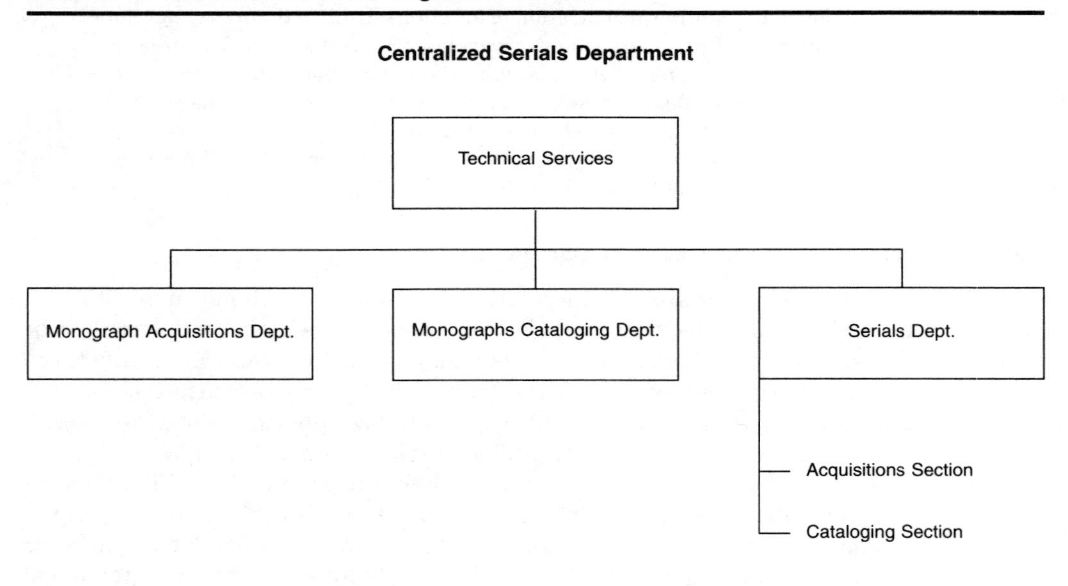

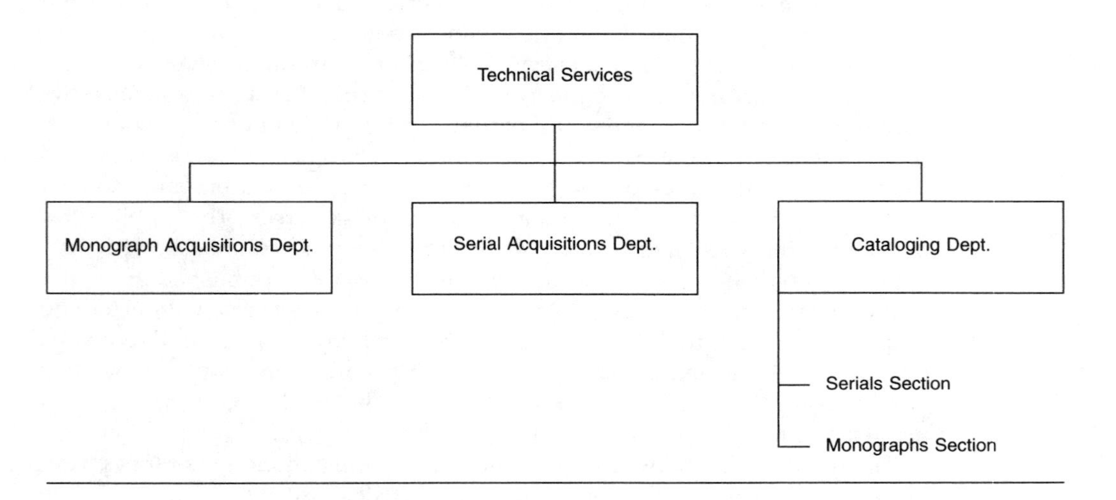

eliminated if both acquisition units share the same database and updating is prompt.

In the division of cataloging responsibilities, it is likely that serials catalogers will handle only open-entry cataloging, such as periodicals, newspapers, and annuals. For monographic series, if one record is required for the whole series title, it is the same as other serial cataloging, but if analytical cataloging is required for each individual title in the series (each title is cataloged as a monograph), then monograph catalogers are best equipped to handle them. Loose-leaves and multiple-volume monograph sets are cata-

FIGURE 1. *(continued)*

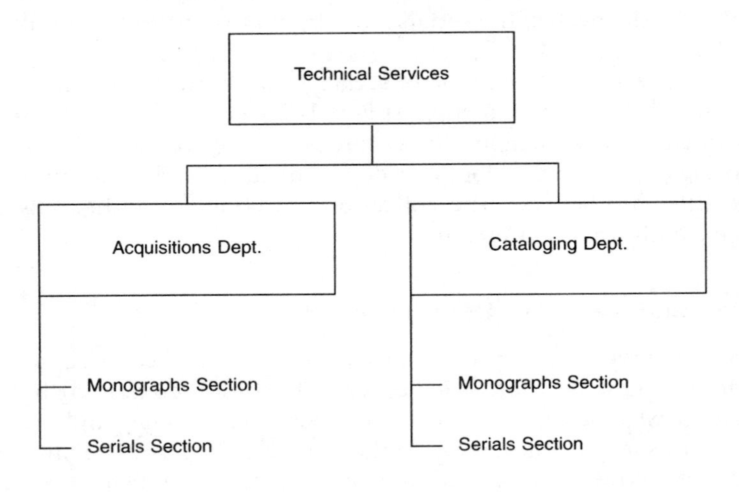

Total Decentralization

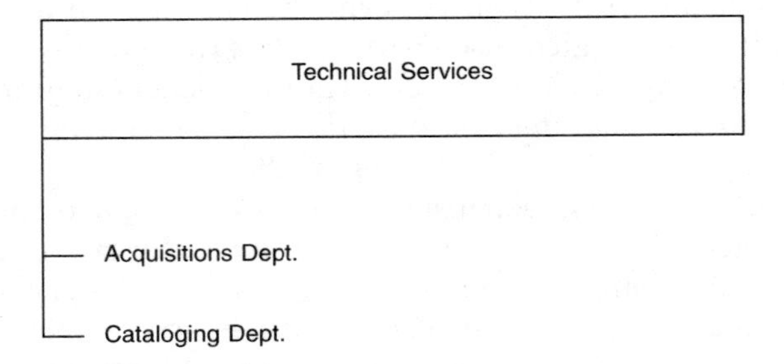

loged as monographs, but pseudoserials are in the gray area and could go either way.

If serials acquisitions are recognized as the only function requiring total specialization, libraries will have a serials department handling only this function. Still, there are a variety of ways of organizing this department and different choices of which acquisition activities are to be included in the department. A serials department can handle all activities related to the acquisition operation—searching, ordering, receiving, routing, paying, claiming, maintaining records, binding—or only some of them. More detailed discussions about serials acquisitions appear in chapters 5 and 6.

Collection Development and the Serials Department

It is not a common practice to include collection development in the serials department because it is a function that focuses more on information content than publication format. In addition, the library materials fund usually is divided first according to subject disciplines, then subdivided by material formats. However, if a library chooses to allocate funds first by format—into monographs and serials—before dividing by subject, it is possible for the head of the serials department to control the serials fund and the selection of serials.

Even when the selection of serials is not performed in the serials department, clerical tasks to support serials collection development may be performed there, especially when there is no support staff to perform such tasks in the collection development department. More discussion on the working relationship between the collection development and serials departments appears in the next chapter.

Public Services and the Serials Department

Public services areas that may be included in the serials department are managing the current periodicals reading room (containing both periodicals and newspapers), managing the microforms room, and handling public inquiries for locating serials in the library collection. The obvious advantage of having the serials department manage the periodicals reading room is to speed up the availability of current periodicals. The latest issues are shelved directly in the reading room by the serials staff as soon as the receiving work is done. It is faster than sending them to another department (e.g., the circulation department) to perform the shelving. In addition, serials staff members are motivated to keep the reading room in good order because they view every periodical issue received as the result of their hard work. A messy reading room generates more work, such as tracing missing issues and answering more inquiries from the public.

Asking the serials department staff to respond to public inquiries by locating serials is logical because they have the latest status information, such as title changes, temporary suspensions, bindery status, claims, the latest issues received, and when the next issues may come. It is more efficient for them to answer inquiries directly, rather than serve as information supplier to the public services unit. Getting involved with public services also is a good way to become more aware of user needs and, thus, to improve technical services. If the serials department is responsible for public inquiries, it is important to have a mutual agreement with the public services unit on the division of responsibility. In principle, the serials department should be limited solely to questions about locating serials in the library collection, and all other reference questions should be handled by reference librarians.

Many libraries also include microforms room management in the serials department when the majority of the microforms collection is serials. The advantage of this arrangement is similar to having the serials department manage the current periodicals reading room. However, managing the microforms room is more complicated because users often need assistance in using microform readers and staff members have to handle mechanical work, such as changing bulbs, adding toner, and solving paper jams. When materials in the microforms collection are not limited to serials (other materials may include monographs, government documents, and large research collections), staff members also must deal with nonserial materials.

Serials Management in Branch Libraries

It is common for a large academic library or public library system to have a main library and several branches. Branch libraries may be established to serve users in different locations, which is a popular practice of academic libraries with multiple campuses and of public libraries that serve people in a large city or county. Branches also may be devoted to subject disciplines, such as the science library, the art library, the East Asian library. In such systems, there also is a choice between centralization and decentralization for branch libraries' serials management. Centralized service means the main library handles the serials management for branches; decentralized service means each branch library handles its own serials management.

There is little controversy about public services being decentralized because such services can be effective only when performed on the location of both the collection and expert librarians. Centralization is an economical choice for collection development in branch libraries established for the purpose of serving users in different physical locations unless they serve user groups that have different needs from those of the general population, such as a public branch library in an area with a heavy concentration of one ethnic population. Collection development may be decentralized for subject libraries or branch libraries that have a mission different from that of the main library because librarians with the appropriate knowledge of subjects and user needs are in branch libraries.

For technical services, there is greater controversy about whether centralization or decentralization is a better choice. Like other issues, the choice is influenced by local policy and environment. Generally speaking, centralization is more economical because only staff members in the main library must be trained to perform serials duties; it also offers better quality control because the training is apt to be uniform and practices follow the same procedures. Centralization also promotes good-quality work because the central staff concentrates on serials work and handles a large number of serials; therefore, the staff has the opportunity to gain better understanding and experience with serials. The advantage of decentralizing is that having both technical and public services performed on site in the branch library provides better local coordination, which may improve efficiency. When technical services are carried out in a branch, it eliminates the need for checking with the main library to find out the status of various operations or titles or to wait for the serials staff in the main library to take action on local requests. Decentralization also offers more efficiency and flexibility in accommodating local user needs because decisions made and actions taken locally are easier to customize.

Within technical services, serials cataloging has a tendency to be centralized. In principle, while a serial title requires continuous receiving work, it only needs to be cataloged once unless there are complications caused by title changes, merges, and splits. Therefore, it is not cost effective for branches to master the serials cataloging. Nevertheless, for branches containing materials for which subject or language knowledge is essential for efficient cataloging, such as music recordings or Asian language materials, decentralized cataloging may be the logical choice in using the subject and language expertise of branch librarians.

The real agony of centralization versus decentralization lies with serials acquisitions. Timely receiving of periodical issues is critical for public services, especially for science, technology, and medical libraries. Centralization may be economical and offer better quality control, but it delays the receiving of current periodical issues, which are received in the main library and then forwarded to the branch. This makes centralization of serials acquisitions an unwelcome practice for branch libraries. Another disadvantage of centralization is the need to maintain duplicate receiving records in both main and branch libraries. The main library needs the record for proper acquisitions operation, and the branch library needs it to perform accurate public services. However, this problem only exists with manual serials operations. In automated serials control, both main and branch libraries share the same database, eliminating the need to maintain twin check-in records.

To complicate the matter further, some libraries choose to do centralized ordering in the main library mixed with decentralized receiving in branch libraries. This practice gains some advantages of centralization and avoids delaying the receipt of current issues, but it is difficult to make this mixed method into a smooth and effective operation. As discussed earlier in this chapter, centralization advocates emphasize the importance of grouping serial activities together to achieve maximum coordination. The togetherness is especially acute for activities in serials acquisitions because each one has a close tie with others and each action has an impact on others. If they are split between two libraries, staff members in both places need to spend time in cross-training and constant coordination. Without proper understanding and consideration of the impact of one library's actions on the other, costly mistakes in the whole operation and hostilities between the staff members of the two libraries may result. Mixed practice may also pose a problem for smooth working relationships with serial vendors because vendors cannot decide which library is their primary contact and, if there is a difference of opinion between the two, who has the final authority.

Some libraries have departments or collections for special types of materials, such as government documents, audiovisual materials, and local history materials. Different decisions can be made about whether their serials departments should be responsible for their serials activities. The arguments and choices between centralization and decentralization are similar to those between main and branch libraries.

The Role of the Serials Manager

There are a variety of ways to organize serials management, and there is no perfect organization model for a particular type of library. Two libraries with similar purposes and collections may have totally different serials management organizations, yet both will declare the organization works very well. In the opposite case, two similar libraries may share the same organization model, which works wonders for one library but is a disaster for the other. This is because a sound organization contributes only in part to the success of the serials management; the other part depends on a capable serials manager and an effective serials staff.

A serials manager is a serials librarian. In a library with a serials department, the head of the department is the serials manager. In a decentralized serials organization, this title usually goes to the librarian who is in charge of acquisitions. Although the librarian who heads a department covering multiple functions—with a large staff composed of librarians, paraprofessionals, and clerks—has much heavier responsibility than the one who is responsible solely for a small acquisitions unit, there are enough similarities in the nature of their work to call for the same qualities and requirements of a serials manager. A serials manager needs to have managerial skill, knowledge of serials and general librarianship, and a keen business sense.

The Manager

With the exception of original cataloging, well-trained and coordinated nonprofessional staff should be able to handle daily serials operations without constant supervision from the serials manager. Routine work can be performed by trained clerks under the supervision of paraprofessionals, and complex problems can be handled by experienced paraprofessionals in consultation with the librarian. Therefore, an effective serials manager is not tied down by supervision of routine operations but can concentrate his or her energy and time on organizing the operation, setting the work flow, training the staff, finding ways to improve efficiency, and creating a harmonious working environment. At a time when serials librarianship is experiencing many changes as a result of automation and new developments in information technologies, the serials manager also must keep up with the present status, plan for the future, and prepare the serials organization and staff to face new challenges.

Managerial skill may be obtained through training and experience, but some lucky people possess it as a natural talent. For a new serials librarian with little or no supervisory experience, reading management books and articles is a good start. There are basic fundamentals for good management. One is having genuine concern about the staff's well-being. The manager should understand each staff member's skill, potential, and attitude toward the job assignment and find suitable matches between people and responsibilities. Some people prefer handling repetitive tasks, but others like new challenges and creativity. There are suitable serials jobs for both types. An effective manager should develop and use the staff's capabilities to the fullest.

A second fundamental of good management is maintaining open communications. The manager should keep staff members informed of new developments in the organization and their jobs and listen to staff feedback. A free flow of informal discussion should be encouraged. The manager should also maintain close coordination with other departments by informing them of changes in serials procedures and policies that may have an impact on their work and by learning about implementations relating to serials in other departments.

A third basic principle of management is delivering strong leadership and consulting with staff. Strong leadership gives the staff a sense of security that their well-being is in good hands. Nevertheless, leadership without proper staff consultation can turn into unbearable dictatorship. It is up to the manager to plan and implement changes to improve efficiency or to accommodate a new development, but appropriate staff members should be consulted for their input before a final decision is made. For instance, before implementing a new procedure to improve the efficiency of a task, ask the staff member who is responsible for the task to check the draft procedure to make sure it is workable and can achieve the desired goals. The motto of a serials manager is to never forget that staff is the manager's most valuable asset; an efficient, content, and devoted staff is the basis for a manager's success.

The Serials Specialist

A serials manager must be knowledgeable about serials to be effective in organizing tasks, supervising work, solving problems, and serving as a resource person. Knowledge of serials may be obtained from library education, the serials literature, job training, and work experiences. For serials knowledge, on-the-job training and experience weigh heavily, but there is no need for new serials librarians to panic. All experienced librarians started as novices. There are ways to act effectively, even if you are a new serials librarian. Reading this book is a start for gaining a general understanding of serials management practices, and it should prepare the reader to move toward more specialized and advanced literature. Attending workshops and conferences is a good way to meet and listen to experienced serials librarians. Joining professional associations, such as North American Serials Interest Group and the American Library Association and its Association for Library Collections and Technical Services, and attending their conferences provide ways to learn about the latest developments and future trends in the serials field.

At the workplace, the new serials librarian is lucky if there is a senior person in the library to act as trainer. For instance, if the new librarian is in charge of the acquisitions unit under the supervision of the head of the department, this person will be the most valuable serials knowledge and local practice resource person for the new librarian. Otherwise, the new librarian has to find a quick way to understand the local serials operation and get acquainted with staff members. The first step may be interviewing staff members to learn about their responsibilities and how they execute them. This is followed by working with the staff to gain some solid hands-on experience by actually checking in periodicals, sending claim letters, processing invoices for payment, etc., and following through the whole operation's work flow. Reading written procedures is also important, as they give step-by-step instructions of current practice. If there is no written procedure, writing such procedures not only helps the new serials librarian gain an understanding of current practice but also may be used as a way of reviewing efficiency. Besides becoming familiar with the work flow and routines in the serials unit, it is essential for the new librarian to understand the library's organization and environment, particularly with regard to the working relationships of serials management.

It is unwise to evaluate a serials operation and plan for improvements without first gaining a thorough understanding of current operations. If improvements are called for, it is preferable to start with small-scale changes as test cases before jumping into a major reorganization or job reassignment. Seeking input from the staff before implementing a change can avoid mistakes and gain staff support. For large-scale changes, the advice and approval of superiors should be sought. Be sure to coordinate with other departments in the library if the change has an impact on departmental working relationships. Two good pieces of general advice to a new serials librarian are never underestimate the value of experience and do not hesitate to seek and treasure advice from your superiors, colleagues, and staff members who have substantial working experience with serials.

Besides serials knowledge, it is also important for a manager to keep up with new developments and general trends in other aspects of librarianship because serials management cannot operate in a vacuum. Although the serials manager may be responsible only for technical services functions or acquisitions, it is essential to keep up with serials-related events in the library, such as a serials cancellation project being planned by the collection development unit, a comparative study of commercial-article delivery services being run by reference, or a LAN for CD-ROM being considered by the system office. In this rapidly changing field, only the well-informed serials manager can anticipate the impact of changes and help the organization and staff adjust to meet new challenges.

The Businessperson

Managing serials acquisitions requires dealing with vendors and publishers who are profit-making businesspeople. Faced with a depressed economy, increasing operation costs, and diminishing library funds, their work is becoming tougher. To stay competitive, they are offering a variety of deals and packages to attract library customers, and there is room for negotiation. Serials managers have to sharpen their business sense and shop for the best deal to cope with increasing user demand, escalating serial prices, and limited budgets. For a new serials manager, this may be the hardest part of the job. Fortunately, there is a lot of literature covering vendors, publishers, and serials pricing. The library budget crunch and rising materials costs combined with the impact of new technologies on vendor services have turned discussion toward the value of vendor services and pricing issues. Chapter 4 will discuss how to negotiate and work with vendors. With the cost of serials being a major library budget issue, library administrators have become knowledgeable about price studies and vendor evaluations. This increases chances that a new serials librarian looking for advice will get it from library administrators. Besides making business deals with vendors and publishers, serials managers also deal with numbers and dollars in managing the serials budget with selectors. This topic is discussed in chapter 3.

Characteristics of Serials Managers

It is not necessary to stereotype serials managers, but either by chance or by virtue of their work with serials, they seem to share certain characteristics that turn the complexity of working with serials into a pleasure. They tend to be flexible enough to deal with changeable serials governed by no rules of how and when changes should occur; they tolerate details required in keeping meticulous serials records; they like to play detective to investigate, analyze, and solve problems. They are people-oriented and enjoy dealing with staff members, colleagues, vendors, and users; they are practical people who can accept the best solution possible without insisting on perfection. Last but not least, they have a good sense of humor. New serials librarians may be frustrated by the complexity of the work. A positive reaction to it is treating complexities as stimulating challenges; then the job is never boring and the joy of being able to solve a complicated problem is rewarding. Serials management is addictive. The more one works with serials, the more one enjoys them.

Reorganization

Reorganization is a common phenomenon in serials management. It is caused mainly by the choices between centralization and decentralization and by the various decisions that can be made regarding which functions to include in a serials department. These choices make reorganization tempting whenever a change in the library or a new development in the serials world occurs. These changes might include, for example, the hiring of a new director in the library, the resignation of a serials manager, a budget cut, a new library building, the implementation of a new automation system, new increases in serials prices, or the coming of electronic publishing. Reorganizations generally are limited to shifts from centralization to decentralization or vice versa, or the expansion or contraction of departmental responsibilities.

A potential trigger for a reorganization is the problem caused by rising serials prices and decreasing serials budgets. If a library with a serials department finds serial activities have been decreased by many canceled titles and few new titles, a separate department may no longer be justified. However, the budget problem has made serials the focal point of collections in some libraries because the monograph budget is sacrificed to compensate for the serials budget or because new subscriptions are allowed on condition that current subscriptions of equal value are canceled. Eventually it may result in creating a serials department to handle the major collection of the library.

Automation can also trigger reorganization. In fact, a wave of technical services reorganizations has been caused by automation. Libraries are discussing and implementing technical services reorganizations to realize the advantages of automation. Cataloging was the pioneer of library automation, followed closely by monograph acquisitions; both have experienced the full impact of automation. Unfortunately, serials departments are at the tail end of library automation, and some libraries are still in manual mode. Serials management is dragged into this reorganization wave as a part of technical services, although it is not always on equal footing with cataloging and monograph acquisition functions, which have reached the maturity of automation.

With the development of new information technologies and the changing serials acquisition methods—including licensing of CD-ROM products, purchasing of serial articles from information vendors, accessing of electronic journals via networks, and other methods expected to come in the future—there are many potential reasons for a serials reorganization. Serials managers and staff members are kept running from one organization model to another.

Human factors may also contribute to serials reorganizations. From dealing with changeable publications, serials librarians learn to be flexible and adapt to changes with ease, which makes reorganizations less intimidating. They are often eager to try new organization models, hoping to achieve greater efficiency. Nevertheless, reorganization is a costly process because it takes time to plan and energy to implement; it disrupts the work routine and changes the work flow; and it involves job reassignments, staff reallocations, and retraining. Unless the reorganization can truly improve efficiency and cost effectiveness, the action should not be undertaken lightly.

Notes

1. Peter Gellatly, ed., *The Good Serials Department* (Binghamton, N.Y.: Haworth Press, 1990). Also published as a special issue of the *Serials Librarian* 19:1/2, 1990.
2. Michael Gorman and Paul Winkler, eds., *Anglo-American Cataloguing Rules,* 2d ed., 1988 rev. (Chicago: American Library Association, 1988), 274–98.
3. J. Harris Gable, "The New Serials Department," *Library Journal* 60 (1935): 867–71.
4. New York University Libraries, *Report of the Director 1939–40* (New York: the Libraries, 1940), 16.
5. Mitsuko Collver, "The Role of the Central Serials Unit in an Automated Library," in *The Serials Collection: Organization and Administration,* ed. Nancy Jean Melin (Ann Arbor, Mich.: Pierian Press, 1982), 28.
6. Ibid.
7. Andrew D. Osborn, *Serial Publications: Their Place and Treatment in Libraries,* 3d ed. (Chicago: American Library Association, 1980), 57.

Chapter 3

Collection Development Issues

Collection development, the process of determining materials to be owned and accessed by a library, is a major library function, and entire books are devoted to the topic. The purpose of this chapter is not to teach readers how to be collection development librarians but to prepare serials librarians to aid in collection development activities by providing basic concepts of collection development and discussing issues that require special consideration for serials collection development.

Serials librarians usually are not assigned responsibility for making serials selection and deselection decisions. Only in very small libraries where professional librarians have multiple-function responsibilities or serials librarians participate in collection development due to special subject knowledge is this likely to happen. However, serials librarians always have the responsibility of supporting collection development activities, such as providing information needed in making selection or deselection decisions, producing fund-expenditure reports to assist in controlling the budget, and following up on selection or deselection decisions with actions that turn them into realities. Therefore, to develop an effective working relationship with collection development librarians, it is vital for serials librarians to understand serials collection development and local collection development policy and practice.

Basic Concepts of Collection Development

Collection development is the function responsible for the intellectual content of the library. In their book, *Acquisitions Management and Collection Development in Libraries,* Magrill and Corbin state:

> In one sense, collection development includes assessing user needs, evaluating the present collection, determining selection policy, coordi-

nating selection of items, reevaluating and storing parts of the collection, and planning for resource sharing. However, in a broader sense, collection development is not only a single activity, or a group of activities, it is a planning and decision-making process.[1]

Ownership and Access

Once, collection development meant expanding the library collection by adding volumes. As new publications continue to proliferate, library budgets shrink, and storage spaces fill up, no library can afford to continue adding volumes as the only method of satisfying user needs. Librarians not only have to find ways to best use limited budget and storage space to provide a collection that can serve user needs but they also must take advantage of modern technology to obtain materials not owned by the library but needed by users. Sharing resources among libraries with interlibrary loan (ILL) agreements is a common practice for obtaining materials not owned by the library. Purchasing articles on demand from information vendors, such as Dialog, UMI, and CARL, has also become a popular practice. The new concept of collection development is not simply adding more materials in the library, but also enhancing information accessibility. The aim of collection development has changed from pure ownership to a mix of ownership and accessibility.

Librarians with collection development responsibility may be referred to as selectors because selecting materials is their important task. In research libraries, librarians who devote most of their time to collection development work are often referred to as bibliographers. In large academic libraries, collection development work is divided according to subject disciplines, with each bibliographer responsible for the development of certain subject areas, such as social sciences, humanities, engineering, Latin American studies. It is quite common for bibliographers to have advance degrees in their designated subject areas in addition to an MLS.

Selectors' main responsibility is building library collections. They make decisions on material selection and deselection. Decisions are based on factors such as user needs, strengths and weaknesses of existing collections, collection-sharing agreements with other libraries, publishing trends, and materials budgets. Selectors also participate in the generation of collection development policy, stating the goal and scope of collection development. The policy may also provide guidelines for collection development activities. In an academic library it is essential for selectors to maintain close contact with academic departments in order to assess the faculty's teaching and research needs. It is expected that teaching faculty will have a substantial influence on library collection development decisions. They are the primary library users and also knowledgeable about their subject areas and student needs. To ensure that faculty members have appropriate input on library collection development decisions, a common practice is for each academic department to appoint a faculty member as the library liaison to work with selectors. Selectors should also be aware of changes in academic programs. If a new program is being established, relevant subject materials need to be acquired to support it. When a program is in the process of being phased out, then material acquisitions may be cut to the minimum.

Organization of Collection Development

The organization of collection development varies with the size and traditional practices of libraries. In smaller libraries, the library director or reference librarian may be responsible for collection development, or the responsibility may be shared by several librarians, each with knowledge of certain subject areas. In large libraries, there may be a collection development department with several librarians. A common model in libraries is a collection development coordinator working with a group of librarians with collection development as a part of their responsibilities. Collection development responsibility is typically combined with reference responsibility. Since direct contact with users is an effective way to assess user needs, and the selector's subject knowledge enhances user service, this combination is viewed as beneficial to both functions. In a library with a collection development group, the acquisitions librarian and the serials librarian may be invited to be members of this group. They may also serve as selectors in their areas of subject expertise.

Serials Collection Development Information Sources

The decision-making process for selecting a serial title is more complex than for a monographic title because a serial is a continuous publication. Selectors and serials librarians have to work as a team during the process of identifying and verifying information for selection decisions. Selectors initiate the information-search process for titles under consideration, then pass the information to the serials staff for further investigation and verification before the order is placed. The amount of information supplied by selectors varies with each selector's working habits. Some selectors do a thorough search and obtain all information required for acquisition, while others give only sketchy information. In establishing information for collection development, the division of responsibilities between selectors and serials staff is not absolute. Even if library policy requires selectors to submit a formal order request with complete bibliographic and holding information, there is no guarantee all selectors will comply with the requirement. As a rule, serials staff should always verify information supplied by selectors before placing orders. Although serials staff may use different information sources for verification, knowing the selector's information source makes follow-up work easier. In many libraries, the serials staff also supports selectors in collection assessment activities. Therefore, it is important for serials librarians to have a general understanding of information sources used by selectors.

The following subsections provide brief descriptions of several types of information resources available for serials collection development. There is no intention to provide a list of serials-selection tools because such a list quickly becomes obsolete. The publishing scene is constantly changing, influenced by new technologies and unsteady economics. Information-distribution methods are improving rapidly and serial publications are also being introduced, changed, or ceased at a fast rate. Therefore, instead of remembering a list of titles as selection tools, it is better to have a basic understanding of different types of information sources available for serials collection development activities. If a list of specific selection tools is needed, readers should consult the latest edition of the *Guide to Reference Books,* and its latest supplement, both published by American Library Association.[2]

Publishers

The best and fastest information source for new serial publications is publishers' promotion flyers and catalogs. With today's aggressive marketing and sales techniques, no library can escape publishers' mailing lists. Sophisticated marketing research can also differentiate libraries' needs and provide appropriate types of materials to fit each library's collection scope. For example, promotion flyers and catalogs for research journals are sent to academic libraries but not to small public or school libraries. Some publishers send unsolicited sample issues to promote new periodicals, or they may supply sample issues on request.

Vendors

Serial vendors are good information sources for new and current serial publications. Major vendors maintain comprehensive serials information databases that include full bibliographic records and acquisitions information. For business purposes, vendors keep in close contact with publishers and constantly update their databases with the latest information. Vendors regularly distribute current and new serial title listings to customers and provide access to their databases for information verification. For example, Faxon distributes *Librarians' Guide to Serials,* which is an alphabetical listing of all the titles in Faxon's databases. Likewise, EBSCO supplies *Librarians' Handbook.* Access to a vendor's database may be free, or it may require an access fee. Vendors provide announcement services by sending libraries notification forms containing new publication information. A library desiring such service has to set up a profile with the vendor indicating which types of materials in what subject areas should be included in the service. This service is popular with monographs, but the profile can include serials if the vendor handles both. Vendors also provide customized lists catering to a library's specific request, such as supplying a current periodicals list in a certain subject area. This service is useful for building a new collection or evaluating the strength of an existing collection.

Trade Bibliographies

Trade bibliographies consist of publications by major reference publishers, such as Bowker's *Ulrich's International Periodical Directory,* Oxbridge's *The Standard Periodical Directory,* and EBSCO's *Serials Directory.* Entries in these reference tools include all the vital information useful for both selection and acquisition verifications. Major bibliographies in this group may be available on CD-ROM and online. For instance, Bowker offers *Ulrich's Plus* in CD-ROM; it is also available online through Dialog and BRS. Serials directories in CD-ROM versions are good tools for collection building and evaluation because they provide varied ways of sorting that help selectors gather information by subject, language, publisher, etc.

National Bibliographies

National bibliographies have long-standing value as a record of publication. Since publishers and vendors are mainly interested in pushing sales for current publications, the value of their catalogs is short-lived, and they are regularly superseded by newer catalogs. National bibliographies, such as *New Serial Titles* published by the Library of Congress, are comprehensive publication records of a nation, and they have a permanent value for the library. They are valuable for retrospective collection development in verifying a publication's history and may be used to check new titles as well. Some national bibliographies are also produced on CD-ROM.

Shared Databases

Shared bibliographic databases, such as OCLC, RLIN, WLN, are rich information resources. They contain both the Library of Congress and their member libraries' constantly updated cataloging records and provide the efficiency of computer searching with multiple keys. Shared databases also list libraries owning a title. This is valuable information for resource sharing considerations in collection development and interlibrary loans.

Reviews

Some serials are devoted to reviews, such as *Choice* and *Booklist.* Some journals, while not devoted entirely to reviews, have a section for reviews of publications in the relevant subject areas; for example, *Contemporary Psychology* reviews publications in the field of psychology. While most reviews are of monographs, occasionally they include serial titles as well.

Indexes and Abstracts

Indexes and abstracts are keys to reaching periodical articles and are essential reference tools for serial users. There are general indexes and abstracts, such as *Magazine Index,* and subject indexes and abstracts, such as *Engineering Index, Art Index,* and *Library & Information Science Abstracts.* Selectors may use the list of periodicals covered in indexes and abstracts as a guide to building a new subject collection or to evaluate the strengths of an existing serials collection by comparing the library's holdings with the titles covered by a relevant index or abstract.

Core Serials Lists

Core serials lists are compilations of serial titles considered to be essential to a subject area or a particular type of library. Titles are chosen according to set criteria that determine the importance of the title. These lists are useful in building a new collection or evaluating an existing collection.

User Input

User input is valuable, especially in academic and research libraries. As discussed earlier in this chapter, selectors in academic libraries may be expected to keep in close touch with faculty members to solicit their input.

Serials Collection Development Considerations

Serials are a vital component of a library collection. They are essential tools for conveying current information to users. This is especially true with newspapers and periodicals. Therefore, serials are most valuable for fast-paced scholarly research, particularly in the fields of science, technology, and medicine. The fundamental difference between serials and monographs is their publication pattern. For a monograph, the acquisition decision can be based on known facts, such as the credentials of the author and the publisher, the length of the book, and the price. Yet for a serial, there are past, present, and future considerations. The past needs investigation and the future is unpredictable. The fact that serials are continuous publications makes the selection and deselection decision more difficult and the acquisition process more complex. The following subsections describe extra considerations and efforts needed in the serials acquisition decision-making process that are not required for monographs.

Making a Long-Term Commitment

A monograph acquisition decision commits to a one-time purchase because a library is acquiring a single volume or a set with limited multiple volumes, but a serials acquisition decision is a commitment to purchase all the future issues until either the library cancels the order or the serial ceases publication. In theory, selectors should regularly review serial orders to weed out unsuitable titles, but in reality, very few selectors have time to perform this duty. Usually, serials are reviewed only when there is an urgent cause, such as a budget crunch or stack space shortage, or when something happens to the title calling for attention, such as a large price jump or a title split. The decision to acquire a serial should be made with careful consideration and extra caution because a serial order is a long-term commitment of budget for future purchases, staff effort to receive and manage issues that continue to come, and shelf space to hold growing numbers of volumes of the title.

In making a serial selection decision, an important step is to check whether a periodical is indexed. Library users rely on indexes and abstracts as the key to access articles in periodicals; therefore, a periodical included in indexes and abstracts is a confirmation of its value and utility. Checking shared bibliographic databases to see which libraries own the title is another way to measure the quality and importance of a serial, especially for libraries with similar user groups and collection scope. For example, a law library might check other law libraries' holdings. Another purpose for checking the shared database is for resource-sharing considerations. However, caution should be exercised to avoid overlooking small-press publications and unusual scholarly association publications that are not indexed or popularly owned by libraries but that might be valuable for local user needs. Checking a serial's past publication history can shed light on the consistency of its quality and stability.

When reviews are not yet available, examining a sample issue is a common practice among selectors making a serial acquisition decision. For new titles, publishers may send unsolicited sample issues; otherwise, selectors can request that the serials librarian obtain a free sample issue from the publisher. Some publishers require payment for sample issues, especially for high-priced scientific and medical journals. If the price of a sample issue is high, an issue might be requested through interlibrary loan. Otherwise, the serials librarian should consult with the selector before ordering the sample issue so the charge does not come as a surprise.

As an extra precaution in placing serial orders, many libraries have a screening process. In such cases, selectors are not the final decision makers for serials acquisitions. After a selection decision is made by a selector, the recommendation has to be reviewed and approved either by a committee or the selector's superior, such as the head of the collection development department, the coordinator of the collection development group, or the library director.

Gift and exchange programs are a well-established method for acquiring materials that are not easily obtainable through regular commercial channels. Accepting a serial gift or entering into an exchange agreement for a serial title is also making a long-term commitment. Therefore, the same considerations used in placing a serial order should be applied to gifts and exchanges. Thinking that serial gifts and exchanges are free is a misconception. Although there is no charge for a gift serial, staff time and effort are needed to manage it. A donor usually has less commitment to supplying the serial faithfully to the library than a publisher who accepts payment for the order. As a result, serials staff members have to spend time claiming and searching for missing issues. For exchange titles, the staff has to maintain double records for materials being received from and sent to exchange partners. In addition, both supplying exchange materials and paying shipping charges impose costs on the library or its parent institution.

Additional Decision Requirements

After a selector has made an acquisition decision, some titles may need further investigation and decisions to take care of order details. This is unique to serials because of their continuous publication pattern and complexity. Following are examples of areas needing decisions.

Should previous volumes be acquired? For a new publication, there is no question about starting the order with volume 1, but for an ongoing serial, the decision has to be made whether to order back files. For example, if the current volume is volume 10, should the library back order volumes 1 through 9? If the library wishes to back order when earlier volumes are out of print but available in microform, what is the selector's choice? What is the serials librarian's recommendation? The serials librarian can search for back files from vendors specializing in out-of-print materials, but the result is uncertain, and the cost may be much higher than the price for the current volume. Back files in microform may be available at a reasonable cost, but splitting holdings into two formats may confuse readers.

What will the retention decision be for the title? If a decision is made to keep the title in the collection permanently, action must be taken to preserve the material. The choice may be to bind the paper issues or to add a microform subscription for the title and discard its paper issues on the receipt of the microform version. For annuals and yearbooks, new volumes may supersede old volumes. If so, should the library keep only the latest volume or keep all volumes? Should the latest volume be kept in the reference room?

When multiple formats are available, which one should the library choose? As discussed in chapter 1, a serial can be available in different formats. Before making a choice, it is important to understand the advantages and disadvantages of each format to decide which is most suitable for the library environment and user needs. Since both paper and microform formats have been available for a long time, the formula for choosing between them is well established in most libraries, or a decision may be made during discussion between the selector and the serials librarian. Electronic publishing is a new and developing alternative, and decision-making processes for this format are evolving. Libraries may set up a committee to study the feasibility of moving to an electronic version before making a choice. With the relatively high subscription cost and the need for computer equipment, the library director and the system librarian are likely to be involved in the discussion in addition to selectors, reference librarians, and the serials librarian.

How should supplementary and accompanying materials be treated? If a newsletter is included with the subscription of a journal, should it be kept permanently or for a limited period or be discarded on receipt? The selector has to review the newsletter and make a decision based on its value. How should a library treat maps that come with *National Geographic?* Should a pocket be made on the issue to store the map, or should all maps be kept with the map collection? If a disk comes with a journal, should it be left with the journal or kept behind the circulation counter? Keeping accompanying materials with the serial is convenient for the user, but this method carries with it the risk of losing the materials; keeping them in a different location may provide proper care but is inconvenient for the user.

If an association offers subscription discounts to members, should the library join or ignore the discount offer? It may depend on whether the membership fee offsets the discount. If the library subscribes to several journals published by the association, making the combined discount higher than the membership fee, and if there are other membership benefits for the library, then it should join the association. Otherwise, the library should not be tempted by a small advantage of the discount because keeping a subscription on a membership is more complicated than maintaining a regular subscription.

Should monographic series be ordered as monographic or serial orders? The answer depends on the selector's wish. If the selector wants to purchase every volume published in the series, the series should be ordered as a serial on standing order. If the selector wants to pick and choose random volumes, then each one has to be acquired by a monographic order.

These issues reconfirm that serial orders are more complex than monographic orders and that selectors and serials librarians have to maintain a close working relationship and consult with each other. The serials librarian should provide technical information to assist selectors in their decision-making process, such as whether there is any hope of obtaining out-of-print back volumes or what methods are available in treating accompanying materials. The selector should avoid making unreasonable demands and unwise decisions, such as insisting on purchasing paper back files when the out-of-print search has failed and the material is available on microform at a reasonable cost.

Deselections

Collection development responsibility is not limited to adding information sources to the library; it also includes weeding out obsolete and unwanted materials. Proper weeding or deselection can free up precious library space for new acquisitions and save staff the burden of maintaining useless materials. Deselecting serials has become a very popular library procedure in recent years, and serials cancellation projects have been undertaken at many libraries. Unfortunately, libraries are not canceling unwanted titles, but they are losing wanted serials because they can no longer afford to pay for them.

Making deselection decisions under the pressure of a budget crunch is a tough task. There is no perfect formula or reasoning that can please all users. Selectors have to develop a policy for deselection and ways of setting priorities that will minimize the negative impact on user needs. Obvious steps include weeding unwanted titles, canceling duplicate orders, identifying titles of minor importance, reviewing high-priced titles, consulting faculty members, and negotiating resource sharing with neighboring libraries.

While selectors are going through the decision-making process, the serials librarian and staff are often required to supply information, such as compiling lists of titles for deselection considerations. For example, selectors may need to know all the library subscriptions costing more than $500 or request a list of subscriptions in a certain subject area or a list of library subscriptions from a particular publisher. After deselection decisions are made, serials staff have to process cancellations. Therefore, the serials librarian and staff are also involved in deselection projects.

In working with selectors on deselections, the serials librarian has to remind them to pay attention to the following matters.

Selectors should not cancel a title unless the decision is absolutely certain. It is not uncommon for a selector to request that a canceled title be reactivated, especially when a cancellation project is done in a rush. This is costly for two reasons: (1) both cancellation and order processing are time consuming; (2) issues or volumes published during the cancellation period may be out of print, so the library has to either pay a high price to acquire these back files or suffer a gap in its holdings because missing issues are no longer obtainable. Reasons for reactivating can vary, e.g., the selector was not aware the canceled title is useful for multiple subject areas and considered the cancellation from a single-subject perspective only, thus raising objections from selectors responsible for other subjects; the selector did not consult with all relevant faculty members and was not aware the title was important for a professor's research project; the selector relied on a neighboring library's collection for resource sharing without realizing that that library also was planning to cancel the title. In all three cases, better communications can help. To avoid such mistakes, libraries may set up a review procedure to screen cancellations. The process may include having the cancellation list reviewed by fellow selectors, relevant faculty members, and a screening committee of a library's usual resource-sharing partners. As a rule, cancellations should be done with the same caution and care as placement of new orders.

It takes time for cancellations to be processed and to go into effect; therefore, requests should be submitted before renewal time with sufficient lead time for the cancellation to reach the publisher. Generally speaking, cancellation requests for January renewals should be submitted before October, and if the list is long, earlier submission is required to allow the serials staff sufficient time to process them. Of course, telephone and fax can speed communications with vendors and publishers, but these are more expensive methods and should be reserved for emergency cases.

When submitting a cancellation request, the selector should also consider the treatment of back files. Should they be retained or discarded? If the cancellation is a result of weeding, back files most likely should be discarded. Otherwise, they may still have value and should be retained.

Budget Allocation and Control

Two essential elements in collection development are identification of titles to be acquired and allocation of funds for acquisitions. The first element has already been discussed. The following subsections discuss the second element—the serials collection development fund.

The library fund allocated for materials acquisitions is called the book budget or more appropriately, the materials budget or acquisitions budget. It may be divided into different categories according to subjects, such as humanities, social sciences, or sciences; according to material types, such as monographs, periodicals, or annuals; according to formats, such as paper, microform, or computer file; or according to usage, such as bindery or replacements. A library follows its collection development policy and stated goals to determine fund categories and their allocations. Since dividing the budget into categories is a method of managing the fund to ensure appropriate allocations and expenditures, the larger the fund is, the more detailed the divisions are. In allocating funds to different categories, libraries usually follow a formula based on an established group of facts. For instance, the formula for allocating funds to subject disciplines in an academic library may consist of the number of students and faculty members, the importance of the program, the strength and weakness of the existing collection, the average cost of serials and monographs in the discipline, and the number of publications produced annually.

Dividing budget categories, developing the budget allocation formula, and allocating funds are selectors' responsibilities. The serials librarian is involved in helping to plan the serials budget by supplying information on current serials expenditures and predicting future expenditure trends. After the budget is approved, the serials librarian is instrumental in controlling the serials budget by supplying serials financial reports. Therefore, it is essential for the serials librarian to have a basic understanding of the serials budget.

Serials Budgets

Funds spent on serials can be divided according to different purposes.

Current subscriptions and standing orders. The fund carrying the expenses of existing serial orders is referred to as the *fixed cost* because it is already committed to purchases. Both subscriptions for periodicals and standing orders for continuations are long-term orders. Once an order is placed, invoices for new and future publications will continue to arrive until the order is canceled or the publication ceases. Each year an appropriate amount of money has to be put aside to cover the fixed cost. The fixed cost increases with the addition of new orders and decreases with cancellations and cessations. In contrast, the fund for monographs can vary according to the library's needs and desires and is referred to as the *variable cost.*

New orders. If the fixed cost is budgeted only for existing orders, new orders are not covered. The cost of new orders must become part of the next year's fixed cost because by then new orders will have changed into existing orders. Some libraries may allocate extra fixed cost to include an allowance for new titles, so the cost of new titles immediately becomes part of the fixed cost.

Bindery costs. Funds allocated to bind periodicals must be repeated each year for existing periodicals; the amount increases when new titles are added or decreases when titles are canceled, ceased, or microform subscriptions are placed to replace binding.

Back files. Funds for serial back files are different from the fund for subscriptions and standing orders because back file funds are not for a continuous commitment but for a one-time purchase only. Acquiring back files is similar to purchasing monographs, and such acquisitions are executed by firm orders instead of open orders.

Replacements. Replacement orders for missing or damaged serial issues and volumes are like back file orders, they are also one-time purchases and handled as firm orders.

Planning Serials Budgets

Serials budgeting is a focus point in a library's materials budget. The proliferation of serial publications plus inflation in serials prices have elevated the serials budget to the fastest growing portion of the total materials budget and a main concern of library administrators. Planning for the serials budget is essential in controlling collection development funds.

The main concern in planning for the serials budget is the fixed cost for current serial orders. In the case of monographic orders, budgeting is flexible because the number of orders to be placed can be adjusted according to available money. If there is enough money, all desired orders can be placed; if funds are short, orders may be reduced by holding back some titles. This can also be done for the bindery and for serial back files and replacement orders. Delaying back orders and bindery work may lower the quality of the collection; nevertheless, it is a way of preventing a budget disaster—not being able to pay for what has been ordered. Not allocating enough funds to cover the current serial orders may truly create a financial disaster—not being able to pay serial invoices when they are due.

Three factors should be considered in allocating the fixed cost:

the total amount paid for the fixed cost and new orders in the previous year minus the cost of cancellations and cessations

the estimated inflation rate for the current year

foreign currency fluctuations

The first amount is easy to calculate if the library keeps finance reports with accurate serials payment records. This amount is used as the base budget for the new year. However, irregular serials, such as monographic series, can be troublesome in predicting the new year's budget. Using the amount spent on monographic series standing orders during the last year as the base for this year's budget allocation is not necessarily accurate because the number of volumes published in a series and the price of each volume can vary from year to year. Standard reasoning is that some titles may publish more volumes than last year, but others may publish fewer, and at the end of the fiscal year things may just even out. Some libraries exclude monographic series from the serials fund and charge their payments to the monographs fund. This practice solves the problem for the serials budget control, but it creates a problem for the monographs fund. Firm orders can be held when the fund is short, but standing orders will continue to supply newly published volumes with their invoices that must be paid.

The second factor is an estimate of the average inflation in percentages imposed by publishers. Multiplying the base budget by the inflation rate produces an estimate of the dollar amount required to meet inflation. This inflation cost is then added to the base budget. A good information source for the inflation rate is the annual publication of "Periodical Price Index" and "Serial Services Price Index" sponsored by the Library Materials Price Index Committee of the Association for Library Collections and Technical Services (ALCTS), a division of the American Library Association, to assist librarians who prepare annual budgets for serials or analyze serials pricing trends. They provide price analyses for serials in different subject categories, but the scope is limited to domestic serials. Both indexes have been published in *Library Journal* but have appeared in the May issue of *American Libraries* since 1993. They are also published in the *Bowker Annual.* The British counterpart of these indexes is "Periodical Prices," published annually in the May issue of the *Library Association Record.* This study is prepared by Blackwell's Periodicals Division and is not limited by language or country of origin of the titles included in the study. It provides price analyses for country of origin in three regional groups, Great Britain, the United States and Canada, and all other countries.

In addition to these studies, major serial vendors, such as EBSCO, Faxon, and Readmore, also provide serial price analyses and predictions to assist customers in planning their serials budgets. An excellent information source for librarians who are responsible for serials budget planning is the electronic *Newsletter on Serials Pricing Issues,* edited by Marcia Tuttle. It is available through Internet and BITNET.[3]

For libraries with no foreign serials or very few foreign titles, foreign currency exchange rate fluctuations are not a serious concern, but for libraries with many foreign serials, currency fluctuation can have a big impact on budget. For instance, if the exchange rate between the U.S. dollar and the British pound was $1.90 to £1.00 in the previous year's invoice payment time and the rate dropped to $1.50 to £1.00 this year, the library needs to pay less for British titles. In the reverse case, there will be a large increase in the dollar amount to be paid for British titles. Unfortunately, currency exchange rate fluctuations are unpredictable and beyond the control of librarians, thus creating problems in budget planning. Vendors, as the intermediaries between libraries and publishers, are also affected by the exchange rate in paying bills to foreign publishers. Some vendors are trying to provide a solution by buying foreign currency when they feel the exchange rate is favorable before renewal payments are due and asking their library customers to use the same exchange rate in paying renewal invoices. However, there is no guarantee that the rate will not change and make the agreement unfavorable for the library at renewal time.

Before placing new serials orders, in addition to ascertaining that there is sufficient funding for the current year, it is important to consider whether there will be continuous funding to sustain these orders in the future. A library may receive temporary funding from time to time, such as a grant or a gift donation, that it might use to initiate new subscriptions. In such cases, it is unwise to enter new serials orders because there is no continuity in these funds to cover future costs.

Calculating the bindery budget is done by using last year's bindery cost, adding binding costs for new titles subscribed to last year, and subtracting the binding costs for canceled titles and new microform subscriptions replacing print back files. If the binder imposes a cost inflation, it should be added to the total budget. In deleting the cost for canceled titles and microform titles, do not forget the binding operation has a delayed reaction—when a title is canceled for this year, the volume published in the previous year needs to be bound this year; therefore, the saving will not be effective until the following year. Libraries usually have a separate bindery budget that includes funds for both serials and monographs.

For back files and replacements, budgeting is flexible and may vary each year with acquisition needs and fund availability. It is sensible to exclude back files and replacements from the serials fund because they are one-time firm orders as opposed to long-term serials orders. They should not be treated as a part of the fixed cost; they belong to the variable cost.

A controversial subject in library budgeting is that of having a separate fund for nonbook materials and their reading equipment, such as microfilm, microfiche, and their readers, and CD-ROMs and their workstations. Libraries have used materials funds to cover the purchase of microforms and CD-ROMs, but reading equipment has been covered by equipment or automation funds. Separating materials and their reading equipment into different funds may create problems for collection development when there is a shortage in one fund but surplus in the other. For instance, if the collection for periodical microfiches grows but no new readers are added in proportion to this growth, users may have difficulty finding available readers to use the collection. If the materials fund can afford a serial in CD-ROM but the automation fund has no money to purchase a workstation, users cannot use it. With the growing popularity of CD-ROM, the problem caused by separating funding for materials and equipment has become more obvious. Since selectors may control only the book fund, they are left to find funds for the workstation after a selection decision has been made for a CD-ROM title. Libraries are beginning to change fund allocation policies and consider materials and their reading equipment as one unit in acquisition.

Budget Control

Good budget control neither overspends nor underspends allocations. Well-planned budget allocations are needed as the base for achieving good budget control, followed by close monitoring of expenditures. In monitoring expenditures, selectors have to rely on budget reports supplied by the serials librarian.

The main purposes of producing budget reports are to plan and control the budget and to request appropriate funding for collection development. Reports may be produced with different information contents to suit the purpose. The report to assist selectors in controlling expenditures should include information on the original allocation, current commitments, amount spent, and the cash balance for each of the fund categories. Libraries use fund codes in budget reports to represent different categories. Fund codes may be alphabetic or numeric symbols or a combination. There is no standard formula on how to construct a fund code. A library is free to decide how detailed the fund divisions should be as well as how to construct the codes to represent them. For example, the fund for American history periodicals in microfiche may be constructed as "shapm," "41123," or "sha23." In the first example code, *s* represents social sciences, *h* represents history, *a* represents American, *p* represents periodicals, and *m* represents microform; in the second example, numbers represent the subjects, material types, and formats; and in the third example, both alphabetic characters and numbers are used. Fund codes should be formulated consistently in both collection development and acquisition functions. Selectors should assign a fund code with each order request, and the acquisition staff should attach the fund code to the order and the invoice payment. Using fund codes consistently and faithfully is essential for accurate record keeping and producing budget reports.

An automated serials control system with fiscal control capability can produce budget reports in different ways. Libraries with such systems are lucky. If a library is still in the manual mode for serials control or if the automated system cannot produce budget reports, then the library has to find other alternatives. A budget report for monitoring serials expenditures may be produced on a personal computer by using a commercial software program. Vendors can also produce different management reports from their databases as a service to their library customers. A discussion with the vendor may produce useful results for budget control.

Cooperation between Selectors and Serials Librarians

Effective cooperation between selectors and serials librarians is the key to successful serials collection development. The preceding discussions described the interrelations among selectors, serials librarians, and the serials staff. Following are some suggestions to promote smooth working relationships and improve effectiveness in collection development.

Agreement on the division of responsibilities. Each library follows its local policy in deciding the division of responsibilities among selectors, the serials librarian, and serials staff members. The division can vary in many ways. For instance, in performing the searching function, one library may decide the selector is responsible exclusively for all searches and the serials staff is responsible only for placing orders. Another makes the serials searching staff responsible for both exploratory searches and preorder searches. Yet another has the selector do the exploratory searches and the serials staff do the preorder searches. A mutually agreeable division can prevent duplicate effort, incomplete work results, and constant questioning, even arguing, about who should be responsible for what tasks.

Working procedures. Developing working procedures for handling routine processes is a way to improve efficiency. For instance, instead of the selector and the searcher asking questions to verify information, an order request form can be designed for the selector to supply information for an order search, which can be returned to the selector after data are verified and completed by the searcher. Instead of having selectors pass order requests to the serials librarian in person with oral instructions, selectors can drop requests with written instructions in a box marked *Orders* in the serials department. Then the staff members responsible for searching and ordering can pick up requests directly from the box or, if preferred, the serials librarian can review requests and set priorities for the staff.

Working procedures for each library will vary according to its local policies and environment. Although there is no uniform standard procedure that fits the needs of every library, a few basic guidelines can be followed by librarians in developing the procedure. The procedure should cover all the routine processes, such as how order requests are submitted, what information is required on the request, and what steps in the routine are needed for review and approval of requests by a higher authority. The procedure should avoid consultations in person as much as possible by giving instructions for the different possibilities. For instance, adding an item in the order request form for back-file-order instructions may replace the personal consultation with selectors. A personal consultation takes more time and effort than following an instruction on a form. The procedure must be discussed and agreed on by selectors and the serials librarian. Then it must be understood and followed by serials staff members. Good procedures improve efficiency in collection development work and promote appropriate coordination among selectors, the serials librarian, and the serials staff.

Close coordination. Since serials collection development is more complex than that for monographs and requires many extra considerations, close coordination between selectors and the serials librarian is a must. Positive attitudes are important in promoting good coordination. The serials librarian and staff members must play a faithful supporting role to selectors; in return, selectors should appreciate the value of these services and be considerate and modest in their demands. A positive attitude is the base for developing mutual respect and pleasant working relationships.

Notes

1. Rose Mary Magrill and John Corbin, *Acquisitions Management and Collection Development in Libraries,* 2d ed. (Chicago: American Library Association, 1989), 2.
2. The latest edition published at this writing is Eugene P. Sheehy, ed., *Guide to Reference Books,* 10th ed. (Chicago: American Library Association, 1986). The latest supplement is Robert Balay, ed., *Guide to Reference Books: Covering Materials from 1985–1990, Supplement to the Tenth Edition* (Chicago: American Library Association, 1992). The eleventh edition, edited by Robert Balay, is due to be published in 1996.
3. For more information on this newsletter, see Marcia Tuttle, "The Newsletter on Serial Pricing Issues: Teetering on the Cutting Edge," *Advances in Serials Management,* 4 (1992): 37–63. To subscribe to the newsletter, send a message on the Internet: LISTSERV@GIBBS.OIT.UNC.EDU saying "subscribe Prices" and your name. If there is a problem, contact Marcia Tuttle: TUTTLE@GIBBS.OIT.UNC.EDU

Chapter 4

Serials Vendors

In performing serials acquisitions, librarians may choose to place orders directly with publishers or go through an intermediary, referred to as a vendor, dealer, jobber, or agent. According to Katz and Gellatly: "For a library with more than one hundred periodical titles on order, it is generally a good idea to employ an agent. This is so even in the case of an agent whose service charge is from 5 to 20 percent."[1] According to the survey done by Katz and Gellatly, 95 percent of libraries use vendors.[2] The fact that most libraries use vendor services may be viewed as recognition of the vendor's value.

Vendor Services

The major benefits of using vendors are saving staff time and simplifying acquisitions processes by dealing only with the vendor instead of a large number of individual publishers. For instance, if a library has 5,000 serial subscriptions published by 500 publishers, when the choice is direct ordering, the library receives 500 renewal invoices from and sends 500 payments to different publishers. If a vendor is used to handle all 5,000 subscriptions, there is only one renewal invoice from and one payment to the vendor. Paperwork is reduced with this simplified renewal process through the vendor service.

In addition, vendors are willing to accommodate a library's requests to suit its local needs, while publishers are not likely to alter their business practices for a library's convenience. For example, if a library needs triple invoice copies for payment processing, the vendor is often willing to comply, while the publisher may supply only two copies according to its business practice and leave the library staff to duplicate the third copy.

Vendors also provide information on new publications, changes in existing publications, statistics and trends in publishing, and analysis and predictions of serials costs. A major vendor's database is a good source for acquisitions and bibliographic information and is capable of producing management reports for libraries, such as a library's subscription list sorted by title, library fund code, country of origin, or subscription price. When a library is in the process of automating, the vendor also can provide assistance by extracting the library's subscription records or MARC records from its database to be downloaded to the library's system, thereby eliminating the need to build the database for the library from scratch. At a time when libraries are troubled by high serials pricing, vendors serve as mediators to improve understanding and cooperation between publishers and libraries. A good vendor is a valuable ally of a library's acquisitions operation.

Vendor Selection

Once a library has decided to use vendors, the next step is to select the right ones. Each vendor has its own business scope and emphasis, strengths, and weaknesses. General vendors handle all types of materials, while special vendors handle only certain types, such as serials, government documents, art materials, audiovisual materials, or materials from certain geographical areas. There are domestic vendors and foreign vendors. Vendors in the United States tend to specialize. Their business scope may concentrate only on monographs, serials, special types of materials, or publications from certain geographical areas. Foreign vendors tend to handle all types of materials. With the advances in communication technology and the globalism of modern business, major vendors may be international vendors, able to handle multinational materials and do business in different parts of the world.

The library vendor business is labor intensive and highly competitive with a low profit margin. One can well believe that people in this business are there for the love of books more than for the desire to get rich. With the increasing use of automation in the library world, vendors have to invest heavily in automating their business operations and information databases. They also have to keep up with new information and communication technologies to improve the efficiency of services. Many smaller vendors are driven out of business because they cannot afford to keep up with the fast pace of modern technology. They have either disappeared or been acquired by larger vendors. The sale of Faxon, one of the largest serials agents that had acquired smaller vendors in the past, to Dawson Holdings PLC of Folkestone in the United Kingdom in 1994 sent a shock wave through the serials world. The message seems clear: sometimes even a large established vendor cannot survive the business pressure. *Guide to Magazine and Serial Agents* by Bill Katz and Peter Gellatly, published by Bowker in 1975, lists quite a few vendors that are no longer in existence.

In addition to the *Guide to Magazine and Serial Agents,* a useful guide to vendors is *International Subscription Agents,* published by the American Library Association. The sixth edition, compiled by Lenore Rae Wilkas and published in 1994, is the latest. This book lists agents alphabetically by name within an alphabetical arrangement by country in which they are based. The description of each agent includes address, phone and fax numbers, date established, countries/geographic areas covered, branch offices, types of materials supplied, services offered (including computerized services and ability to interface with library systems), participation in library and library-related associations, and business details.[3]

An effective way to find suitable vendors is to visit the exhibition hall of the American Library Association's annual and midwinter conferences. Vendors with exhibition booths there are very willing to provide information on their companies and services to potential new customers. However, unless the vendor offers a flat service rate to all customers, most vendors will not provide a firm service charge rate at this time because charges may vary with the library's serials collection size and subject areas. If the librarian shows enough interest, the vendor can arrange for the regional sales representative to visit the library for further discussion.

Another valuable source for vendor information is acquisitions and serials librarians in other libraries. With BITNET and Internet in use in libraries, communication among librarians is instant. Acqnet and Serialst are newsletters in these networks that may be used for vendor information inquiries. Christian Boissonnas of Cornell University started the Acqnet. The current editor is Eleanor Cook of Appalachian State University. Her Internet address is COOKEI@CONRAD.APPSTATE.EDU. Acqnet provides discussions of library acquisitions, collection development, and related subjects. To subscribe to Acqnet, send the message SUB ACQNET-L <your name> to LISTSERV@APPSTATE.EDU on the Internet. Serialst, owned by Birdie MacLennan of the University of Vermont, provides discussions related to serials. To subscribe, send the message SUBSCRIBE SERIALST <your name> to either LISTSERV@UVMVM on BITNET or LISTSERV@UVMVM.UVM.EDU on the Internet.

Selection Criteria

Selection criteria will vary among libraries, but some fundamental criteria apply.

Service A library's vendor selection criteria should be a combination of commonly recognized criteria plus local requirements. Most important among commonly recognized criteria is good service. High fulfillment rate, speed, accuracy, and responsiveness are the elements of good service. A vendor should fulfill orders and handle claims and invoices with accuracy and speed. A vendor also should be responsive to library requests for acquisition information, management reports, special invoice requirements, automation assistance, etc., and be communicative during the problem-solving process.

Cost A second important criterion is cost, which is a combination of discounts and service charges. Years ago, vendors received sufficient discounts and commissions from publishers to be able to serve libraries and earn a profit without charging more than the stated subscription rates. This is now history because commissions have disappeared and discounts are diminishing.

Today's vendors rely heavily on service charges to defray their operational costs. Negotiating service charges with vendors is a complicated process. For the subscription service charge, vendors usually add a certain percentage of the total subscription cost. For instance, for a total annual subscription cost of $100,000, a 4 percent service charge is $4,000. Some vendors have a flat service-charge rate that applies to all customers. Other vendors determine the service charge according to the total amount of business and the mix of titles on the library's order list. A customer that orders more-lucrative titles may negotiate for a lower service charge. Lucrative titles include those journals in science, technology, and medical fields that are published by reputable major publishers at a high subscription price but require relatively low maintenance. On the opposite side, a humanities journal with a low subscription price published by an academic department that has a tendency to miss publication deadlines is a title that yields poor or negative profit for vendors. For instance, a $1,000 medical quarterly that yields a $40 service charge at a rate of 4 percent and that requires low maintenance because the publication is always on schedule is a lucrative title; a $50 literature monthly that yields only a $2 service charge but that requires constant claims because the publication is often late is a low- or negative-profit title. Titles from publishers offering good discounts to vendors are also lucrative. Some vendors provide libraries with a list of publishers whose significant discounts to the vendor contribute to the reduction in service charges. This list may contain different titles from year to year following the change in publishers' discount policies. Librarians should be able to judge whether a service charge is a fair one by knowing the vendor's service charge formula.

To simplify calculation of the service charge, it is preferable to use the same service charge rate for all subscription invoices—the main renewal invoice, supplementary invoices, new order invoices, and credits. Vendors usually send the main subscription renewal invoice to libraries around October, when most major publishers have notified vendors of their new prices for the next year. For titles with no new price available at renewal time, vendors usually quote their current prices plus an estimated adjustment for inflation. When the new price is known, if there is a discrepancy with the price charged in the renewal invoice, the vendor issues a supplementary invoice for the underpayment or a credit for the overpayment. Libraries may also receive credits from vendors for cancellations and cessations. For new orders placed before renewal time, subscription charges are merged into the main renewal invoice. If new titles are ordered after the renewal invoice is issued, the invoices come separately whenever orders are received by the vendor. With such a variety of invoices and credits coming to the library, it is important to have a clear-cut service charge agreement that applies the same rate to all types of subscription invoices, and credits should include the refund of service charges. Otherwise, it is difficult for the serials librarian to calculate the bottom line.

Vendors traditionally deal with periodical subscriptions and continuation standing orders as two separate groups. Serials on standing order are either not included in the subscription renewal invoice or listed as "bill later" orders with no price given. Their invoices usually accompany the shipment of materials or come shortly before or after the shipment. Their service charge may not be the same as subscriptions, and some vendors offer a discount from the publisher's list price.

Making the service charge issue more complicated are vendors' various payment methods. Some vendors offer libraries interest or discounts on their service charges for early payment of the main renewal invoice. The earlier in the year the payment is made to the publisher, the larger the interest or discount due the library. This is a good offer if a library's book fund is available before the regular renewal time and if the fund yields no interest or lower interest than the vendor is offering. When a library chooses the early payment plan, the vendor supplies either an estimated renewal invoice or a one-line invoice with just the estimated total renewal cost but no title listing. The amount paid by the library will be compared with the true renewal cost at regular renewal time, when the library will either receive a credit for the overestimate or pay the balance for underestimate.

Another payment method offered by some vendors is to send only the main renewal invoice with no supplementary invoices or credits to follow. This is done by adding to the renewal invoice the estimated inflation cost for the next year agreed to by both the vendor and the library. This is like gambling for the library and the vendor. If the estimate is too high, the library loses; otherwise, the library wins. This method has the definite advantage of eliminating all the work of handling supplementary invoices and credits for both parties. With this advantage, a vendor usually can afford to predict the inflation on the low side by giving the library a better price. Therefore, it is most likely a game where both parties may come out as winners.

Libraries with a large number of foreign subscriptions should choose vendors who accept payment in U.S. dollars. Otherwise, libraries or their institutions will have to buy various foreign currencies. There also should be an agreement between the vendor and the library on how and when the conversion of foreign currencies is done. The price for foreign titles is a tricky business because of unpredictable foreign currency exchange rate fluctuations. The exact dollar amount paid for foreign titles can vary, depending on when the currency conversion is done. Vendors may bill foreign titles either in dollars or in foreign currencies. If they are billed in foreign currencies, the conversion is usually done by the library at payment date. If they are billed in dollars, then the conversion is done by the vendor either at the invoice date or when the publishers set their prices. As an ethical practice, the library and the vendor should follow the agreed conversion time faithfully. There is no sure way for either party to pick a winning date because neither librarians nor vendors can accurately predict the future exchange rate. The rule seems to be that you win some and you lose some.

Negotiating for service charges is a complicated process. For a novice serials librarian the best way is to ask the vendor to provide all options with detailed explanations, then study them carefully before negotiating the agreement. What the librarian should be looking for is not a low charge that leaves no profit for the vendor, but a fair charge for services. To provide good services to the library, vendors need profits to run an effective operation and invest in developing new services.

Establishment Status

Besides service and cost, the last but not least criterion is what might be called the wholesomeness of the vendor, such as the business's reputation, financial stability, automation facilities, and future plans. Libraries likely will be able to maintain a long-term partnership by selecting vendors with established service records and sound financial status. They should also look for vendors who keep up with automation and advances in information technology so that the services keep pace with the times.

A common mistake in selecting vendors is putting heavy emphasis on low cost over good service and wholesomeness. Selecting a vendor offering a low service charge but with a poor service record may cost the library more than another vendor offering excellent services with a higher service charge. To compensate for the vendor's inefficiency more library staff time and effort are needed to maintain an effective serials operation. Choosing a shaky vendor is risky because the vendor's business may fold and put the library's serials operation in jeopardy. Unfortunately, some libraries are forced by legal requirements to select vendors by lowest bid, thus leaving the library little room to judge other criteria besides low cost.

Consolidation versus Multiple Vendors

In addition to the criteria discussed previously, a library has to consider its local conditions in choosing the most suitable vendors. An obvious consideration is matching the library's acquisition needs with the vendor's business scope. In doing so, a library may choose one vendor or several vendors. Although each library has different reasons for its choice, there are a number of theories about whether a library should consolidate all orders under one vendor or use multiple vendors.

Consolidation has the advantages of simplifying the acquisition processing by dealing with only one vendor and of possibly receiving better services and paying lower service charges for being a larger customer. The sole vendor's management reports can represent the complete library serials order, which makes those reports more valuable. Disadvantages are whether one vendor is capable of supplying all orders wanted by the library, whether placing all eggs in one basket is a safe practice, and whether lack of competition will decrease the quality of the vendor's services and increase the rate of service charges. Without a close comparison between vendors, it is hard to evaluate whether a vendor is providing good service at a fair price. The first disadvantage is a valid concern; the second may be avoided if the vendor is selected with a careful evaluation process. With decreasing library budgets causing many serials cancellations, and with the high cost of keeping up with new developments in automation and communication technology, serials vendors are in a tight business. They value their customers more than ever and are unlikely to risk the chance of losing consolidated customers by providing inadequate service or overcharging them. Therefore, for a small- or medium-sized library, if a serials vendor is capable of supplying all its orders, there is no compelling reason to maintain specialized vendors or multiple vendors with similar business scope. Consolidation is a good choice.

Large academic, research, and public libraries may feel there is a need to deal with several vendors for their foreign publication orders and special types of materials. For libraries with a large number of foreign titles, especially those with eccentric publications from small press or local organizations, materials from developing countries, or materials in non-Romance languages, a vendor from the publication's country of origin or a vendor specializing in certain geographical regions may have better fulfillment rates. These libraries may also need to employ other vendors for different types of publications. For instance, a library with a substantial documents collection may wish to use a vendor specializing in documents, or a library with a large art collection may wish to use a vendor specializing in art materials.

Alternative Supply Sources

There are a number of alternative supply sources to vendors.

Direct Ordering

In theory, libraries should switch all direct orders with publishers to vendors because using vendor services is more economical; but in reality, it is difficult for libraries totally to avoid direct ordering. Ironically, one reason for direct ordering is to be economical. Since vendors charge a service fee by percentage of the material cost, this practice makes the service charge for a high-priced title very costly. For instance, the 4 percent service charge for a $5,000 title is $200, which is likely to be more costly than processing a direct order by the library staff. However, the need for this type of direct ordering may be eliminated if libraries negotiate with vendors to set a service charge ceiling for high-priced titles. For example, both parties may agree on the maximum service charge per title as $50; then the charge for the $5,000 title is $50 instead of $200. Another reason for direct ordering is that some publishers prefer dealing directly with libraries without the vendor as the intermediary and reward libraries with discounts for direct orders. In such cases, librarians have to evaluate the economy between the discount and the vendor service. The size of the discount can make the difference. There also are cases when direct ordering is unavoidable, such as when publishers sell only through direct ordering, local publications are not available through regular commercial channels, or materials are received through gifts and exchange programs.

Some major publishers of reference materials prefer direct orders and send sales representatives regularly to libraries to promote publications and solicit sales. Usually each representative covers a geographical territory and works on commission. Libraries deal with these representatives for orders, renewals, and service requests. Commerce Clearing House and Prentice-Hall are examples of such publishers.

Local Suppliers

When a library chooses vendor consolidation for serials acquisitions, it still may need to maintain local suppliers for newspaper subscriptions. The most important considerations in choosing a newspaper supplier are the speed of delivery and the ability to respond to claims instantly. Some users come to the library first thing in the morning just to read the newspapers of the day. If newspaper delivery is tardy or issues are missing, libraries need immediate response from the supplier to correct the problem. A local newspaper service is able to make a special delivery for claimed issues in the same day, while an agent located far away may be unable to do so.

For local newspapers, a small local delivery service may be excellent. However, for out-of-state and foreign newspapers, libraries probably will have to use a large delivery service that handles multilanguage and different geographical area newspapers. Some major newspapers often have their assigned agencies in various geographical areas. If no suitable service agency is available, the library may have to use a subscription vendor or place direct orders.

Magazine Fulfillment Centers

Fulfillment centers provide circulation services for magazine publishers. Their main responsibility is producing mailing labels, not distributing issues to subscribers. Labels are sent to printers for the distribution of magazine issues. Subscribers are directed by either an advertisement or information in a magazine to communicate with fulfillment centers for new subscriptions and cancellations, although many subscribers may *think* they are dealing directly with the publisher. With this arrangement, subscribers are totally cut off from contact with publishers. Since fulfillment centers work with popular magazines, which rely on personal subscribers as their main customer base, their procedures often neglect libraries' need to maintain the integrity of the collection. When fulfillment centers first start to work with publishers, libraries experience a surge of problems, such as getting poor response to claims, receiving duplicates, or having subscriptions dropped at the beginning of the new volume. Thanks to the continuous effort of the well-known serials librarian Marcia Tuttle and cooperative serials vendors, fulfillment centers are beginning to understand libraries' needs and are gradually improving services. For example, many now keep some back issues for library claims and pay more attention to vendor orders. In the meantime, serials librarians and vendors also are acquiring the knowledge of which magazines are associated with fulfillment centers and how they work with libraries. This knowledge enables librarians to plan better methods of dealing with subscriptions handled by fulfillment centers.

Vendor Evaluation

A library may wish to go through a formal evaluation process to select its vendors. It is a good idea to have an evaluation committee instead of relying on one person's judgment. The key committee member should be the librarian responsible for serials acquisitions; other members also should have basic knowledge of serials acquisitions and the vendor trade. The committee's first action is to analyze local serials acquisition needs to decide on vendor selection criteria. The second step is to identify vendors whose business scope and practice match the selection criteria. It is preferable to limit the final deliberations to two or three candidates to avoid excess evaluation work that burdens both the committee and the vendors involved. Then it is time to invite each potential candidate for an interview in which the library's needs are outlined and the vendor's business and services are explained. Using the interview as an elimination process, the committee then solicits written proposals from the vendors with the highest potential. The proposals detail the vendors' services and charges to suit the library's requirements and provide some customer names as references. After reviewing proposals and checking references, the committee may wish to contact candidates again for further negotiation on services and prices before making a final decision. When the selection is made, it is essential to have a written agreement detailing services and costs. This agreement should be updated regularly.

Libraries may also wish to evaluate their current vendors' services and costs. This may be done as a formal evaluation involving outside vendors, similar to the one previously described for selecting vendors, or as an internal comparison study among current vendors. If a formal evaluation is done and the result shows an outside vendor is superior to current vendors, then the library may switch to a new vendor for better services and lower costs. With the internal comparison study, a possible result is consolidation to eliminate weaker vendors. To proceed with the internal comparison study, a library usually chooses an equal number of subscriptions handled by each vendor to compare their services. This comparison might include such factors as responsiveness to claims, problem-solving ability, and rate of service charges and discounts. When selecting sample titles for comparison, the librarian should keep in mind that as an intermediary, the efficiency of vendor services and the rate of the service charges are influenced by differences among publishers and publications. It is unfair to compare a $500 medical periodical published by a major commercial publisher with a $30 literature title published by a small nonprofit association; it is also unfair to compare an annual publication with one published weekly.

Vendor evaluation should be done for specific reasons and with careful planning because it is a time-consuming and costly process for participating vendors and for the library. A well-planned and executed vendor evaluation certainly yields positive benefits for the library, but only the chosen vendor among all those who participate in the evaluation benefits from this process. To be ethical, librarians should screen vendors carefully and only invite those with high potential to participate in the evaluation. It is also important to burden vendors as little as possible during the evaluation process. Finally, an acknowledgment letter to each participating vendor is a proper conclusion.

Switching Vendors

Switching vendors is a complicated and costly process. It consists of a massive twofold process: canceling all orders with the old vendor and starting them with the new vendor. It involves the library, two vendors, and numerous publishers. All parties involved have to alter their records to reflect the change. If coordination among all parties is not done precisely, the most common errors are duplicate orders supplied by both the new and the old vendors or missing orders that are dropped by the old vendor but not picked up by the new vendor. Therefore, vendor switching should be done only when it is truly justifiable. If vendor switching is desired because the library is not satisfied with its current vendor, a thorough discussion with the vendor may improve the situation and avoid the need for switching.

Successful vendor switching requires a good plan, the right timing, and close coordination with both vendors. A good plan includes writing a switching procedure and discussing its feasibility with both vendors, setting the time frame for each step in the procedure, and training the staff who will do the processing. A good time for switching is approximately three months before renewal confirmation time. This will give sufficient time for the old vendor to cancel orders with publishers, the new vendor to initiate new orders, and publishers to alter their records for vendor changes. The old vendor usually will provide the library with a list of its current orders indicating each title's expiration date, which it can give to the new vendor to pick up orders accordingly. As a courtesy to the old vendor, a polite service cancellation notice should be sent in time for it to prepare for the cancellation process. Reasons for switching should be explained if possible. The old vendor also should be asked to contribute as little work as possible to the switching process. The new vendor should be responsible for solving any problems and errors that occur as a result of the switching process. Some publishers may require a letter from the library to authorize vendor switching. The new vendor should be able to deal with publishers on the library's behalf.

Working with Vendors

When a library chooses a vendor, it is entering a long-term partnership with the vendor. Establishing an effective working relationship is beneficial to both parties. Some guidelines for achieving an effective working relationship are offered in the following sections.

The Working Agreement

The foundation of a sound partnership is a mutually recognized working agreement. The basic agreement between libraries and vendors is that vendors help libraries in serials acquisitions and libraries pay a fee for these services. The specific details of the agreement should be discussed, agreed on, and followed by both parties.

Understanding Each Other

To establish a proper working relationship, a library needs to have a basic understanding of how the vendor conducts its business. The people in the vendor organization who work closely with libraries are the sales and customer service representatives. The sales representative is the key person who sells vendor services to the library. This person maintains an ongoing relationship with the library by keeping in close contact with the serials librarian, visiting the library regularly, informing the library about new services, and soliciting input and suggestions for improvement. Sales representatives also attend serials-related conferences and workshops and mingle with their library customers at such occasions.

The vendor's customer service representative is the library's regular contact for conducting daily acquisitions business. This person works closely with the serials staff in performing acquisition duties, such as receiving orders, processing claims, sending invoices, answering inquiries, and solving problems. If there are inquiries that cannot be handled by either the sales representative or the customer service representative, librarians and staff members should be connected with the appropriate resource person in the vendor's organization. For instance, if the library is implementing serials automation and needs information on whether the vendor might provide automation assistance, a member of the vendor's automation staff may conduct direct discussions with the serials librarian or with a representative of the library's automation group.

On the other side of the working relationship, the vendor's sales representative and customer service representative also need to have a basic understanding of their customer's serials organization and operation. The sales representative needs to know about the library's local environment and collection scope to improve services and suggest suitable new services. The serials librarian should provide names and responsibilities of a few key serials staff members, such as the serials supervisor, the claim staff, and the invoice staff, to the vendor's customer service representative.

Communication

Initial acquaintance has to be followed by continuing communication to keep the vendor-library partnership effective. An important rule to remember is that when a title is ordered through a vendor, all the business and communication related to the title should be conducted with the vendor, not the publisher. Otherwise, the vendor cannot be effective in representing the library, and confusion will be created for all parties involved—the publisher, the vendor, and the library. Occasionally, a publisher may contact the library to verify information for claims or other problems. In some cases such direct communication may be necessary in solving a complicated problem, but the vendor should always be informed.

Sales representatives provide ample opportunities for communication with librarians. They call and visit serials librarians; their business cards have all sorts of contact numbers; they are at ALA conferences, North American Serials Interest Group (NASIG) conferences, and other serials-related occasions. It is important for the serials librarian to maintain close contact with the vendor's sales representative to ensure the library is receiving quality services and timely information on new services. As a positive customer, the serials librarian should also suggest to the vendor new services or ways to improve services. If the librarian is visible and concerned, the library is likely to receive more-responsive service. It should not take long for the serials librarian and the sales representative to treat each other as old friends. After all, they have the mutual interest in serials and share the same goal of delivering good services to the library.

In a large and busy serials acquisitions operation, it is common for the library staff to have frequent contact with the vendor's customer service representatives and their staff. It does not take long for the participants to start addressing one another by first name, and it is common for the serials staff to learn the vendor's customer service telephone number by heart. Since vendors provide free 800 numbers, communications between the library staff and the vendor's customer service representatives are mostly conducted by telephone.

Electronic mail and telefacsimile are gaining popularity between libraries and vendors who have the capability. The serials librarian should train staff members who communicate with vendors in the appropriate communication skills and provide general guidelines for choosing different communication methods. A cardinal rule in making an inquiry to the vendor is that the staff members should always prepare themselves first by gathering all relevant information and analyzing it to know exactly what needs to be asked. Telephone and electronic mail communications should be precise and courteous. Standardized forms can be developed for certain routine inquiries.

Cooperation

Vendors generally are willing to accommodate their customers' specific requests as much as possible. In return, libraries should also accommodate vendors' requests. Cooperation improves the working relationship, business efficiency, and cost effectiveness. Examples of being cooperative are paying invoices on time, checking renewal confirmation lists on receipt, and sending cancellations and order change notifications promptly. Delaying payment creates more work for everyone because the vendor has to generate statements of overdue invoices and the library has to check them. Likewise, late notification of cancellations and changes may need special rush processing or cause other complications in processing.

Librarians have to understand that the quality of vendor services is influenced by publishers' behavior. An unsuccessful claim may occur because the publisher is ignoring the claim. An unfulfilled order might not be the result of the vendor's forgetting to process it, but rather that the publisher failed to respond. Library staff members often complain about the vendor's inefficiency. They need to be reminded that complaints yield few positive results and create an unpleasant working relationship; the best solution is to cooperate with vendors in getting a positive reaction from publishers.

Business Sense

Librarians have to recognize that vendors are profit-making organizations, and their profit comes from selling services. Vendors need income to sustain their operational costs and to develop new services. A vendor with a good income and low operational costs can afford to lower the service charge and invest more in developing new and better services, both of which are beneficial to libraries. In many ways, libraries can help vendors increase their income and lower their operational costs. For example, libraries can provide positive references to other libraries in the process of selecting a vendor, which may increase the vendor's income. Being a considerate customer may lower the operational costs. Being a considerate customer means paying each invoice on time, requesting rush services sparingly, and not generating unnecessary claims. It also means not occupying customer service staff time unnecessarily by carrying on long and chatty telephone conversations during a business inquiry or taking unneeded free services offered by the vendor. Considerate customers do not expect the vendor to throw fancy parties during the ALA conventions or take clients to expensive restaurants for business discussions.

Being a considerate customer may sound like putting too much emphasis on vendors' interests, but it is really for the libraries' benefit. A good example is not taking unneeded services from the vendor to save the library's operational cost. Vendors often refer to services such as providing management reports, automation assistance, and extra copies of invoices as "no extra charge" services, but in truth *all* customers, whether or not they demand them, share the charge for these services. It is common sense that providing management reports requires staff time to extract data from the database, computer time, paper to print the reports, and postage to mail them. All of these become part of the vendor's operational cost that must be covered by the service charge. Therefore, librarians should be reasonable in asking for services and should not request unnecessary services just because there is no extra charge. Eventually, increasing demand on services pushes up the vendor's operational costs and, therefore, the service charges to the library. To be a shrewd customer, a library should choose only useful services.

If a library uses very few vendor services but pays the same rate of service charge as libraries using many services, the librarian should question if the vendor is out of step with the library's service needs or whether the library is failing to use the vendor's service capacity because of ignorance. In any case, a discussion with the sales representative may yield some positive results. Good business sense is knowing what the library is paying the vendor for, and neither over- nor under-taking its share of services.

Notes

1. Bill Katz and Peter Gellatly, *Guide to Magazine and Serial Agents* (New York: Bowker, 1975), 3.

2. Ibid., 33.

3. Lenore Rae Wilkas, comp., *International Subscription Agents,* 6th ed. (Chicago: American Library Association, 1993).

Chapter 5

Serials Acquisition Methods

Serials acquisitions—the process of ordering, claiming, receiving, and controlling an inventory of serials—is at the center of serials management and the subject of this chapter. A serial acquisitions operation that uses sound methods is the basis for effective serials collection development and user services.

Due to the unique continuous publication pattern of serials, their acquisition methods are different from monograph acquisitions. While the monograph acquisitions process consists of a definite string of actions—ordering, receiving, paying, and sending for cataloging—the serials acquisitions process is an indefinite string of actions. It starts with ordering, followed by the repetitive process of receiving and paying for new issues, claiming issues that have failed to come, altering records to accommodate changes, preserving loose issues by binding or using other alternatives, and sending information to cataloging for the initial cataloging and whenever changes occur. The string only ends when the library cancels the order or the publication ceases. Thus, the long and limitless serials acquisition journey is more complex than the short and more limited monograph acquisition journey.

The emphasis is different when working in monograph acquisitions and serials acquisitions. The main work in monograph acquisitions is placing new orders, and the workload is measured by the number of new titles acquired in a year. In serials acquisitions, the main task is the maintenance of orders; therefore, the amount of work is measured by how many current orders are being maintained in the library. If a library has no new order requests for the year, there is no work for monograph acquisitions; however, the serials acquisitions work does not diminish as long as there are current orders existing in the library.

Since technical services work is generally pattern and rule oriented, developing procedures and rules to be followed is required to maintain the work's quality and consistency. Being a part of the technical services work, the serials acquisitions process does require and follow procedures. However, there are many unexpected occurrences in serials acquisition that are not covered by procedures. In performing serials acquisitions, it is vital to follow procedures faithfully, but it is also necessary to be flexible in dealing with unexpected exceptions and changes. Therefore, the processing of serials acquisitions needs a set of definite procedures plus a variety of remedies for unpredictable occurrences.

There are various methods used to acquire serials. In addition to the most commonly used methods of subscriptions and standing orders, there are a few other alternatives. The serials acquisitions librarian has to match the most effective and economical method with each type of material. The following sections explain different acquisition methods and how they are used.

Subscriptions

Subscription is the acquisition method used for acquiring periodicals that require prepayment. Publishers demand prepayments before periodical issues are dispatched to libraries. The payment covers issues to be published over a certain period of time, referred to as the *subscription period.* In the majority of cases, the subscription period is one year because most periodicals are published one volume per year. However, newspaper publishers often have different prepayment requirements. They may prefer a shorter subscription period, such as monthly or quarterly.

In this acquisition method, a publisher considers a library to be committed to an order solely for the paid subscription period. If payment is not made in time for the coming volume, the publisher may consider the subscription canceled and stop sending issues. However, many publishers give a grace period for late payment by continuing to send issues for a limited period of time. (Please note that newspaper publishers are very unforgiving and rarely give grace periods.) Sending payment confirms the renewal, and timely renewal is very important to avoid lapses in subscription. Libraries usually choose a common expiration date for all subscriptions in order to have a uniform subscription period. This practice not only simplifies the renewal process but also lessens the possibility of missing the proper renewal time for each order. The sensible choice for the common expiration date is the end of the year because the majority of periodicals have a publication cycle from January to December, although some publications have different publication cycles. For instance, a volume may stretch to two years or only take six months to complete, and some periodicals have a volume that covers July to June instead of January to December. In such cases, some publishers may accept January to December as the subscription period; otherwise, the renewal process becomes more complicated.

Some publishers offer bonuses for longer subscription periods, such as lowering the total cost for prepayment of two or three years or guaranteeing no price increases for the years covered in the period. The advantages to publishers in making such offers are that they have locked in the subscription for a longer period and received larger advance payments. However, not all libraries can take advantage of such offers because their budgets are allocated annually and local accounting systems may not permit advance payments for future fiscal years. This may not be a serious disadvantage for libraries, since committing payment annually makes it easier to plan and control budgets. Besides, if a publication ceases, libraries may encounter difficulty recovering extended prepayments.

Standing Orders

A standing order requests that the publisher send to the library a title's future volumes with invoices as soon as they are published. This method is used for continuations, such as numbered monographic series, multiple-volume monograph sets, pseudoserials, loose-leaf service updates, annuals (including yearbooks), proceedings, advances, and reports. Payment usually is processed after the volume is received by the library, but some publishers may require prepayment. Standing orders ensure complete coverage and prompt delivery and are more efficient than acquiring each volume after its publication with a firm order.

Unlike subscriptions that need to be renewed at the end of the subscription period, standing orders are valid indefinitely until the library issues a cancellation or publication ceases. For irregular serials, a title may have no new volumes published for a long time. The order may stay dormant during the nonpublication period but will automatically resume when a new volume is published. For standing orders vendors usually receive materials from publishers and then reship them to libraries. Most vendors send the invoice with the shipment, which makes the receiving process and invoice payment easier for libraries.

Firm Orders

Although subscriptions and standing orders dominate serials acquisitions, not all serials orders are continuous orders. Replacement and back-file orders require a one-time order; therefore, they are acquired by firm orders, as in monograph acquisitions. These orders are not for future publications but for specific volumes or issues that have already been published. Although both replacements and back files require back orders, there is a technical difference between the two. Replacement orders are for missing materials that the library once owned. It is not uncommon for a library to lose a bound periodical volume, to have a current issue disappear from the reading room, or to discover that pages are torn from an issue. Missing materials must be replaced to maintain the integrity of the collection. Sometimes a replacement order may aim at a serial issue that has been paid for but never received by the library—a failed claim turns into a replacement order. When a publisher insists it has sent the claimed issue and refuses to supply another copy free of charge, or when it declares the claim period has expired, the library has no other option but to buy the issue as a replacement order. Back-file orders are for serials volumes that the library has never owned but now wants. This usually happens when a library orders a new periodical subscription and wishes to back order published volumes or when a library wishes to fill a gap in its serials title holdings.

Occasionally, a firm order is used to purchase a single serial issue devoted to a special topic that has a distinctive issue title, such as when a selector wishes to obtain the special issue to serve as a monograph but has no interest in subscribing to the journal. The issue is ordered under the journal title, whether or not it has its own distinctive title, by indicating its volume and issue number. However, cataloging it under the journal title does not make the issue stand out as a monograph and may lead users to the false expectation that the library subscribes to the journal. Therefore, if possible, it should be cataloged under its distinctive title with a note linking it to the journal title. A cataloging treatment note, such as "catalog as monograph under the distinctive title," must be put in the order record to ensure the proper treatment.

Acquiring Electronic Serials

Acquiring serials in electronic format is a new challenge to serials librarians. The acquisition methods used in acquiring serials in paper and microform do not always strike a perfect fit with the electronic format, and there seems to be no standard method of dealing with this new format. There are three major causes of this phenomenon. One is the departure from the tradition of owning materials in the library after the acquisition. Serials in electronic format may be owned or just made available for access by the library. The acquisition process is not always purchasing the physical material but may be leasing the right to use it for the duration of the subscription, after which all materials revert to the publisher. A second cause is the need for computer equipment, making the acquisition process more complex. The third cause is a lack of consensus among publishers on the methods of merchandising their products. Some want to sell; others prefer to lease. Some market the serials only; others combine the computer software and hardware with the serial title as a package deal. Some charge a subscription fee; others require an access fee, a combination of both subscription and access fee, or various extra charges. To make the matter even more complicated, besides the regular players in the acquisitions game—the publisher, the vendor, and the library—there are additional players in the electronic game—telephone companies providing the telecommunication, networks relaying access, or information brokers retailing information assembled in their databases.

At this point, acquiring serials in electronic format may be loosely categorized according to different types: online databases, CD-ROMs, and electronic journals. Acquiring information in databases usually requires three fees: subscription, access, and purchase. Libraries first pay an annual subscription fee, or membership fee, for the right to access the database. When the database is being used, libraries are charged the access fee, including the telecommunication fee charged by the telephone company, according to the length of the connect time. If a library wishes to obtain a copy of an article, there is a purchase fee that includes a copyright fee charged by the copyright holder. There may be variations in charging methods. For instance, frequent users may be offered the purchase of a block of searching/processing time at a discount price.

Most CD-ROM publishers lease their products to libraries. The subscription fee pays for the lease, not ownership of the material. When an update is received, libraries have to return the superseded disc. If a library stops the subscription, it has to return the last disc, leaving no information in the library's possession. After much protest from libraries, some publishers have begun to allow libraries to keep their last disc if the cancellation follows a continuous minimum subscription period. Local area networks (LANs) increase the accessibility to a CD-ROM from a single user to multiple users. However, this also increases the complexity of negotiations for acquisition because publishers want to charge extra fees for multiple access. If CD-ROMs are loaded into the local online public access catalog or if remote access is involved, the price goes up further. The complexity of negotiations for CD-ROM acquisitions is due to the various potential combinations of merchandise, services, access rights, and price structures.

Acquisition for online journals is more confusing than that for CD-ROMs because the online journals are a less mature format than databases and CD-ROMs. Access to online journals may be directly from the publisher's database or through networks. Some scholarly journals provide free access on the Internet and BITNET; others charge a subscription fee with unlimited access, a base fee plus access charge, or an access fee alone.

Serials in electronic format are still developing and constantly changing. It is hard to pin down set patterns for acquisitions. Serials librarians have to treat each title as a unique case and study publishers' offers carefully to make a wise decision. Most libraries have systems librarians or institutional computer support staff from whom librarians should seek assistance in selecting software and hardware or in choosing the best access method. In the meantime, it is very important to keep up with the new developments in this format by reading the literature; attending relevant conferences; and communicating with publishers, vendors, and fellow librarians.

Alternative Methods

In theory all serials may be acquired by either subscription, standing order, or firm order, but in reality there are other acquisition methods. Alternative methods are used either for achieving better efficiency and economy or for obtaining materials that are not available otherwise. In a negative sense alternative methods add more complexity to serials acquisitions. It may not be wise for a small serials acquisitions operation to use alternative methods. However, for large libraries with demanding collection development programs, the following methods provide more options and opportunities to obtain desired materials and may yield advantages and benefits.

Gifts

Gifts to the library may be solicited or unsolicited. Libraries solicit gifts of materials that are valuable to the collection but are not available for purchase or are very expensive to acquire. Unsolicited gifts may come in a variety of ways. Some donors contact the library first to express the wish to donate materials; some send materials without previous warning. Although these gifts are not sought by the library, they may contain valuable materials. Unsolicited gifts should be reviewed by selectors to determine their retention value.

Serials gifts may be divided into three categories: back files, continuous donations, and miscellaneous materials. Back files usually are obtained when a person donates his or her personal collection. Continuous donations may come directly from institutions that publish serials titles. A library may be selected by the institution, or it may ask to be included in the gift mailing list. At other times, a donor may choose to pay for subscriptions of certain periodicals or to provide a gift fund to acquire serials. The third category consists mainly of dumping-style gifts. These often come from someone who is cleaning out a house or office and finds some useless serials but has no heart to throw them away, so he or she thinks the library is the place to donate them. Although librarians may find some useful materials, dumping-style gifts are the least likely to be truly productive.

Gift acquisition decisions usually are made by selectors following the same criteria as for commercial acquisitions. Solicitations may be done by the acquisitions unit if they only require routine requests for inclusion on a mailing list, but unique and special gift collections may need different approaches. The library director or subject selector may have to carry on a lengthy and delicate negotiation with the potential donor. Once a gift serial is accepted, its receiving and processing follow the same procedures as for purchased serials, except that no payment is involved. Libraries that deal with gifts regularly need to have a policy to guide the soliciting, screening, and handling of gifts. In general, the policy will rely on an external document that describes the scope and acceptance conditions of gifts to the library. This is used to attract potential donors and to avoid getting unsuitable gifts without offending the donor. A common condition in accepting gifts is that libraries reserve the right to discard, sell, or give away donations that are not suitable for their collections.

Correspondence plays an important part in the gift program. Acknowledgments to donors and letters to solicit gifts or to reject unwanted donations need to be handled appropriately. Gift claims may need to be done more tactfully than claims to paid orders. If an unsolicited serial title is not desired by the library, a polite letter requesting the removal of the library's name from the donor's mailing list may be necessary to save staff time in handling unwanted materials. Although gifts are free of payment, they can be expensive in terms of administration and staff time. If a serial title is available commercially at a reasonable cost, the economy of the gift should be evaluated before choosing the gift over the order.

Exchanges

Exchange programs are established between libraries for the purpose of exchanging materials. This method is used mainly for acquiring materials that are not available for purchase or are extremely difficult to obtain. There are two types of exchange programs: regular exchanges and barter exchanges. A regular exchange program uses materials available to the library without cost, such as library or institutional publications, duplicates, or unwanted materials. If the library does not have for exchange free publications or publications desired by the partner, then it has to opt for a barter exchange. In barter exchange, the library has to purchase materials requested by the partner and trade them for wanted materials, such as subscribing to American journals for the foreign exchange partner. These journals are either not available or are too expensive for the foreign library to purchase.

Setting up an exchange program is a complicated and time-consuming process. A library must identify the suitable partner, decide on the titles to be exchanged, and balance the value of exchanges. After the exchange agreement is settled, maintaining the program requires double record keeping—one set for receiving and the other for sending materials. The library also has to keep a file for exchange partners and agreements. Similar to gift programs, correspondence plays an important role in exchange programs; therefore, libraries traditionally group gifts and exchanges together in one working unit. The distribution of exchange-program responsibilities may vary from library to library. Popular practices are sharing the responsibilities between the collection development and acquisitions units or setting up a separate gifts and exchanges unit. After an exchange agreement is reached, incoming serials issues may be processed as regular orders by the serials staff, but sending materials to exchange partners requires a different procedure. Reversing the familiar receiver's role, libraries are required to act as suppliers who oversee the timely delivery of materials to exchange partners and respond to their claims. In barter exchange, vendors may be used in placing serial orders for exchanges. To eliminate extra work imposed on the library staff handling exchange titles and to avoid confusion in mixing library orders with exchange orders, some libraries prefer to request that publishers send exchange titles directly to partners.

The cost of exchange programs is escalating due to the continuous increase in serial prices and shipping costs. When libraries are forced to cut serial subscriptions, it is difficult to justify or find funds for exchange subscriptions. Traditionally, university press publications are used heavily in exchanges. With most university presses no longer enjoying financial subsidies from universities, libraries also lose the privilege of receiving their publications free or at large discounts.

Exchange programs are complex and expensive, especially in barter exchanges. Therefore, this acquisition method should be used only when there are no other alternatives for obtaining desired materials. For research libraries, exchange programs are necessary to acquire certain research materials not available through commercial channels. Programs are established primarily with foreign libraries from geographic areas that have no diplomatic or trade relations with the United States or whose publications are hard to obtain by the outside world. Now that the Cold War is over and the world is opening up to global communication, the need for exchange programs may diminish.

Memberships

Libraries may join associations and societies as institutional members when such memberships are offered. There are two main reasons for them to do so: first, to receive publications available only to members, and second, to receive free publications, discounts, or other benefits. Libraries also may join associations vital to librarianship, such as American Library Association. Sometimes memberships are automatically given to libraries, whether they desire them or not, when they purchase publications from certain societies and associations.

Serials received through memberships require more record keeping than regular orders. It is essential to have a membership file containing information on each membership, including the organization's name, address, and contact numbers; membership conditions and benefits; serial titles received through the membership; and payment records. For each serial title received with the membership, an individual check-in record has to be established for receiving purposes. This record should refer to the membership file that provides a trace to the payment record for claim purposes. Cross references between the membership and its affiliate serial titles are vital in maintaining the integrity of the serials record. For instance, if a membership's benefits change or the library cancels the membership, all related records must be altered. Tracing these records relies on cross references.

The serials librarian has to ensure that the library takes full advantage of the membership. For example, if benefits include a discount for monograph purchases, this information has to be shared with and used by monograph acquisitions staff. It is common for libraries to receive free reports, directories, newsletters, pamphlets, charts, and maps from memberships. All freebies need to be reviewed either by selectors or by the serials librarian for appropriate treatment. After the reviewing process, a decision record should be established for each serial title to avoid having to repeat the process for future issues of the same title. For example, if the selector decides to keep a newsletter for a year, a check-in record is set up with reference to its retention period; if the decision is to discard the newsletter, a record with disposal instructions is also needed so that staff can handle future issues without further consultation.

Depository Programs

Depository programs are used for distributing government publications free to designated depository libraries. The most notable program is the U.S. Federal Depository Program, which distributes documents to depository libraries in the United States and its territories from the Superintendent of Documents in Washington, D.C. The program includes both monographs and serials. Libraries may select desired documents from the publication list provided by the Superintendent of Documents. For serial titles, the initial selection serves as a standing order and future issues and volumes will continue to arrive. Depository libraries are obligated to make documents available for public use and to retain accepted documents in the collection for at least five years. State governments also provide depository programs for designated libraries in the state, and some international agencies may also have depository programs.

The serials unit usually is not responsible for managing the depository program, but it may be responsible for processing document serials after they are dispatched to the library, especially if there is no government document unit in the library. Receiving and processing document serials is similar to handling regular orders, but claims are quite different. Since the Superintendent of Documents distributes documents according to the selections submitted by libraries, it has very few copies available for claims. If claims are not submitted immediately after the distribution, hope of getting a missing issue is very slim. If the claim fails with the superintendent of documents, a library has to submit a request to the issuing agency or send a request to the Document Expediting Project, popularly known as Doc. Ex., managed by the Library of Congress. Another resource is a nearby regional depository library. A regional depository library permanently keeps all government publications in its collection and is obligated to provide interlibrary loan and reference services to other libraries.

Approval Plans

An *approval plan* is an acquisition agreement between a library and its vendor. The plan is based on an agreed-on profile indicating the types of materials and subject areas desired by the library. The vendor selects new publications that fit the profile and sends them to the library with an invoice. After reviewing the materials, the library may exercise the right to reject a certain percentage of publications and pay only for accepted materials. Rejected materials are returned to the vendor. Approval plans offer libraries timely delivery of new publications, complete coverage, and staff time savings by eliminating order work for individual titles.

Approval plans mainly are designed for monographs and managed by monograph acquisitions. Periodicals are excluded from such plans, but continuations such as annuals, numbered monographic series, pseudoserials, and multiple-volume monographic sets may be included. For instance, the approval plan vendor may supply volumes in a monographic series as they are published. A rule to remember is that standing orders for continuations and inclusion of continuations in the approval plan are mutually exclusive. Otherwise, duplicates will be received from both acquisition methods. A library has to decide whether it wishes to receive continuations through the approval plan or standing orders. It is hard to judge which method is more efficient because they are influenced by the vendor's performance and local practice. Including continuations in the approval plan may save the work of setting up and maintaining individual standing order records, but standing order records provide better inventory control.

Blanket Orders

Some publishers offer blanket orders to supply to the library all or part of their publications as they appear. Unlike the approval plan, which is managed by the vendor and includes multiple publishers' publications, with blanket orders the library deals directly with one publisher, and there is no option for returning unwanted materials. However, the advantages are similar. Both provide speedy delivery of new publications, ensure complete coverage, and save order work for individual titles.

If a blanket order includes mainly serials, it should be managed by the serials unit. Managing blanket orders is similar to managing memberships: a record summarizing the order profile, a receiving record for each serial title in the order, and cross references to link the two records. The payment method may vary with different publishers. It may be treated as a subscription with fixed prepayments, or payments may be required when volumes are sent to the library. Some popular blanket orders are offered by international organizations such as the United Nations and the Organization of American States, as well as research organizations such as the Brookings Institution and the Rand Corporation.

Chapter 6

Processing Serials Acquisitions

This chapter explains the essential steps involved in processing serials acquisitions and serves as the basic guide for developing a library's serials acquisition working procedures. *Guidelines for Handling Library Orders for Serials and Periodicals*[1] and *Serials Acquisitions Glossary,*[2] both prepared by the Serials Section, Acquisitions Committee of the Association for Library Collections and Technical Services of the American Library Association, are highly recommended as consultation documents for preparing serials acquisitions procedures. When developing a library's working procedures, it is important to consider the local environment in addition to following basic guidelines. A library's organization, staffing, budget, serials control system, and vendor agreement may all influence the procedures. If a library uses a vendor, the vendor's customer handbook often contains explanations and instructions relating to the processing of serials acquisitions. That also may need to be incorporated into the local procedures.

New Orders

There are three types of serials orders: new, renewal, and back-file orders. New orders start the acquisition process for current and future publications, renewals extend current orders, and back-file orders are for specific published issues and volumes. New orders initiate the long-term order commitment and recurring actions that comprise the main work of serials acquisitions.

Searching and Verification

When a serials acquisitions unit receives an order request, the first step is to perform a search of a library's serials order records to determine whether the library already has a current order for the title. If a current order exists, the request is disregarded unless the intention is to place a duplicate order, such as an additional copy of a popular title or a copy for a branch library. If a library has no current order, the search proceeds to verify order information. General library practice is to prepare a search card to record the verified order information. The verification search first determines whether the title is being published and is available for order. Then it identifies the title, ISSN, publisher, publisher's address, commencement date, frequency, and price. Any features and conditions attached to the order offering are noted, such as availability in both paper and electronic formats or offering only through a membership. In addition, accompanying materials are not to be overlooked. When the publisher supplies title pages for binding, cumulative indexes, supplements, etc., the search card should include such information and indicate whether these materials are included in the subscription cost or are optional on payment of extra charges.

If selectors rely on the search card to make the final acquisition decision, they may request the inclusion of information that influences selection decisions, such as where the title is indexed and who else holds the title among the library's potential resource-sharing partners. The searcher may discover that the library has no current order for the title but holds some back volumes (e.g., it could be a monographic series with some individual volumes ordered through firm orders or a periodical with some back files from a gift). These discoveries should be noted, as they may influence the selector's decision on back orders. A search card also includes the selector's acquisition instructions, such as the fund code and the starting volume and year. Adding the searcher's name provides the source for information verification, especially when there is more than one staff member performing searches. Since the information may change over time, noting the search date is important. After the selector makes a final decision, the serials librarian has to review the search card for accuracy and completeness of information and determine the most appropriate supply method and source.

To sum up, a search card may include information on title, ISSN, publisher's name and address, commencement, frequency, price, indexing information, back-file holdings, holdings in collections of resource-sharing partners, selector, fund code, order starting date, back-file order instruction, supplier, searcher, searching date, and a note area for whatever other information may be required or useful. This may appear to be an overwhelming amount of information for a search card, but a thorough and accurate search can prevent errors in ordering and eliminate extra work to correct the errors later. The selector, the serials librarian, and the order staff all rely on the search card to obtain a clear understanding of the requested title, to make the correct acquisition decision, and to process an accurate order. Not all libraries need to include all these items of information on their search cards; a library's local policy and practice influence the inclusion and exclusion of information. Libraries usually design a search card that caters to their information requirements to improve efficiency and contribute to the quality of the search. After an order is placed, the search card may become a part of the order file and be kept for future reference. Figures 2 and 3 demonstrate the differences between a complex and a simple search card.

FIGURE 2. Complex Search Card

Serials Search Form

Title/Commencement: Clinical Microbiology Reviews, v.1, no.1, Jan. 1988–

Publisher: American Society for Microbiology, 1325 Massachusetts Ave. NW, Washington, DC 20005

ISSN: 0893-8512 **Frequency:** Q **Price:** $121

Index: Biol. Abstr., Chem. Abstr., Ind. Med., Sci. Cit. Ind., etc.

Holding libraries: NYCM, NYCX, PAUM, CTYA, etc.

Order: S.O. v.8, 1995– , B.O. vols. 1–7 (Microfiche/UMI) **Supplier:** Ebsco

Selector: ACS **Fund:** sbmpp **Searcher:** KBC **Date:** 3/15/95

Approved: CD Committee **Date:** 4/5/95

Notes: Available in microform from UMI. DCLC record attached. Cat. to Per.

FIGURE 3. Simple Search Card

Serials Search Form

Title/Commencement: School Librarians Workshop, v.1, Sept. 1980–

Publisher: Library Learning Resources, Inc., 61 Greenbriar Dr., Box 87, Berkeley Heights, NJ 07922.

ISSN: 0271-3667 **Frequency:** M (except Jul.–Aug.) **Price:** $42.99

Order: S.O. v.15, 1994+ **Supplier:** Publisher

Approved: B. Smith **Date:** 9/15/94

The best sources for searching are publishers' fliers and catalogs. If these are not readily available, cataloging records in a shared database, such as OCLC, RLIN, or WLN, can be checked and will supply information on indexing and holdings in other libraries. Libraries connected with the Internet have access to all the catalogs available in this network. The Internet serves as a vast bibliographic and holdings information source. Trade bibliographies, vendors' catalogs and databases, and national bibliographies also are good information sources. If the searcher fails to acquire sufficient information from these sources, an inquiry letter to the publisher or an appropriate vendor should produce a positive result.

Placing Orders

Orders are prepared according to the information and instructions on the search card. An order should clearly indicate the library's request and give instructions on delivery and invoicing. A typical order consists of the following information:

Identification. This part of the order may include author and title, ISSN, publisher's name and address, order date, and a library-assigned order number. When a vendor is used, there is no need to supply addresses for trade publishers or well-known organizations because they are available in the vendor's file. Providing addresses for obscure presses or organizations may avoid delays in processing. Libraries traditionally assign each order a unique number to avoid misidentification. Orders produced by automated systems bear unique record numbers assigned by the system. Some vendors assign a title number to each title in their file and request that their customers quote the number in all orders, claims, and correspondence. These numbers are available in vendors' databases, catalogs, or handbooks distributed to libraries. They also serve to avoid confusion and errors. When a library orders multiple copies for a heavily used title or for branch libraries, it is a good practice to assign a separate order number for each copy, especially when copies are sent to different locations, to eliminate confusion when processing claims or cancellations.

Starting volume/date. Since serials are continuous publications with past, current, and future volumes, the order has to specify what volumes are to be included in the order. For a new serial title, libraries always start the order with volume 1. For an ongoing serial with back files, it is not a simple matter to decide what to include in the order because the library's request, the vendor's supply policy, and the publisher's stock are involved. Based on user needs and budget allowances, a library can choose to start the order with the current volume without ordering any back files, to include some back volumes, or to include complete back files. Some vendors accept only orders starting with the current volume, some allow the inclusion of limited back volumes, and others handle all back files, including out-of-print materials. Although very few domestic serials vendors handle out-of-print materials, most foreign vendors do, and they provide their customers with the convenience of placing one order for all issues. Publishers consider the latest published issue as the current issue and all previous published issues and volumes are back files. Most publishers keep an inventory of two to three years of back files and can supply them as long as they are available in stock. However, some mass-circulation magazines do not even keep back issues for the current volume.

It is a safe practice for libraries starting a new serial order to begin with the current volume and give separate consideration of and instructions for back files. One might ask if the vendor handles back orders and whether desired back files are still in print. Libraries may prefer to deal separately with vendors who specialize in serial back issues and out-of-print materials for their back-file orders. If back files are to be included in the initial order, instructions should separate the subscription and standing order from the back order. A sample instruction is "Start the subscription with volume 3, 1995, back order volumes 1–2, 1993–94." In this case, volumes 1 and 2 have already been published, and volume 3 is the current volume.

In general, publishers are able to supply current issues very quickly but are slower with back issues. When they are unable to supply back issues included in an order, they may or may not inform the vendor or the library. Often a library has to make a claim to discover it. If the subscription vendor also handles out-of-print materials, it will search for missing issues for the library. Otherwise, to complete the volume, the library has to order the back issues from out-of-print materials vendors or other sources. Details of handling back-file orders will be discussed later in this chapter.

Price. It is good practice to quote the price for regular serials, such as periodicals and annuals, indicating how much the library is committing. However, the quoted price often differs from the price on the invoice. Prices are constantly changing, which makes it difficult for searchers to pin down the current price. The invoiced price often is higher than the quoted price because shipping and handling charges are added. Libraries usually accept the difference if it is within a certain predetermined percentage. If the difference is too large, the supplier may send an inquiry to confirm whether the library wishes to fulfill the order at the higher price. Price quoting is not commonly done for irregular serials.

Address. Libraries have to provide the supplier with the correct addresses for delivering materials and sending invoices. These are commonly referred to as the *ship to* and *bill to* or *sold to* addresses. Depending on a library's local policy, the ship to and bill to addresses may be the same or different. If a main library handles its branch library's orders and processes those invoices for payment, while the periodical issues are shipped directly to the branch, the addresses will differ.

Notes. Notes may be required to explain some special features and conditions, such as an order attached to a membership, a request to exclude supplements from the subscription, or a rush order. For microform orders, notes must be made to explain choices of microfilm or microfiche: positive or negative; silver halide, diazo, or vesicular; and 16 mm or 35 mm for microfilm. If a serial is offered in multiple formats, the note can be used to specify format choices.

Internal notes. Since libraries always keep copies of orders in their file for internal reference, there may be a need to record some local information, such as fund codes or special processing instructions. This information should be placed in a section clearly marked "for internal use only." Otherwise, it may confuse the supplier and create errors and delays in processing.

All of the preceding order information may not be needed or suitable for electronically transmitted serials. Typically, ordering electronic serials requires sending requests through computer networks to the editor or publisher's electronic mailing address. Sometimes, an order request has to use the exact command for the publisher to recognize and register the order. Since electronic serials are part of a new format that still is unsettled, there are no uniform rules to follow in ordering them. A valuable reference tool for ordering electronic serials is the *Directory of Electronic Journals, Newsletters, and Scholarly Discussion Lists,* published by the Association of Research Libraries.[3] This annually updated directory provides specific instructions for electronic access to each publication.

If a library uses a vendor and has a preagreement on order format and conditions, it should be followed consistently. Some vendors supply forms to their customers so that orders are prepared according to vendor information requirements. Since this practice is intended to improve efficiency and service, libraries should comply and cooperate as much as possible. If a library uses an automated serials system that prints orders, it should discuss the order format with the vendor before sending orders. Some serials control systems and serials vendors' systems allow ordering online or by using magnetic tapes and disks. This also should be discussed and the feasibility tested before implementation.

When there is an urgent need, a library may request a rush order. This means both the library and the supplier give priority to the order and apply the fastest communication and shipping methods in processing it. For instance, instead of using the regular postal service, the library may use fax, express delivery services, or electronic mail for ordering, and express mail or commercial services such as United Parcel Service (UPS) and Federal Express (FedEx) may be used for delivery. The library should be ready to pay the extra cost incurred in such rush processing. Vendors may absorb some costs for rush orders as a service feature. If so, libraries should not abuse this service and should reserve it only for truly urgent requests.

After an order is sent to the supplier, the library should always keep a copy of the order on file to serve as a reference for verifying proper receipt and payment. There are various ways to arrange the order file; a library has to choose the arrangement most suitable for its local needs. Common choices are filing according to order numbers, titles, or suppliers. In automated systems the order record is stored when the order is placed. Multiple access points to computerized order records eliminate the agony of choosing the absolute best filing arrangement.

Receiving

To speed up the delivery process, publishers send subscription issues of periodicals directly to libraries even when subscription agents are used. With the direct-shipping arrangement, subscription agents have no information on their customers' receiving status and assume all is well unless libraries send claims to report problems. For standing orders, agents receive materials from publishers, then reship them to libraries. Most vendors send the invoice and shipping list with the shipment, which makes the receiving process and invoice verification easier.

Establishing a Check-in Record

Since serial orders are received continuously and there are possibilities that the supplier may forget to send some issues, drop the order by error, or send the wrong materials, a check-in record for each order has to be established to track its receiving record in detail. A check-in record may be established at the time the order is placed or when the first issue/volume arrives at the library. In a manual system, a copy of the order is kept in the check-in file until the first issue/volume arrives. This enables the receiving staff to identify the arrival of a new order. In automated systems, the order record is automatically linked to the receiving record.

In a manual system, libraries use visible files for check-in records. Each order has a separate record. If a library orders more than one copy for a title, each copy should have a separate order number with a separate check-in record to eliminate confusion in receiving and claims. Libraries usually use preprinted cards to record receipt. The receiving cards, or Kardex cards, provide information to identify the order, notes for processing, and space for recording the receipt. The filing arrangement of check-in cards is controversial. Some libraries file according to main entries and others use titles. Using a main entry has the advantage of maintaining consistency with cataloging records. Actually, the majority of serials' main entries are titles. If a corporate body is used as the main entry, a title reference card may link it to the main entry record. In an automated system, check-in records are designed by the system, and there is no filing controversy.

A check-in record may typically consist of the following elements:

Order information. The detail level of order information depends on the size of the serials collection. A large collection needs more information than a small one. Title, ISSN, and order number are the basic elements required to identify the order. Frequency, supplier, and the starting volume/date of the order are important to guide proper receiving and claiming. The publisher's name is useful in differentiating publications with the same title.

Check-in provisions. This section provides space to record the receiving status in detail. The design of this space should provide flexibility for recording various numbering systems used by publishers. Usually there are different designs catering to periodicals and nonperiodicals: periodicals use a box format and nonperiodicals use a line format. Figure 4 shows a manual check-in record, and figure 5 is an automated record from the Innopac serials control system. Figures 6 and 7 are examples of a box format check-in screen for periodicals and a line format for annuals.

Location and processing instructions. Location should include the permanent location, such as a call number or the periodical stack for bound periodicals, and the temporary location, such as the reading room for current periodical issues. If each volume in a monographic series standing order receives analytical cataloging, then the location note should be something like "cataloged separately" or "sent for analytical cataloging" to indicate its treatment. Location notes serve as processing instructions for the receiving staff. A periodical reading room location indicates that current periodical issues are to be sent to the reading room, and a "cataloged separately" note indicates that monographic series volumes are to be sent to the cataloging unit.

Retention decisions. If a serial is not kept in the collection permanently, there should be a note to indicate its retention period. Some sample notes are "Keep until microfilm is received"; "Latest year only"; and "Do not bind, keep latest year only," which is used for materials that lack permanent value for the collection and will be discarded after a year.

FIGURE 4. Manual Check-in Record

	Faxon: 017203	Order# P-07328	S.O. v.20, 1988-	
CALL NO.	NOS. PER VOL.	VOLS. PER YEAR	FREQUENCY	TITLE PAGE
US GS4 .23	4	1	Q	INDEX
	BOUND: Bd each vol. standard #375			
	PREPARED: Per RR	IN BINDERY		
				DEMCO

YEAR	SER.	VOL.	JAN	FEB	MAR	APR	MAY	JUN	JUL	AUG	SEP	OCT	NOV	DEC	T.P.	I.	CLAIMED
1993		25			1 / 3.8.93			2 / 6.9.93			3 / 9.1.93			4 / 12.3.93 bd			
1994		26			1 / 4.2.94			2 / 6.5.94			3 / 9.9.94						

INC.		JAN | FEB | MAR | APR | MAY | JUN | JUL | AUG | SEP | OCT | NOV | DEC	BIND
		Prologue: Quarterly of the National Archives	

Source: Demco, Inc.

FIGURE 5. Summary Screen of a Title with Multiple Copies and Locations

```
B1901345        BIBLIOGRAPHIC Information
TITLE           The Quarterly review of economics and finance
PUBLISHER       Champaign, Ill.: Bureau of Economic and Business Research,
                University of Illinois, c1992-

                Summary of Attached Records
CHECKIN         1 > COPIES: 1; LOCATION: klmr; CHECK-IN=Card: Status is current, 12 bo
CHECKIN         2 > COPIES: 1; LOCATION: alex; CHECK-IN=Card: Status is current, 24 bo
CHECKIN         3 > COPIES: 1; LOCATION: dana; CHECK-IN=Card: Status is current, 16 bo
CHECKIN         4 > COPIES: 1; LOCATION: camdn; CHECK-IN=Card: Status is current, 47 b
ORDER           5 > LOCATION: klmr; FUND: bupk; STATUS: f; PAID=Inv# 089606 Dated: 10-2
ORDER           6 > LOCATION: dana; FUND: ecpd; STATUS: f; PAID=Inv# 089708 Dated: 10-2
ORDER           7 > LOCATION: alex; FUND: ecpa; STATUS: f; PAID=Inv# 089646 Dated: 10-2

To see a particular attached record, Key its number
E > EXAMINE BIBLIOGRAPHIC                    A > Create CHECKIN Record
Z > MOVE Records                             O > OTHER options
Choose one (1-7, E, Z, A, P, R, Q, O)
```

Source: Innopac Library System–Serials

FIGURE 6. Check-In Screen of Record 2 from Figure 5

C1081585 Last updated: 05-26-94 Created: 10-28-92 Revision:
TITLE The Quarterly review of economics and finance
LABEL PER LOCATION alex
NOTE RR, B#571-BD EA V.-G92-S1388

Boxes 1 to 14 of 24

Spr 94	Sum 94	Fal 94	Win 95	Spr 95	Sum 95	Fal 95
ARRIVED 05-25-94 34:1 1	ARRIVED 08-30-94 34:2 1	ARRIVED 11-30-94 34:3 1	EXPECTED 02-28-95 34:4	E 05-30-95 35:1	E 08-30-95 35:2	E 11-30-95 35:3
Win 96	**Spr 96**	**Sum 96**	**Fal 96**	**Win 97**	**Spr 97**	**Sum 97**
E 02-29-96 35:4	E 05-30-96 36:1	E 08-30-96 36:2	E 11-30-96 36:3	E 02-28-97 36:4	E 05-30-97 37:1	E 08-30-97 37:2

C > CHECK in 34:4
O > Check in some OTHER issue
F > Scroll FORWARD
M > MAINTENANCE mode options
E > EDIT Checkin Record
A > ADDITIONAL options
Choose one (C, O, F, M, E, S, P, Q, A)

Source: Innopac Library System–Serials

FIGURE 7. Annual Check-In Record

C1017032 Last updated: 10-26-94 Created: 07-06-92 Revision:
TITLE The Annual review of anthropology
LABEL GN1.A623 LOCATION alex
NOTE CIRCULATES

Boxes 1 to 5 of 24

box # 1
ARRIVED on 10-24-91 20 1991

box # 2
ARRIVED on 10-26-92 21 1992

box # 3
ARRIVED on 11-10-93 22 1993

box # 4
ARRIVED on 10-24-94 23 1994

box # 5
EXPECTED on 10-21-95 24 1995

C > CHECK in 24
O > Check in some OTHER issue
F > Scroll FORWARD
M > MAINTENANCE mode options
E > EDIT Checkin Record
A > ADDITIONAL options
Choose one (C, O, F, M, E, S, P, Q, A)

Source: Innopac Library System–Serials

Notes. Permanent notes include bindery instructions, routing notes, etc. Temporary notes include those concerning the need to notify a recommender upon receiving the first issue, the need to consult the selector to make the retention decision, a publisher's announcement of temporary suspension, a claim note, etc. With serials being so changeable and problematic, many notes are needed. Temporary notes should be made in pencil on the manual receiving card so that they may be erased when they are no longer applicable. An automated system should allow notes to be deleted.

Check-In

Newly received serials being prepared for check-in in a manual system should be sorted alphabetically by title so the receiving staff need not move around the Kardex file to locate different alphabetical sections. Sorting is not necessary in an automated system because check-in records are stored in the database.

When the first issue/volume of a new order is received, it is sent for cataloging. For serials with open-entry cataloging, such as periodicals and annuals, one cataloging record covers all the past, present, and future issues in the title. For serials needing analytical cataloging for individual volumes, such as monographic series, each volume with a distinctive title is sent for cataloging.

To record receipts in a manual system, use pencil to allow for possible corrections. In addition to recording the chronological and numerical sequence of each issue/volume, it is a good practice to record the date of receipt. The relationship between the sequence and the date of receipt illustrates a serial's general receiving pattern. For instance, one periodical has a prompt publishing schedule, so the library receives the January issue in January; another periodical has a consistently delayed schedule of approximately three months, so the January issue normally arrives in April. The receiving pattern is useful in predicting the arrival of future issues and determining when a claim is due. In recording monographic series, each volume's author and title should be recorded in addition to the series number. Since a series volume is often identified by its distinctive author and title instead of its series number, this information is useful in tracking the receiving status of each individual volume.

Processing

After serials are checked in, they should be marked or labeled with their location designations and should receive property and date stamps. Magnetic security tapes may also be inserted at this time. A word of caution: never stamp, mark, or tape a serial before it is properly checked in. If for some reason materials are to be returned, suppliers do not accept copies that have been irreversibly marked by libraries. After processing, issues should be distributed to their appropriate locations. Some may be sent to their permanent locations; others may go to an interim location (e.g., periodical issues to the reading room, monographic series volumes to the cataloging unit, annuals to the stacks, paperback volumes to the bindery unit, microfilm to the microforms room, CD-ROM to the reference room) and some issues are routed to designated readers according to a routing list. Routing slips have to be attached to issues being routed. These slips contain the title, volume/issue number, a list of names to whom the issue will be routed, and instructions on the disposal of the issue after it has been read by the last person on the list.

Receiving Electronically Transmitted Serials

Serials in paper, microform, and off-line computer formats (such as CD-ROM, disk, and tape) all come to the library as physical objects. Although there are minor differences, the receiving process is similar. When serials arrive via telecommunication, they are not corporeal objects but are visible only on the computer screen. How to receive, store, and deliver them to the user are matters of special consideration and handling. Libraries are exploring different methods to deal with this new format. According to the Association of Research Libraries, "The decade of the 1990s will continue to be an era of experimentation, with research libraries individually and collectively involved in providing local and remote access to electronic journals."[4]

The receiving staff needs specific training on accessing electronically transmitted serials from publisher's databases. Typically, receiving is done by checking the database regularly, according to frequency. Some publishers send an electronic mail message to subscribers alerting them to the distribution of a new issue. Publishers may not distribute the full contents but may inform libraries to use a file transfer protocol (FTP), such as Gopher server, to obtain them. There are a variety of methods for processing receipts. Issues can be stored in the institution's mainframe computer database, downloaded to a disk, or printed on paper. Since scholarly electronic journals generally are published by academic institutions and distributed on the Internet free of charge, libraries may include their access command in the cataloging record for patrons to have remote access via the Internet. Serials librarians may want to consult ARL SPEC Kit 201, *Electronic Journals in ARL Libraries: Policies and Procedures,* when preparing procedures for processing electronic journals.[5] Although libraries may use different methods when receiving and distributing electronic information, it is important to establish a check-in record, similar to the method applied to other serials, for the arrival of each issue.

Renewal

To maintain the order continuously without interruption, subscriptions require renewal before the current subscription period has expired. The renewal process usually starts at least three months before the expiration date. If a library does not use a subscription agent, renewal is a time-consuming and complex task. Serials librarians must keep a record for each order's renewal status and take appropriate action in due time. Setting a common expiration date for all orders, such as the end of the year, is an essential step in coping with this complex task. Communicating with numerous publishers and sending renewal payments to each of them are time-consuming tasks. Since publishers have different renewal policies and payment requirements, the process gets complex.

When vendors are used, they are responsible for processing renewals in a timely manner. A library should have an agreement with its vendor indicating whether to renew all subscriptions automatically or first to obtain approvals each year. Being cautious, most vendors send renewal lists for their customers to review and check prior to renewal time. If libraries wish to cancel titles or make any order changes, they should notify vendors before the deadline. Otherwise renewals will be processed without change. Some publishers have the annoying habit of sending renewal notices to libraries even though subscriptions are handled by vendors. This practice makes librarians nervous about whether vendors are renewing orders properly. If a library has a reliable vendor, there is no need to waste time calling the vendor to verify a subscription's status.

Claiming

Claims are made when a library fails to receive issues of ordered serials on time. The most common claim is for skipped issues. This type of claim usually is detected by the receiving staff during the check-in process. As the current issue is received, they notice that the last issue has not yet been received. The second type of claim is for a complete breakdown in receiving. This can happen when a new order fails to show up, an existing order ceases to come, or back-file and replacement orders receive no response from the supplier. There also are claims for damaged or defective issues that arrive in mutilated condition or come with missing pages, upside-down pages, etc. The last type of claim is for wrong shipments when the supply does not match the order. Publishers usually allow only a limited grace period for claiming. Once this period is exceeded, the publisher may charge for the missing issue or declare that it is no longer available. Check-in records should be reviewed regularly, and claims should be sent as soon as the delinquency is discovered.

Identifying the Need for Claiming

Identifying the need for claiming in a manual serials operation system is a time-consuming task, especially when there is a complete breakdown in receiving. While skipped issues, damaged or defective materials, and wrong shipments come to the receiver's attention in the normal course of operations, a complete lapse can be discovered only by reviewing the receiving records. Sometimes a lapse may be discovered when users fail to locate wanted materials in the library and request the title. To discover receiving lapses, libraries must develop a method of reviewing the check-in records. One feasible method is reading the Kardex file at scheduled intervals according to publications' frequencies: weeklies need more-frequent review than monthlies, monthlies need more than quarterlies, etc. Libraries may use color codes to indicate different frequencies, attaching a colored dot at the bottom of the Kardex card where it is easily visible in scanning the file to guide the reading schedule. For example, the librarian may decide that weekly periodicals, coded in red, need to be reviewed monthly; monthly periodicals, coded in green, are reviewed quarterly; quarterly journals, coded in blue, are reviewed twice a year; annuals, coded in brown, are reviewed annually.

The efficiency of claiming takes a giant leap with an automated serials control system. The system can produce a claim-alert list by screening check-in records and listing titles that are overdue. This provides better claiming control than with manual systems and reduces the staff workload. However, the list has to be reviewed carefully to eliminate unnecessary claims. Titles may appear to be overdue but not really need claiming for various reasons, such as when the publisher has announced that the publication is temporarily suspended or delayed, a payment check is lost and no issues will be supplied until payment is received, the title has already been claimed and the vendor is working on a solution, or the title tends to fall behind schedule. For irregular serials, such as monographic series, determining the need to claim definitely requires human judgment. When irregular serials records are created on the system, predictions for expected receiving can be only loosely estimated. In addition, irregular serials are often published out of numbering sequence. Therefore, a system-produced claim list must be reviewed carefully by an experienced staff member who is familiar with publication schedules and receiving patterns. Otherwise, excessive claims may be generated that unnecessarily burden the library, the vendor, and the publisher.

To determine when a claim is due, libraries should set up a claim cycle for each title. A claim cycle is the waiting period, or grace period, for the late arrival before a claim is issued. It is set according to the publication's frequency. For example, a library may claim a monthly when it is fifteen days late, but a quarterly is allowed thirty days before a claim is issued. Setting the claim cycle is a tricky business. If it is too short, premature claims are generated; if it is too long, the claim period allowed by the publisher may be missed. With faster deliveries and shorter grace periods for claiming, libraries are setting shorter claim cycles. If a librarian is not sure what a reasonable cycle is, the vendor or publisher can suggest a realistic time frame for claiming.

Claim cycles only send signals to alert the librarian that a claim may be due. Further investigation is required to confirm the need to claim. Paying attention to order coverage, frequency, enumeration and chronology, publication pattern, receiving pattern, payment status, and supplier's reports is important in reviewing the need to claim. Order coverage provides limits for claiming. If the order starts with volume 2, the library has no right to claim volume 1. Frequency, enumeration, and chronology guide receiving expectations. Monthlies should come once a month, number 3 should come after number 2. However, this logical expectation can be upset by irregular publication patterns. Some serials follow publication schedules and numbering sequences faithfully, but others have uncontrollable patterns that pose difficulty in determining when a claim is truly justified. For instance, instead of publishing one issue a month at the beginning of each month, the January issue is published at the beginning of the month, February is published at the end of the month, there is no publication in March because the March issue is published with the April issue as a double issue and appears at the beginning of April. No one knows for sure when the May issue will be published and when the library should claim it. This periodical's past receiving pattern may shed some light on its wild publication pattern. In such a case, the claim staff may be wasting a lot of time in claiming each late issue systematically according to the claim cycle. A better method is to wait a bit longer to allow the expected issue to arrive. Payment status also influences the claim decision. If a library is late with a payment, it is better to hold the claim until the supplier has received the payment and can dispatch issues to the library. The claim staff has to pay close attention to suppliers' reports. There is no point in claiming an expected issue on a regular claim cycle when the supplier has already reported that publication is delayed or is suspended, or that an issue is being published out of sequence. Finally, always send the claim to the correct supplier. If an order is placed directly with the publisher, the publisher receives the claim. If a vendor is used, then claims are sent to the vendor. Pay close attention when an order is switched from the publisher to the vendor or from one vendor to another. If an order is switched from vendor A to vendor B starting with volume 11, the claim for volume 10 goes to vendor A, not vendor B.

Current events may also influence claiming. For instance, if a country has a postal service strike, a newspaper's workers are on strike, or the country is at war, publication and delivery of materials will be affected. Awareness of current events may save unnecessary claims.

Processing Claiming

After careful reviewing and screening, legitimate claims are sent to suppliers. Claims can be sent by telephone, fax, electronic mail, magnetic tape, disk, online, or postal or delivery service. The library's claim policy, the urgency of the claim, the library and supplier's communication facilities, and the agreement between the library and the supplier may influence the choice of method. Libraries and their vendors usually have a claiming routine; thus, working with vendors is easier than sending claims to numerous publishers. For efficiency and simplicity, claim forms are preferred over letters. Forms spare the library staff the need to compose individual claim letters, help suppliers identify precisely who is claiming what, and determine whether the claim is legitimate. A typical claim form includes the following information:

Library identification. The library's name and address are needed for the supplier to identify the customer and send claimed material to the correct address. To validate the legitimacy of the claim, the name and address have to correspond with those given in the order. If the library has a customer or account number assigned by the supplier, quoting it may speed up the customer-identification process.

Order identification. Title, publisher, ISSN, and order number are helpful in identifying the order. Some vendors may want libraries to quote the title number assigned by the vendor. If the publication being claimed is part of a membership, be sure to note it and include the membership number.

Materials being claimed. Clear indication of the numerical and chronological sequence of the material being claimed is essential to avoid the wrong response.

Payment status. If the payment has been made, inform the supplier and quote the invoice number as verification. If the invoice has not been received, this may be an indication that the order has been dropped by the supplier. In this case, request both the invoice and the material.

Claim date and the claim number (first claim, second claim, etc.). The claim date is important not only for monitoring the claim but also for relating it to the publisher's grace period. If there is no response to the claim, the library may send follow-up claims after a predetermined waiting period of one to three months. Foreign publications need more time than domestic ones to respond.

Notes. As with everything associated with serials, there may be possible exceptions and unpredictable facts that need to be explained in the note area.

Supplier's response. Blank space should be provided to record the supplier's response.

In a manual system, claim forms are usually produced in multiple copies. Two copies are sent to the supplier so that one can be returned to the library with the response; the library keeps the third copy in its claim file. Some libraries keep two more copies in the file to accommodate the possible need for second and third claims when there is no response to previous claims. After a claim is sent, a note about issues being claimed and dates is recorded on the check-in record as a status reference. A claim file should be maintained for monitoring purposes. Arranging the file by claim date, and then by title, allows chronological review for timely follow-up actions. When a claim is fulfilled, its form is pulled from the file, the note is deleted from the check-in record, and the case is closed. When a claim gets no response during the preset waiting period, the library should send follow-up claims. Libraries routinely process three claims. If there still is no response, the library may give up on the claim and try to order the missing volume/issue or take more-aggressive action by calling the supplier or sending an inquiry signed by the serials librarian. There really is no set formula for dealing with claim problems. At times, it may not be worthwhile to invest too much time and effort in chasing a hopeless claim. It may be more economical to give up the claim and pay for the missing issue, especially when the issue is urgently needed by a user and is not expensive or is on the verge of going out of print. If the material being claimed is expensive then persistence and aggressiveness in claiming are definitely called for.

Automated serials systems should be able to print claim letters or even communicate claims with the vendor's system online or by tape or disk. There is no need to keep a separate paper claim file because the system records the claim status automatically and generates reclaims as needed.

However, for complicated claim problems a small file may still be needed for correspondence, proof of payment, etc.

Receiving Problems

Besides making claims for missing materials, libraries also have to deal with the problem of receiving damaged, defective, or wrong materials. Libraries should contact the supplier to explain the problem, request the proper replacement, and ask for permission and instructions for returning the unwanted material. If the problem was not caused by the library, the supplier should bear the postal cost for returned materials. Some publishers supply return mailing labels to eliminate having to refund postage to the library and to ensure that returned materials are received by the proper operational unit.

Libraries also may receive unrequested duplicate copies of their orders. These may result from a premature claim: one copy is the regular shipment, the second copy is the supplier's response to the claim. Other reasons could be that the publisher or the vendor entered the library's order twice, the fulfillment center produced duplicate mailing labels with slight variations, or the packing staff made a mistake. When a duplicate is received, a timesaving strategy is to hold the duplicate and wait. If no more duplicates appear and there is no invoice asking for payment, consider the case closed. To play it safe, a duplicate should be held for a while just in case the supplier requests its return. If the duplication continues or an invoice comes, then the supplier has to be notified about the error and asked to investigate the cause and solve the problem. The library may assist with the investigation by supplying clues, such as copies of mailing labels and information about the invoice. However, before blaming the supplier for the mistake, an internal investigation should be done to determine whether a library error initiated the duplication. The library may have to bear the consequences of the mistake and offer a reasonable solution.

Invoices and Payment

Various types of subscription invoices and credits have been discussed earlier in this chapter. As a rule, subscription invoices always precede the shipment of materials, and prompt payment of invoices is important to receive materials without delay. Invoices for other types of orders usually come with the shipment. When publishers want to receive payment before dispatching materials to libraries, they send prepayment invoices. Such an invoice is also known as the *proforma.*

Invoice Verification

Verification is the first step in processing invoices for payment. Invoice staff checks the invoices against orders and receiving and payment records as necessary to verify that the charges are legitimate and accurate. When an invoice comes with a shipment, it should be checked against the materials received. If it comes with a partial shipment, payment usually is held until all the materials charged on the invoice are received. As a general rule, an invoice is ready for payment only after proper verification. However, verification of a large subscription renewal invoice consisting of thousands of titles can be very time consuming. It is not practical to hold payment until every title is checked. After a general review, if there seem to be no major errors, the invoice usually should be paid as is. The invoice staff will then proceed with title-by-title verification and solve problems with the vendor later if errors are found.

Usually the serials unit does not actually pay the invoice after verifying it. Payment is handled by either the library's or the parent institution's accounting office. Each institution has its own rules and regulations for processing payments. The invoice staff must understand and follow the procedures set by the accounting office. In general, the invoice staff links payments to the proper fund codes assigned by selectors and provides that information on invoices. This information is entered in the accounting records to produce proper expenditure reports and to track each fund.

Payment Records

Before a verified invoice is sent to the accounting unit, details are entered on a payment record. Payment records are used for tracking payments, verifying invoices, and issuing claims. A typical payment record contains the supplier's name (either the publisher or the vendor), order number, title, fund code, and a space for recording payment details. These details include the invoice number and date, processing date, amount paid, and subscription period or volumes covered by the payment. A note area is useful for recording invoice problems or complex payment plans, such as a problem about duplicate invoices or an order shared by two fund codes.

Invoice Files

An invoice file contains copies of paid invoices. The file usually is arranged according to the fiscal year, then by the supplier's name and invoice numbers. The accounting office maintains this file as its working records and to comply with local auditing requirements. Since this file is useful in verifying payments to solve invoice problems, some serials acquisitions units also keep such a file. For auditing purposes, this file has to be kept for a period designated by the auditor, but for problem solving, invoices older than two years are rarely consulted. A well-kept payment record is usually sufficient for solving most invoice problems. In addition, if the accounting office regularly produces financial reports providing references to payments and invoices, there are few occasions when checking copies of paid invoices is required. Unless the serials acquisitions unit has difficulty in obtaining information from the accounting office, it is not worth the effort of keeping an extra file that is rarely used. Some serials units maintain the invoice file to produce serials expenditure reports. However, this need is diminishing as sophisticated financial systems capable of producing a variety of reports are installed in accounting offices.

Invoice Problems

Invoice problems occur often, but they may not necessarily be caused by libraries. The keys to success in solving invoice problems are keeping good invoice and payment records, using analytical skills, and communicating effectively with suppliers. Following are explanations of how to handle some common problems.

Statements. When payments are overdue, suppliers send statements listing delinquent invoices. Some institutions are consistently slow in processing payments due to backlogs or cumbersome accounting procedures. In the meantime, suppliers or publishers have automated accounting systems that are exceptionally efficient in producing statements. An experienced staff member often knows which statements can be ignored and which should be checked carefully. If the institution is slow in processing payments, the first statement of overanxious suppliers may be ignored because payments are most likely on their way. If statements continue to come, then the payment records, the accounting reports, or even the invoice files have to be checked to verify the payment status. If an institution pays invoices promptly and the supplier has a reasonable statement schedule, then even the first statement needs attention.

A statement usually lists invoice numbers and the amount of each invoice, but not the materials it covers. A common method in dealing with statements is checking the accounting office records to decide whether a payment was sent and the check was cashed. If the payment has been sent but the check has not been cashed and a sufficient amount of time has elapsed, the accounting office may assume the check is lost and request that the bank stop payment for the lost check. It should then issue a new check to the supplier. However, to avoid unnecessary work and expense for the accounting office, before the library requests that the accounting office cancel the check, it should ask the supplier to review its internal records to make sure the check has not been received. If the accounting record shows that the check has been cashed, then a proof of payment may be required by the supplier. Usually the proof is a copy of both the front and the back of the returned check. Sometimes, when checking the statement, the library may discover that an invoice has never been received or has been lost during processing. In such cases, a replacement invoice has to be requested from the supplier.

Tardiness in payment not only generates statements but also delays receiving wanted materials. While checking statements is time consuming for libraries, sending statements also costs suppliers time and money. The best way to avoid statements is to improve the efficiency of the invoice and payment processing procedure and to handle incoming invoices promptly.

Invoice errors. There are a variety of possible invoice errors, such as overcharges, undercharges, and duplicate charges. When an error is discovered, the library may not make corrections on the invoice and process it for payment as corrected unless there is a written agreement with the supplier or special permission to allow such corrections. Without sufficient proof of such agreement or permission, an accounting office will not pay the corrected invoice. There are two commonly used methods for dealing with invoice errors. One is asking the supplier to issue a new invoice. In this method, the library has to make sure the supplier cancels the incorrect invoice; otherwise, the library is stuck with two invoices and a larger problem. The other method is paying the incorrect invoice and asking the supplier to issue a credit for the overpayment or send a supplemental invoice for the underpayment. When this method is chosen, the library has to make sure the supplier issues the credit immediately after the overpayment is received. This method should be reserved for suppliers who deal with the library regularly and have good credit. The advantage of the latter method is to speed up the receipt of materials when the supplier is holding the shipment due to the unpaid invoice.

Wrong shipments or duplicates. Libraries should not pay an invoice for the wrong shipment or duplicates due to a supplier's mistake. A library has to report the problem to the supplier, ask permission to return the unwanted materials, and request that the invoice be canceled. Each step taken in solving such problems has to be coordinated with the supplier. Copies of correspondence and other records should be kept in a file for problems. It is good practice to keep the problem file for a period of time after the problem has been solved. Sometimes, if the supplier neglects to cancel the invoice, a statement may come asking for payment. This starts another round of problem solving. Records from the previous problem-solving process may speed up and simplify the new one.

Back Orders

Serial back orders include replacement and back-file orders. Replacement orders are often for a single issue or volume, and orders are processed routinely by staff members. Back-file orders are usually for several consecutive volumes, and the order process should receive close attention from librarians.

Replacement Orders

Missing serials discovered by the staff when collecting current issues for binding, or by users failing to locate wanted library materials, may be false alarms when serial issues are temporarily misplaced and show up after a search through the reading room or around the library. Libraries usually have a missing-materials report procedure that provides instructions and sets a time limit for searching before declaring the materials lost. After a missing-materials report is verified and confirmed, the next step is to decide whether the missing serial should be replaced. Libraries replace materials that will be kept permanently in the collection. If paper issues are to be replaced by microform or if they have a limited retention period, it is not cost effective to spend time and money to replace them.

If replacements are for microforms or electronic formats, they should be obtainable from the publisher because copies are easily made to fulfill the order. Since paper editions have limited printings, once the publisher runs out of stock, the replacement order process can become complex. Various sources for replacement orders include publishers, vendors, back-issue dealers, and exchange groups. For domestic serials, if the issue is not out of print, the publisher is the best source. With the exception of mass-circulation popular magazines, most periodicals publishers maintain back files for two years or more. Since most missing issues are discovered at binding time, the chance of getting a replacement from the publisher is quite good. If the publisher is unable to fulfill the order, the library may place the order either with back-issue vendors or other exchange sources. Most back-issue vendors' main business interest is supplying volumes of back files, not single issues. They may handle a single issue for their regular customers as a favor, but the charges can be very high. For out-of-print serials, exchange groups are good sources for replacement orders. The Universal Serials and Book Exchange (USBE), a nonprofit organization located in Washington, D.C., was once used by member libraries to send their duplicates and request replacements and back files. Unfortunately, it went bankrupt in 1989. Zubal, a back-issue vendor, revived it in 1990. USBE now stands for United States Book Exchange and is located in Cleveland, Ohio. Libraries that wish to use USBE must join as members. Faxon provides an automated serials exchange database linking participants who wish to sell, buy, or trade back issues, called Serials Quest. Libraries occasionally circulate lists of serials they plan to discard. Other libraries may request them before the discard deadline. In the fall of 1994, a new list named BACKSERV was created on the Internet as an informal forum for libraries wanting to exchange serial issues. Libraries can post issues as "wanted" or "available" to help each other in fulfilling back orders. This list is hosted by the serials agent Readmore, Inc.[6]

Most domestic serials vendors do not handle replacement orders, but foreign vendors are willing to provide this service to their subscription customers. Because ordering replacements directly from foreign publishers is made difficult by geographical distance and language barriers, the fact that foreign vendors accept replacement orders saves headaches for serials librarians and reduces staff workloads. In addition, most foreign vendors search for out-of-print issues, which makes foreign orders convenient one-stop shopping.

It is important to process replacement orders as soon as the missing status is confirmed. Delay in ordering decreases the chance of fulfillment. When a library fails to obtain a replacement issue, it may search for alternatives in microform or reprint. If replacements are obtained in a different format, sufficient linking notes should be provided in the holdings record to lead users to the replacements. With increased opportunity for purchasing articles from commercial document-delivery services, a library may choose to purchase all articles in the missing issue as an alternative.

The replacement order process is similar to that for new orders. It involves ordering, receiving, claiming, and paying the invoice. The difference is that it does not require a check-in record for continuous receiving. Being a firm order for specific issues or volumes, once the order is fulfilled and the payment is made, the process is complete.

Back-File Orders

Publishers are the best source for back-file orders of materials that are still in print. When materials are out of print, libraries must either deal with vendors who specialize in back issues and out-of-print materials or send a request to an exchange group. If libraries decide to obtain back files when the initial order is placed for a title, it is possible to ask the same supplier to supply both back files and new orders, depending on its business policy. For foreign back files, the best source is a library's regular foreign vendor because this vendor usually will accept back-file orders and search for out-of-print materials.

Unlike current-material vendors who maintain no stock but forward orders to publishers, back-issue vendors maintain their own stocks plus a network of fellow back-issue vendors who cooperate in searching for customer requests in their inventories. By using a single vendor, a library actually reaches a network of vendors. The prices of back files are unpredictable. Usually they are higher than current publications, especially when they are out of print and hard to find. Some back-issue vendors distribute catalogs listing their inventories and selling prices. If the price is unknown, the serials librarian should ask for a price quote before commiting to the order. A common practice in ordering out-of-print materials is sending a "want" list to the vendor, obtaining the result of the search and the price, and making a final purchase decision. After receiving the vendor's report, the library should respond promptly because the vendor may be able to hold the material for only a limited time if there is demand from other customers.

Serial back-file orders can be fulfilled only when the material in demand is available and the price is right. The order process requires the serials librarian's close attention to identify the appropriate supply source and to make acquisition decisions. Some libraries may choose to acquire reprints or microforms instead of chasing after expensive and elusive out-of-print back files. These formats not only are cheaper but also require less time and effort to acquire. Some scholarly journals have begun to convert their back files into electronic formats, which offers another alternative for acquiring back files, especially for titles to which the library already subscribes in electronic format.

Cancellations

Timing is most important in processing cancellations, especially for periodical subscriptions. Once a subscription has been renewed and paid for, it is very difficult to cancel the order and obtain a refund because most publishers do not refund subscription cancellations. Therefore, cancellation decisions have to be made before renewal time. If a vendor sends the library a renewal checklist, the best time and the simplest way to cancel orders is to cross off unwanted titles from the list and notify the vendor to proceed with cancellations. For direct orders, ignoring renewal notices and holding payment for invoices does not equal a legitimate cancellation. A formal cancellation notice has to be sent to the publisher before renewal time.

For standing orders and back orders, an order cancellation should be sent as soon as the cancellation decision is made. Libraries have to accept materials sent by suppliers before the arrival of cancellation notices. However, in some cases it is possible to negotiate for the return of unwanted materials and obtain refunds for any payments made less the shipping and handling charges.

If orders are not placed with vendors or if the library fails to cancel an order by crossing it off a vendor's renewal checklist, the supplier must receive cancellation notices or letters. The notices should include the library's identification, order identification, and effective date/volume number of the cancellation request. It is very important to provide an accurate link from the cancellation request to the proper order record in the supplier's file. When manual order files were kept by suppliers and libraries, a copy of the original order attached to the cancellation notice was the best way to ensure the proper match. With automation, order information has been converted to the supplier's and the library's computer files, and paper copies may no longer exist. If the order has a unique order number assigned by the library and registered in the supplier's file, quoting this number in the cancellation notice is essential. Sending a copy of the mailing label is also good insurance because the mailing label is produced from information in the supplier's file. Furthermore, cancellations have to be sent to the proper supplier. If a vendor handles the order for the library, the cancellation goes to the vendor, not the publisher.

Mail Sorting

"If only the mail would stop coming for a few days to let us catch up with our work!" is a common remark made by serials staff members. The amount of mail coming to a serials department is overwhelming, and sorting it is a mind-boggling and time-consuming task. However, prompt and accurate mail sorting is essential for maintaining an efficient serials acquisitions operation. A guide for separating mail into different categories and distributing it to the appropriate person increases sorting speed and accuracy.

First, mail should be divided into two categories: packages and letters. This can be done by an entry-level staff member. Most packages contain materials ordered by the library; therefore, the receiving staff are the ideal people to open and sort packages. They are familier with titles on order, which contributes to speed and accuracy. Titles that lack check-in or order records may be title changes; periodical sample issues; publishers', vendors', or library suppliers' catalogs; or wrong deliveries. It is not uncommon for the serials unit to receive a mail-order catalog for jewelry and clothing. After the sorting, packages are divided into subcategories of routine check-ins, title changes, sample issues, catalogs, wrong deliveries, and junk mail. Each subcategory is then distributed to the appropriate staff member. For example, serials on order are checked in by the receiving staff; sample issues and catalogs go to the search/order staff who will then distribute them to appropriate subject selectors; title changes go to a paraprofessional who is responsible for the follow-up actions of setting up a new receiving card under the new title, providing linking notes between the new and old titles, sending the new title to the cataloger, etc. Wrong deliveries are sent to the correct receivers and most other materials can be discarded.

Letter sorting requires a well-trained staff member who has a general idea of the serials operation and knows who is responsible for specific functions. The most important letters are from vendors and publishers relating to library orders, claims, and invoices. These should be delivered promptly to the responsible staff members. Other business letters may go to the serials librarian. A large portion of the mail will consist of promotional flyers from publishers, which are distributed to selectors.

The preceding description is only a sample of a mail sorting-and-distribution pattern. The actual guide used in the library must be based on the local organization and its distribution of responsibilities. It is important not to treat mail sorting as a simple clerical task. A lower-level staff member may be able to handle preliminary sorting, but a higher-level staff member should check mail that does not belong to an obvious category listed in the guide. Some mail definitely has to be handled by the librarian. Mail-sorting staff should be cautious and curious. They should avoid being too quick to discard.

Mailing labels provide clues in mail sorting. An experienced sorter often can decide whether something is a library order or junk mail by checking the address pattern on the mailing label. Publishers and vendors use mailing addresses specified by the library orders; some conscientious suppliers even include the order number or customer number on the mailing label. Libraries with large serials operations find that having a slight variation in the address for different mail categories speeds up the sorting process. For example, periodical subscriptions may have "Box P" added after the department name, nonperiodical serials have "Box S," replacement orders have "Box R," claim correspondence has "Box C." However, using personal names in the mailing address should be avoided. Using "care of Mary Smith" for subscriptions because Mary is the check-in staff member is not a good idea. If Mary quits or her responsibilities change, her name in the mailing address will create confusion.

Notes

1. Association for Library Collections and Technical Services, Serials Section, Acquisitions Committee, *Guidelines for Handling Library Orders for Serials and Periodicals,* rev. ed. (Chicago: American Library Association, 1992).
2. Association for Library Collections and Technical Services, Serials Section, Acquisitions Committee, *Serials Acquisitions Glossary* (Chicago: American Library Association, 1993).
3. Michael Strangelove and Diane Kovach, *Directory of Electronic Journals, Newsletters and Academic Discussion Lists,* 1st ed.– (Washington, D.C.: Association of Research Libraries, 1991–). The latest edition available at this writing is the 4th edition, published in 1994.

4. Elizabeth Parang and Laverna Saunders, comp., *Electronic Journals in ARL Libraries: Policies and Procedures* SPEC Kit 201 (Washington, D.C.: Association of Research Libraries, 1994), 2.
5. Ibid.
6. Marilyn Geller, "BACKSERV: The Serials Back Issues and Duplicate Exchange List," *Newsletter on Serials Pricing Issues* 124 (22 Oct. 1994). Geller is one of the list owners and may be reached via Internet: MGELLER@READMORE.COM. The BACKSERV archives may be retrieved by sending a message to LISTSERV@SUN.READMORE.COM.

Chapter 7

Preservation and Bindery

The two types of preservation done for library materials include a process for rare materials that conserves both their contents and physical integrity and a process for ordinary materials to conserve only the contents. The latter is of concern when the items involved are serials.

Serials Preservation Methods

Currently, three methods are used in preserving serials information. One is protecting the paper format by binding; another is photocopying the information or reproducing it in microform; and the third is putting the information into electronic technologies, that is, disks, tapes, etc. The first two methods have long been on the scene, but the third method is a newcomer and is developing and changing.

Each method has advantages and disadvantages. Binding paper issues not only preserves the contents of serials but also maintains the original publications. Compared with the other two methods, however, the binding process is cumbersome. Bound volumes take up a lot of shelf space, and paper continues to deteriorate over time. In addition, the binding process is repeated by each library that wishes to preserve the material, while a one-time preservation process is all that is needed for conversion to microform or electronic media to the benefit of all libraries.

The advantages and disadvantages of replacing bound serial bindings with microforms were discussed in chapter 1. Although the use of microforms is widespread in libraries, binding is also a popular preservation method because users prefer reading paper print.

The new option of electronic preservation has great potential because it offers added features to users, such as portability and easy access to information through computer searching techniques. Electronic versions can be viewed by users at offices or homes with the appropriate computer connections and downloaded to users' personal files or made into printed copies. The new generation of library users, who have become addicted to the convenience offered by computer technology, may be expected to prefer this new format over reading serials in their original paper forms. Currently, CD-ROM is popular with publishers and libraries. As soon as the technology of converting retrospective printed information into computer databases becomes more efficient and less costly, this preservation method may replace both binding and microfilming.

Choosing preservation methods is a local decision that should consider, among other things, users' needs, collection development policies, shelf space, budget, staff, and automated systems. Currently, binding is popular and is the only preservation choice for those serials that are unavailable in microform or on electronic files.

Bindery in Libraries

Libraries with extensive rare-book collections may handle conservation binding internally. Since serial binding is not done by hand but is highly mechanized, almost all libraries use commercial binders. It is simply not economical for libraries to maintain heavy bindery equipment and a trained crew. However, some libraries may maintain a small-scale binding operation for minor repairs.

Although the work is done by the binder, librarians are responsible for deciding what, when, and how serials are to be bound. They also make appropriate preparations for the binder to pick up materials to be bound and to receive bound volumes, pay invoices, and maintain records. Since periodicals generally constitute the majority of bindery work, it is important for the serials librarian to understand the serials binding process, whether or not overseeing the bindery function is specifically his or her responsibility.

A separate bindery department or bindery unit in the acquisitions department, serials department, processing department, or another department may be responsible for binding operations. It is strictly a local organizational choice. For libraries with branches in different locations, centralization or decentralization of the serials bindery function is a controversy with no perfect solution. Centralization appears to be more economical and to offer better quality control because the library needs to maintain only one bindery team, which is well-trained and experienced. It also simplifies the pickup process because there is only one pickup and delivery location. However, centralization requires that branches pack and deliver periodical issues to the central bindery unit, and bound volumes have to be delivered back to branches. The longer delivery process prolongs the time that serials are unavailable to users.

Binding Methods

Binding basically covers pages with a hard cover to extend the useful life. For periodicals, multiple loose issues are bound together to create the volume.

The two basic binding methods are sewing and gluing. Sewing methods include oversewing, sewing through the folds, and side sewing. Sewing through the folds is preferred by most libraries because it gives a sturdy binding, and it does little damage to the inner margin of the text. It is important to protect the width of the binding margin as much as possible because volumes with narrow margins may not be rebindable should the necessity arise. Sewing through the folds also allows the bound volume to be opened flat for easier reading and copying.

In the gluing method, a method known as double-fan adhesive binding is popular because it is cheaper than sewing. Applying strong modern adhesives twice by double fanning holds the binding well. Volumes bound using this method also open flat. Deciding which binding method is appropriate is based on the physical condition of the item, the thickness of the volume, the width of the margin, and the nature of the loose sections. Other deciding factors are the anticipated use and the bindery budget. To obtain a better understanding of different types of binding methods and binding terminologies, consult the *Library Binding Institute Standard for Library Binding.*[1] The commercial binder's sales representative should be willing to explain different types of bindings and their advantages, disadvantages, and costs.

Bindery Selection

General criteria for choosing a bindery include the quality of binding, array of services, prices, and business reputation. A library should choose a commercial bindery that is a member of the Library Binding Institute (LBI), follows the binding standard set by the Institute, and is certified by the LBI. This ensures a level of quality in workmanship and materials. The LBI is an association of library binderies and their suppliers established in 1935. Its main purpose is to formulate and promote standards for library bindings.

Good services are reflected in prompt pickup and delivery of materials, short turnaround periods, open communications, prompt responses to claims and problems, and ability to simplify the bindery process. Prompt service means setting and keeping regular pickup and delivery schedules with short turnaround periods. The turnaround period is the time between pickup and delivery of materials. During this period serials being bound are not available to users; therefore, libraries should negotiate the shortest possible turnaround period. Most binders will make weekly trips to the library for pickup and delivery, but very few can offer a one-week turnaround period. A two- to three-week time lag is common. Automation enables binders to assist libraries in simplifying the binding process, such as supplying preprinted bindery slips and keeping a library's binding instructions and records in the binder's database, using electronic communication to replace bindery slips, or interfacing with the library's serials control system.

Binding prices differ with methods, the quality of materials used, and the types of materials being bound. Sewing is more expensive than gluing. Hand sewing is more expensive than machine sewing. Better-grade buckram is more expensive than lower grade. Periodicals are more expensive than single volumes because of the extra work in collating and attaching multiple sections. Other factors also may influence the price. Rush binding may cost more; a larger customer receives better prices or a volume discount. Binders usually present price lists for different categories of binding. Categories may be divided by physical medium, such as books, periodicals, re-bounds, archival packs, or conservation bindings. Categories are further divided according to binding methods and the quality of materials selected. For instance, in periodical binding there is a choice of class-A binding, standard binding, etc. The price may also include a specification of how many characters or lines are allowed for spine labels; by exceeding the specification the library may incur extra charges. Buckram colors used for covers may be limited, with extra charges for other color choices. In examining the price list, category specifications should be reviewed carefully. Pickup and delivery service is generally included in the price.

In addition to quality, service, and price, a binder's business reputation, stability, equipment, automation facilities, and investment in developing better preservation techniques are important considerations. The process of evaluating and selecting a binder is similar to the method applied to screening other vendors. Libraries should determine local needs, then contact potential binders, make comparisons, and ask for their customers' references. It may be wise to visit the binder's plant before making a final choice.

Similar to subscription agents, bindery sales representatives keep in close contact with customers. Bindery exhibits are also visible at American Library Association conferences and other bindery-related professional gatherings. This may not be true for small local binders who operate in an old-fashioned business style and cannot afford modern practices; however, the local binder should not be overlooked. When a library's main binder is not within close driving distance to the library, a small local binder is helpful for rush bindings, special treatments not easily accommodated by massive binding machines, and other binding business. Libraries can have more than one binder just as they can have more than one supplier.

Bindery Processing

A good library bindery operation has policies in place to guide decisions such as which types of materials are to be bound and the selection of the binder. It also provides processing procedures and records the binding instructions and status for each title.

When to Bind

Nonperiodical serials in paperback usually are bound when they are received. If reference materials are urgently needed by users, then binding may be delayed until their peak use is over. However, paperbacks may not survive prolonged periods of heavy use without binding. Rush binding is a solution for materials in urgent demand with anticipated heavy use. Some reference materials are discarded once they are superseded by new editions. In theory they should not be bound; however, in reality, paperbacks may not survive handling during the retention period. Some binders offer a basic binding that is cheaper than regular binding for materials with low usage or limited retention periods.

Periodical issues of the same volume usually are bound together in one physical volume or into more than one if they are very thick and heavy. (A bound volume should not be thicker than one and a half inches.) Publication frequency and thickness of issues influence this decision. It is reasonable to assume that when the first issue of the current volume is received, it is time to bind the previous volume. When a serial volume needs to be bound into several physical volumes, especially if the publication is a weekly or daily, issues may be bound more frequently to avoid having too many loose issues cluttering the reading-room shelves and risking loss or damage. However, it is important to leave the most recent issue in the reading room because users are anxious to read it and do not want to wait until it returns from the bindery.

Instructions should be issued to cover each title's binding schedule, such as bind each volume or bind twice a year. Determining where to keep the instructions is a local choice. A common practice is to keep them in the check-in record so that the check-in staff can flag items for binding during the receiving process. Some libraries prefer to keep the instructions in a separate bindery file and periodically review it to determine which titles are due for binding.

The binder and the library should set up mutually beneficial schedules and then stick to them as closely as possible. Altering schedules may disrupt the regular work flow for both the library bindery unit and the binder, resulting in congestion in processing after the holding period.

Collecting Issues for Binding

Periodical issues are collected from the reading room according to binding instructions. If all issues to be collected are found, they are put in numerical or chronological order and tied together, then forwarded to the bindery staff for binding preparation. Unfortunately, collectors often find some issues are missing or mutilated. In such cases, replacements have to be ordered. (Details on replacement orders were discussed in chapter 6.) If issues are damaged beyond in-house repair capabilities, a replacement copy must be ordered. Libraries may request missing pages from interlibrary loan or borrow the issue containing these pages to copy them. Since most periodicals are now published with acid-free paper, missing pages should also be copied using acid-free paper to prolong their useful life. Judgment must be exercised to decide whether it is more economical and efficient to copy pages or to purchase a replacement when an issue has a large number of missing pages.

When a library must obtain replacements for missing issues, it faces the choice of either leaving the other issues of the volume in the reading room and postponing the binding until all material is received or binding the volume with issues missing. Waiting can be frustrating because leaving loose issues in the reading room may result in losing more of them or creating messy shelving problems. In addition, once the serial is out of print, fulfilling replacement orders becomes more difficult. Therefore, waiting may never end. Some libraries hold other issues in offices or work rooms while waiting for replacements to arrive. Although this practice provides security, it creates a public service problem because users cannot locate issues either in the reading room or in the bound periodical stacks. If the choice is to bind the volume with issues missing, then the volume has to be re-bound later when replacements are received, or the replacements have to be bound separately from the main volume. It is clear that there is no perfect solution for the situation. A compromise is to set a reasonable waiting period for replacements to arrive; beyond that period, the volume is bound with issues missing. When replacements arrive after the binding, rebind the volume if it is possible; otherwise, bind replacements separately.

Bindery Preparations

Since serials are bound continuously, volumes that belong to the same title should be given consistent treatment in binding quality and physical appearance. Each title has instructions specifying the binding category, frequency, spine label (title, format of numerical or chronological sequence, call number or location symbol), cover color, and any other special considerations. After examining materials to be bound, the staff prepares a slip for each group of issues to be bound together as one physical volume that contains the library's name and address, spine label instructions, color codes, and other instructions as needed. This slip is used by the binder as the binding instructions for the volume.

If the library has an automated serials system that includes the bindery function, instructions can be stored in the system and produced on bindery slips as needed. If the binder has an automated system, this will contain the customer's bindery profile and instructions and may be able to produce preprinted bindery slips for the library to use. These slips usually contain fixed information for each binding title, such as the library name, title, call number, and color code. Library staff only need to fill in variable information, mainly the volume's numerical and chronological sequence. If the library's system can be connected with the binder's system, communications can be done electronically, thus avoiding the use of bindery slips.

An inventory list must be prepared for each batch of materials sent to the binder. Each batch usually is assigned a unique number for easy identification. When bound volumes are returned from the binder, they are checked against this list to verify the accuracy of the returns. Libraries usually keep a copy of the inventory list and each bindery slip sent within the batch in an in-process file.

Binders usually supply boxes for packing bindery materials. Boxes should be reusable for reasons of economy and ecology. Prepared materials are packed with a copy of the inventory list that notes how many boxes are included in the batch. Each box should be marked with the library's identification, which can be its name and address or a customer number assigned by the binder, the batch number, and box sequence number. Boxes now are ready to be picked up. Most binders use trucks for pickup and delivery. Parcel post or other commercial package delivery services may be used occasionally for rush or special delivery when only a few volumes are involved. Libraries usually pack and seal boxes the day before the agreed pickup date. Materials are packed as close to the pickup time as possible because users have no access to materials once they are packed in sealed boxes. If users need materials that are being prepared for binding, they should be allowed to use them with certain restrictions. Such restrictions might include use only in the office and limited time of use.

Receiving

Binders usually return all volumes in the same batch together with a copy of the inventory list. If some volumes are delayed, it should be noted on the inventory slip. The bindery staff must monitor the prompt return of bound volumes according to the agreed turnaround period. If some volumes are missing in the batch without proper explanation from the binder and are still missing in the next delivery, then a claim is due. Claims can be done by telephone or written messages given to the binder's driver for delivery to the customer service unit. A common cause of missing volumes is that one library's material was sent to another library by mistake. The binder also may lose or mutilate a volume during the binding process. In such cases, the binder must replace the volume for the library or pay for the library to obtain replacements.

Binding quality should also be examined during receipt. If libraries find some volumes with poor binding, or there are mistakes such as wrong spine labeling, issues bound out of the numbering sequence, or covers attached upside down, then volumes should be returned for correction.

Bindery invoices usually are issued according to binding batches. Staff should verify the invoice against the receiving inventory list and process the invoice for payment after all the volumes included in the invoice are received in satisfactory condition. A payment record should be maintained to record the binder's invoice number and date, coverage of payment, and the amount. Similar to serial invoices, actual payment usually is handled by the accounting office.

Bindery Records

In addition to the bindery instruction file, inventory list, and payment records, libraries need to keep the in-process record for public services. When serials records provide information about issues and volumes sent to the binder, users and library staff do not have to waste time looking for materials temporarily not available in the library. With manual systems, the check-in card may carry a bindery note to indicate which issues are out for binding. Adding the date the issues were sent to the binder helps to predict return dates, something anxious users appreciate. The binding note is deleted when the bound volume is received by the library. Some libraries avoid this time-consuming practice of updating check-in records by using the batch inventory list as a checklist for materials in the bindery. If a library uses an automated serials control system with a bindery-tracking function, the check-in record should show the binding status.

Note

1. Paul A. Parisi and Jan Merrill-Oldham, eds., *Library Binding Institute Standard for Library Binding,* 8th ed. (Rochester, N.Y.: Library Binding Institute, 1986). Readers may also consult Jan Merrill-Oldham and Paul A. Parisi, *Guide to the Library Binding Institute Standard for Library Binding* (Chicago: American Library Association, 1990).

Chapter 8
Records Control

Libraries contain numerous items and are constantly adding and deleting them. Librarians are accountable to users for knowing what materials are available or expected to be available and how to obtain them. They are also accountable to the administration for how the material fund is used. To fulfill these requirements, librarians must track every movement of every item starting from the time its acquisition action is initiated. Keeping accurate inventory and status records for each piece of library material is essential in maintaining an effective library operation and providing proper user services. Records control is the foundation for library functions. For serials management, there are four essential records: acquisition, cataloging, holdings, and circulation.

Acquisition Records

This group of records shows in detail a library's acquisition activities, that is, what has been ordered, received, and paid. A responsible and efficient acquisitions operation relies on well-kept records.

Essential Records

There are four essential groups of records in serials acquisitions: order, receipt, claim, and payment records. A serials acquisitions operation cannot survive without these records. Their contents and purposes have already been discussed in chapter 6. In this chapter their arrangement and maintenance will be discussed. The four essential record groups are closely interrelated and may need to be consulted simultaneously in performing acquisition functions. For instance, in claiming a serial issue, all four records may have to be checked to verify that an issue has been ordered and paid for but not received or claimed, or that a previous claim has expired. In processing an invoice, the order, receipt, and payment records may all have to be checked to make sure items being charged have been ordered but not paid for yet, and that receipt status is up to date. Therefore, the way a library arranges these records can affect its efficiency.

For convenience, it is ideal to keep all acquisition-related records in one file. It works well with automated systems if each staff member has sufficient access to the database. In an automated serials control system, all records are in one database and cross-checking different record groups is easy and quick. There may be different screens for bibliographic records, order records, receipt records, and payment records (claim status usually shows on the check-in record), but switching screens usually takes only the touch of a key.

Merged files in a manual system may cause problems. If there are several serials staff members, each with different responsibilities, who all rely on the merged file to perform their duties, they may have to take turns using the file. Separating records to different files may require that staff members check several files to complete a task.

There is no perfect file arrangement. Librarians can only choose the arrangement that works best for local circumstances and personal preferences. Generally speaking, merging files may yield more efficiency for a small operation with one or two staff members. For large collections, keeping records requires more details, which may make the combined file cumbersome. If sharing a merged file among several staff members proves difficult, separate files may be a better choice.

Among the four files, the order and claim files are more independent, while the receipt and payment files are difficult to separate. Order information mainly serves as the source to verify whether what is supplied matches the request when the receipt process starts for a new order. Once the order is established and receipts are ongoing, order records usually are checked only to solve problems. Therefore, libraries keep a copy of the order record in the receipt file until the receipt process starts. Then it may be moved to an order file that also contains other materials, such as the search card, the selector's request form, the supplier's confirmation letter, etc. Libraries may maintain two access points for order records: alphabetical access by the title or the main entry (achieved by keeping a copy of the order record in the receipt file permanently) and by the order number. This file is useful in solving mysteries when suppliers send invoices or correspondence with order numbers but illegible titles or different main entries from those contained in the library's records.

The claim file is a transitional file with records being constantly created, updated, and deleted. Since it must be monitored closely, a separate file makes for easier review. It is practical to keep receipt and payment records together because of the large amount of cross-checking done between the two. For instance, both receipt and payment records have to be checked to determine the need to claim, to process invoices for payment, and to solve acquisition problems.

If acquisitions records are kept in separate files, it is essential to provide links between them for cross-checking. For instance, a title's order, receipt, claim, and payment records may contain the order number as the common link and may use the same main entry. To achieve greater efficiency, it is common practice to use the receipt file as the main working file, with abbreviated information from other files added to it. This practice reduces the need to check multiple files while performing serials duties. For instance, brief order information added on the check-in card, such as the order number, the supplier, and starting date/volume, often saves having to check the original order record for verification and problem solving. A temporary note on the check-in card about issues being claimed and the action dates may save the need to check the claim file for basic status information. It is difficult to include payment information on the check-in card; therefore, the best practice seems to be keeping the payment card with the check-in card. Choosing the receipt file as the main working file is logical because it is the most frequently used of the files.

The serials acquisitions unit must have easy access to invoices when there is a need to verify payment status or to work with the auditor. (The invoice file was discussed in chapter 6.) Whether the file needs to be maintained only in the accounting office or also in the serials unit is a local choice. The auditor's basic concern is whether an invoice has been paid for a legitimate order and whether the purchased material has been appropriately received. From a paid invoice, the library should be able to produce a properly authorized order and the purchased material. Keeping order records with properly authorized selectors' order requests is important for auditing. However, with acquisitions automation, some libraries may choose to discontinue the manual order file and rely only on order records in the database to save time and labor. A manual file should be discontinued only after the auditor agrees to recognize the authority of the database.

If libraries use binding to preserve serials, keeping bindery records also is essential. Details of bindery records are explained in chapter 7. The bindery file may not be merged with other files because staff members rarely need to check other acquisition records during the bindery process. Some libraries have a separate unit handling the bindery function, so having a separate bindery file is most convenient.

Records for Alternative Acquisition Methods

As discussed in chapter 5, there are alternatives to purchasing serials through subscriptions, standing orders, and firm orders. Serials acquired through alternative methods need the same receipt and claim records, but payment records are not necessary if they are provided free of charge in gift, exchange, and depository programs. No matter what type of acquisition method is used, each serial title must have an order record. Different acquisition methods can be reflected in supplier information. Instead of a publisher's or vendor's name, which is typical for regular acquisition methods, the record may say "Gift of the John Smith Foundation," "Exchange with Beijing University," "American Library Association membership," etc.

Alternative methods may require additional records and files. Gifts need a donors' file that lists donors' names, addresses, contact numbers, and gift titles. It may also include relevant materials, such as gift conditions, claim method, or correspondence with donors. This file is useful in maintaining relationships with donors, issuing proper claims, and serving as the inventory source when a donor cancels the donation. Exchanges require an exchange partners' file, which contains partners' names, addresses, contact numbers, lists of receiving and giving titles, exchange agreements, and important correspondence. The purpose of this file is similar to the gift donors' file. Exchange programs also need a file for titles sent to partners to track dispatching activities. With depository programs, there may be a need to keep a file for government agencies that dispatch documents to libraries. In the U.S. Federal Depository Program, libraries keep an item cards file. These cards are distributed by the program with brief descriptions of deposit items. Each card is assigned an item number that serves as a unique identification.

Memberships require a memberships file, discussed in chapter 5. Approval plans and blanket orders need profile records to explain their conditions and inclusions.

Optional Records

Libraries with large serials collections that use multiple vendors and alternative acquisition methods often need to set up additional files to control their complex acquisitions processes. These optional files are not needed by every library. Record keeping is time-consuming and labor intensive, especially in manual mode. It takes careful assessment of the local environment and needs, plus good judgment, to decide whether it is cost-effective to keep certain records. Following are samples of optional files used by some libraries.

History file. Changes and problems that occur in a serial's long acquisition journey make the acquisition process complex. The history file tracks each order's acquisition history by keeping information that may answer questions and solve problems. Some libraries expand the order file into a history file. Typically, it includes the original order request and search card, a copy of the order sent to the supplier, the supplier's order confirmation, and any document relating to the order that has retention value, such as a supplier's notice about change in a subscription coverage, records of a vendor change, or a local decision for special cataloging treatment. This file may also be expanded into a problem file by keeping documents related to solutions to problems, such as correspondence with suppliers about wrong shipments or duplicate charges on invoices.

Source file. This is a suppliers' information file, which keeps names, addresses, contact numbers, and other supplier-related information. It also lists the library orders handled by each supplier. Source files are useful in maintaining effective working relationships with suppliers and providing inventory lists for vendor evaluation and possible switching. In the typical filing arrangement orders handled by an individual supplier are filed under the supplier's name by order number or title. To keep the information current when there is a supplier switch, orders have to be moved from the old supplier's file to the current supplier's file. Some libraries may expand this file to also serve as the history file by keeping all documents related to orders in it.

Decision file. This file contains miscellaneous information about titles that are not retained in the collection. Serials departments receive unsolicited samples and gifts, freebies from memberships, and supplementary materials. These samples usually are screened by serials staff members, then reviewed by librarians to make acquisition or retention decisions. Since many appear persistently, a decision record can save repeated reviews for titles already rejected by the library. When the check-in staff member cannot locate a receipt record for a title, a record in the decision file may provide a quick solution. The decision record can contain information on which volume/issue of what title has been reviewed by whom on what date and a note about the disposal decision.

Sample file. Samples play an important role during the acquisitions decision-making process. Some selectors do not make a final decision until a sample issue has been examined. This file may serve to track both sample requests and distribution activities. During the sample request process, this file may contain solicitation documents: letters to publishers soliciting free samples, purchase orders if samples require payments, or interlibrary loan requests for sample issues. Documents are updated with follow-up actions such as the receipt and distribution of samples. This file may also record the distribution of unsolicited samples to selectors, e.g., which issue of what title has been sent to whom on what date. Records are deleted after review decisions are received from selectors. If the decision is to acquire the title, the searcher uses the sample issue as source material. If the decision is negative, a record can be made for the decision file.

Routing file. The routing file keeps a record of the library's routing operation. It contains the names of individuals who receive serials and the titles being routed to them. The file needs two access points: one by personal name and the other by serial title. Both access points are important in keeping the integrity of the routing operation. For instance, if a person leaves the organization or changes jobs, his or her routing record must be deleted or revised by using the name access; if a title has ceased publication or has been canceled, then everybody receiving this title has to be notified.

Problem file. During the problem-solving process, there may be a need to keep relevant documents and correspondence as reference materials. Some libraries prefer to keep these materials with other record files, e.g., the receipt file; others prefer to keep them in a separate problem file for easier filing and review of the status of unsolved problems.

Desiderata file. When a library fails to fulfill back-file and replacement orders, the unfulfilled orders may be placed in a desiderata file. When the library receives other institutions' exchange and discard lists, vendors' back-file catalogs and sale fliers, or publishers' reprint announcements, they can be checked against the desiderata file and the library may be able to fill a gap in its serials collection. Some back-file vendors are willing to check a library's desiderata file against their inventories to provide possible matches.

Tickler file. This file is used to keep the integrity of a few selected, exceptionally difficult orders. It usually is arranged by month with action notes for each month. For instance, a publisher may refuse to accept standing orders for a serial publication and give no announcement for forthcoming new volumes. To capture the new volume in time, a library has to estimate the new volume's publication date, make an action note in the appropriate month as a reminder to make an inquiry, and then place the order for the new volume. If a selector decides to order an expensive reference yearbook only in odd years but a publisher will not accept a standing order with such a condition, the title has to be ordered with a firm order every other year at the time it is published. A tickler file helps libraries deal with these and other problems.

Complex Acquisition Records

Due to complicated or changeable publication patterns, some serial titles need a bit of extra effort to keep their acquisition records straight. There are no set rules for managing complex publications other than using housekeeping ingenuity. The following are sample cases that need extra attention and suggestions for records control. By no means should a librarian's imagination be limited by these suggestions. You may figure out a better way to control them after gaining some working experience.

Serials with subseries. When a serial contains subseries, its order record must indicate whether the library's order includes the subseries. Setting up a separate check-in record for each subseries is a better way to control receipts than mixing them in one record. Separate records provide more space to record the receipt and easier reading for receiving status. If the supplier charges the order as a package including both the main title and subseries, the payment record can be attached to the main series receipt record. Otherwise, the payment record for each series is attached to the appropriate receipt record. To keep all records in the serial title together, the subseries record should bear the main serial title followed by the subseries title.

Annuals published within monographic series. Some annuals are published as volumes in monographic series. With this publication pattern, it is difficult to locate the annual in acquisition records and monitor its receiving status. Mixing annuals with monographs in a series also causes confusion in the processing treatment of the series. While monograph volumes need to be sent for analytical cataloging, annual volumes need only a call number label. One way to handle this mixed-up series is to set up an additional check-in record for the annual title. An annual volume is first checked in as a volume in the monographic series and then rechecked in on the annual card. There should be a cross-reference to link these two check-in records and notes to explain their relationship.

Monographic sets within series. A multiple-volume monograph set may be published gradually in a monographic series. This is similar to annuals published within a monographic series, although annuals continue indefinitely but sets have a definite ending. For large sets, separate check-in cards may be added. For sets with only a few volumes, a processing instruction note on the check-in card should be sufficient.

Supplements and special issues. As explained in chapter 1, supplements and special issues come in a variety of modes, and it is not possible to cover all the varieties with treatment suggestions. Generally speaking, regular supplements and special issues are easier to deal with than irregular ones. Regulars may need separate check-in records to register and monitor their receipt properly. For instance, a monographic series published as supplements to a periodical needs a separate check-in card. When using separate records, there should always be a cross-reference to link the main serial with its supplements. Irregulars should be reviewed by the serials librarian or the appropriate selector to make retention and treatment decisions. In most cases, a receiving note on the check-in card should be sufficient for the acquisition record.

Supplementary materials. Some periodicals supply a cumulative index or table of contents for each volume. These items usually come with the last issue of the volume. If they are to be bound with the volume, a note must be added on the bindery record. Since a volume usually is not bound immediately after the last issue is received, the index or table of contents sheet has to be kept in a file in the office waiting to be bound.

Multiple formats. If a library record bears no format note, most assume the material represented by the record is in paper format. Therefore, if a library orders nonpaper format serials, its acquisition records must bear proper format designations. If a library orders a title in multiple formats, such as in both paper and microfilm, each format needs a separate acquisition record.

Title changes. A serial title change must be reflected in acquisition records. Following current cataloging practice, each new title needs a separate record, and linking notes should be made between the old and the new titles.

Other changes. Some publication changes affect the acquisition process and must be dealt with properly. For instance, frequency changes and sequence designation changes affect the receipt, claim, and bindery processes. These changes have to be updated in their respective records.

Potential duplicates. Some publications appear in multiple roles that cause libraries to receive duplicate copies for one title. For instance, a monograph title can simultaneously belong to two different monographic series; if a library has standing orders for both series, it will receive two copies. The monograph's title page usually carries the titles of both series to which it belongs. If the receiving staff member is thorough, both receipt records should be checked. If a copy has already been received under one series title, the second copy may be rejected, depending on library policies. If the receiving staff is not careful or the book gives no evidence of being published in two series, the duplication may be discovered during cataloging. At this point, the item may have already been property stamped and cannot be returned to the supplier. Additional cases include a monograph published both as an independent title and a volume in a series, a supplement to a serial title, and a periodical issue devoted to one topic. If library policy is to avoid such duplications, both the serials receiving staff and the monograph acquisitions staff must be extra careful in dealing with monographs with multiple roles to make sure they are not being received also as serials orders.

Records Maintenance

The more material and records in a file, the more difficult it is to keep the file in good order. Deleting obsolete materials and records from acquisition record files should be a regular routine. Ceased and canceled titles should no longer be kept in current files. Acquisition records for these inactive titles are either discarded or removed to an archival or history file. One must be certain all activities of a title have ceased before deleting its record from the current file. For example, although a title has ceased publication, a claimed issue may not have been received, a refund for next year's subscription fee may be outstanding, or binding may not be complete. If the library's policy is to discard inactive acquisition records, order and payment records should be discarded only if they comply with local auditing requirements. Auditing needs must be met. For instance, if the auditor checks acquisition activities within the past five years, obsolete acquisitions records have to be retained for five years.

Current titles also require record cleanup jobs. Paper check-in cards fill up quickly, especially for frequent publications. Cluttering the current receipt file with filled check-in cards makes the file unmanageable and slows down the check-in process. Once a periodical volume is bound, check-in records for the loose issues are no longer needed. For the sake of checking a serial's receiving pattern, it is usually sufficient to save one or two years' receiving records. Older check-in cards should be discarded or archived. Filled payment cards older than two years may also be removed from current files and kept in archival files according to local auditing requirements. Claim files should be reviewed constantly and records deleted as claims are fulfilled. It is a common practice for libraries to keep papers containing temporary information, such as supplier's reports, correspondence relating to a problem, or claim responses, with their check-in records. These papers should be weeded out as their information value becomes obsolete.

Records maintenance is equally important in automated systems to save database storage space and speed up the search process. Obsolete records should be deleted and noncurrent records moved to online or off-line archival files, depending on policies and database capacity. Temporary notes should be deleted when they become obsolete to free up space for current notes.

Cataloging Records

Cataloging records are created and maintained by catalogers as access keys to library collections. They are not discussed in this chapter because cataloging is not within the scope of this book. It is important for a serials librarian who is not also a cataloger to understand basic serials cataloging in order to maintain an effective working relationship with catalogers. If you lack the knowledge, reading a textbook on cataloging will help you begin learning about it. You may also consult articles relating to serials cataloging.[1]

Holdings Records

Holdings records show the parts of a serial held in a library collection. Since serials are issued in successive parts and are intended to continue indefinitely, libraries may not hold the complete run of a serial's published parts. Therefore, a library may hold a periodical title requested by a user but may not have the specific issue desired. A serials cataloging record without information on a library's local holdings tells only half the story to the public; a list of the holdings makes the story complete.

Acquisition, cataloging, and circulation records all contain holdings information. Acquisition records need to maintain holdings information to monitor the integrity of the serials collection and to process other activities, such as payments, claims, and bindery processing. Users rely on cataloging records to inform them of serials holdings in the library. Circulation must maintain holdings records related to borrowing and other use. Holdings are discussed separately in this section not only because of their vital importance but also because of complications involving how and where to keep different types of holdings records.

Description of Holdings

There are two ways to describe holdings. One is to make enumerative statements for each physical part of a title being held by a library, referred to as the *detailed level holdings;* the other states only the starting and ending parts and is called a *summary holdings statement.* For example, when a periodical is bound by volume, its detailed holdings statement is v.1 (1993), v.2 (1994), v.3 (1995). If the periodical is a quarterly and its volume 3 is not bound yet because only two issues have been received, then the record for 1995 is v.3:no.1 (1995: Jan.), v.3:no.2 (1995:April). This record will be changed to v.3 (1995) when the volume is completed and bound. The summary holdings statement for this periodical is v.1 (1993)–v.3 (1995). If the periodical still is being published and the library continues the subscription, then the holdings statement is left open as v.1 (1993)– .

Besides the level of detail, there are different options for expressing holdings statements. The previous summary holdings example may be expressed differently as v.1–v.3, 1993–95; some libraries may use a plus sign (+) instead of a hyphen for open holdings. If there are gaps in a continuous holdings listing, one library may express it as v.1–v.10, with gaps; another library may use v.1–v.5, v.7–v.10 to indicate the library lacks volume 6. Furthermore, there can be differences in the inclusion of captions, such as v.1–v.3 or v.1–3.

Detailed level holdings statements show the most-accurate inventories by giving the exact count of individual physical items, but these consume both time and space. This level has the capability of expressing the unique status of each item, such as whether an item is in bindery, in circulation, or missing. Acquisition and circulation records are kept at the detailed level because of the need to track down every item's movement in these processes. Summary holdings usually are used for public information, such as the holdings display in the public catalog and the union list of serials. This level usually is sufficient in serving the needs of the general public. If there is a need for detailed holdings information, such as what the latest received issue is or why a specific item is not in the stacks, acquisition and circulation records can be checked.

Holdings Standards

There are two main standards for recording holdings statements. The National Information Standards Organization (NISO, also known as "Committee Z39") of the American National Standards Institute establishes rules for preparing consistent, standardized records for all serials in all physical forms. Its original standard for *Serial Holdings Statements at the Summary Level* (ANSI Z39.42-1980) was replaced by the *Serial Holdings Statements* (Z39.44-1986), which provides identifications and specifications for holdings at all levels.[2] The standard identifies data areas, data elements, and punctuation to be used in holdings statements and provides specifications for displaying data elements. The Library of Congress publication *USMARC Format for Holdings Data* (MFHD) serves as the standard for coding holdings information in the machine-readable MARC format. It provides variable fields to record enumeration and chronology; through the machine manipulation of data, holdings can be displayed at different levels. MFHD was first published in 1984 as the *USMARC Format for Holdings and Locations* (MFHL), and it has been updated since. The first group of libraries to use this format are eight members of the Southeastern Association of Research Libraries (SEARL) for the purpose of developing a regional resource-sharing system for serials.

Descriptions of holdings may be dependent on local choices. However, considering the popular practice of sharing resources among libraries by forming union lists of serials or viewing each other's serials records in the shared databases, holdings standards must be met to enhance resource sharing. Yet, converting local holdings to the standard frequently is not done for several reasons. The conversion of holdings records to the ANSI standard and the use of MARC format for holdings present libraries with a tough challenge. While bibliographic records are universal and libraries may copy them from shared bibliographic databases, holdings records are unique to each library's local holdings. Serials holdings are changeable and elusive. It is hard to control serials activities in the stacks because items may disappear or appear without reason or warning. Before starting a massive project of converting holdings into the ANSI standard or using the MFHD, libraries usually perform a holdings inventory so that time and effort will not be wasted in converting inaccurate holdings records. This requirement adds more complexity and effort to the conversion project. Since both holdings standards were developed in the late 1980s, libraries still need time to test them. Libraries burdened with a budget crunch, staff shortage, booming demand for electronic publications, and endless effort and money needed to keep up with automation will make converting local holdings to standards a low priority unless required to do so by a union listing or resource-sharing group. Some libraries started to input and display holdings in their OPAC by using their local system-defined format before the development of the MFHD. Now they are faced with the challenge of converting local practices to national standards. Their hope is that their system vendors can provide an algorithm that will automatically convert their records to the standards.

Location of Holdings Records

There are a variety of places in which serials holdings records are stored in a library.

Acquisition Records

A serial's holdings statements first appear in the receipt records. The receiving status of each part is recorded in detail on the check-in record. For periodicals, the check-in record is transformed into the bound-holdings record when several loose issues are bound into one physical volume. A bound-volumes holdings card is usually kept with the check-in card in the manual system to serve as the holdings record. For continuations, the check-in record may serve as the holdings record. Keeping the continuation and periodical bound holdings at the detailed level or the summary level is a local choice. Although updating detailed records takes time and effort, a high-quality acquisitions operation and strong support for public services depend on accurate inventory records and the ability to track the activity of each individual part of a serial title.

Public Access Catalog

Holdings statements in the cataloging records serve the purpose of informing users about which parts of a serial title are held by the library. Where to keep serials holdings for public consultation is quite a controversy. For good public service, the best policy is to include the holdings statements in the public catalog. It not only saves users' time and the frustration of checking a second source for holdings but it also reduces the number of holdings-related inquiries to public service staff members. However, if the library has a card catalog, recording holdings on every serial catalog card filed in the public catalog is a labor-intensive job that not all libraries can afford. There are different local practices to deal with it. For example, holdings may be kept on one or more of the following: the main entry card, the shelflist, the acquisition receipt record, etc. Public catalog records without holdings statements need a reference note leading users to the holdings information source. There are so many different local practices that Lynn S. Smith listed sixty-one serials holdings reference notes in *A Practical Approach to Serials*

Cataloging.[3] Recording holdings in automated catalogs is much less work because they require only one data entry for each title. Including holdings in cataloging records has become important because it also supports resource sharing when libraries check the shared bibliographic database or union list of serials for interlibrary loan requests.

Automated Serials Control System

Automated serials control systems are mainly designed to serve the acquisitions function. However, they may also provide public service in the form of access to serials holdings. Systems with public service modules usually provide a public viewing screen containing a brief bibliographic record; location; summary holdings; information on the latest received issue/volume; and relevant notes about gaps in holdings, multiple formats, volumes in bindery, etc. Figure 8 shows a public access screen of the Innopac system. Libraries may place terminals dedicated to the serials control system in the public service area or link the serials control system with the OPAC to have holdings information as a menu choice. System security usually limits public access to only the holdings display designed for patrons.

Showing detailed holdings to the public instead of summary holdings is controversial. There may be occasions when a user needs to check the detailed holdings, but the majority of users' questions are answered by the summary holdings and information on the latest received issue/volume.

FIGURE 8. Holdings Record for Public Access

```
You searched for the TITLE: quarterly review of economics and f

TITLE          The Quarterly review of economics and finance.
PUBLISHER      Champaign, Ill.: Bureau of Economic and Business Research, University of Illinois,
               c1992-
CONTINUES      Quarterly review of economics and business 0033-5797.
DESCRIP        v. : ill. ; 23 cm.
               Quarterly.
               Vol. 32, no. 1 (spring 1992)-
LIB. HAS       ALEX PER SHELVED BY TITLE v.32- 1992-
               KLMR PER SHELVED BY TITLE CURRENT ISSUES ONLY CDPER 1992- ON:

 1 > KLMR PER
   Latest received: Fall 1994 34:3

 2 > ALEX PER
   Latest received: Fall 1994 34:3

        4 holding records to view — Press 'C' to see more of them

Key NUMBER to see recent receipts, OR
D > Display HOLDINGS                          F > FORWARD browse
M > MORE BIBLIOGRAPHIC Record                 N > NEW Search
R > RETURN to Browsing                        O > OTHER options
Choose one (1-4, D, M, R, F, N, A, C, P, O)
```

Source: Innopac Library System

Cluttering the screen with detailed holdings can make it more difficult for users to sort out information.

Automated Circulation System

The automated circulation system contains detailed holdings statements for serials that circulate. Each title is linked with its detailed holdings. Bar-code information is attached to each item. Holdings are entered in the system-defined field. Besides circulation, these holdings records may be used for other purposes, such as for inventory in collection management and for usage studies for collection development.

Serials List

Some libraries offer a serials list for checking holdings. The list may contain all types of serials or only periodicals. Typical information for each title includes a brief bibliographic description, its location, and holdings. This is similar to entries in a union list of serials. Reasons to offer such a list may vary. The public catalog may not include serials records, or its coverage of serials may be incomplete or lack holdings information. It may be provided as an extra service for users who are interested only in checking the library's serials holdings. The list offers easier and quicker searching than combing the OPAC. If libraries have well-managed automated cataloging records with holdings information, extracting such a list from the OPAC, a shared database, or the database of a participating union list of serials is an easy task; otherwise, compiling and updating a separate serials list is extra work.

Union List of Serials

The main purpose of a union list of serials is to support resource sharing in the form of interlibrary loans. The list contains serials holdings of multiple libraries who have agreed to share resources. Union list participants usually share some common characteristics. They may be located in the same geographical area, share the same subject collections, and have similar collecting levels. A union list of serials may include only libraries belonging to the same library system, such as a university library system with a main library plus branches located at different campuses and subject libraries associated with different academic departments, or a public library system with branches in different neighborhoods. These union lists serve intralibrary loan purposes.

Forming and maintaining a union list of serials requires careful planning, a budget to support operations, and staff time to create and maintain the list. Participating libraries have to agree on how to create, distribute, and maintain the list. They must also work out its scope, data elements, and organization. One group may choose to include records for periodicals only, while another also includes continuations. One group may follow AACR2 and NISO standards, while another does not. However, each group must make such decisions before compiling its list. After the initial list is compiled, each participating library must faithfully update its records of cancellations, additions, and corrections to maintain accuracy. Automated cataloging and shared databases have greatly reduced this work. For instance, the Research Libraries Group sets resource sharing as one of its main goals; therefore, its bibliographic database, RLIN, serves as a union list of serials for its member libraries. With OCLC's union listing enhancement, OCLC member libraries can easily establish a union list of serials by extracting serials cataloging and holdings data from the database. No matter how a union list of serials is compiled, the essential conditions for its success are that participants contribute accurate records and faithfully update changes in holdings.

Circulation Records

Circulation records explain why certain parts of collections are not available in the library. The serials format does not pose problems or call for special treatment in circulation processing. However, in preparing serials for automated circulation, each item in a title must be bar coded separately so it can be handled independently in the circulation operation. Different volumes in the same title may be borrowed simultaneously by different users. Therefore, it is a common phenomenon in the circulation records to have a long string of item records with bar-code information linked to one serial bibliographic record. Libraries that do not circulate periodicals may choose not to bar code periodicals or prepare item records for individual physical pieces unless the information also serves other purposes, such as inventory control.

Routing current periodical issues to a group of individuals who are on the routing list is a circulation issue unique to serials. Although it is a public service, the routing records often are kept as acquisition records because this function is usually carried out by the acquisition staff on receipt. Since acquisition records are internal working records, users may have difficulty trying to locate issues being routed. Keeping routing records as part of circulation records prevents this type of public service problem.

Managing Serials Records

With so many different types of records relating to serials, and with their status and inventories constantly changing, managing them is not a simple matter. To make the matter more complicated, many libraries are in a transition period of converting serials records and operations from manual to automated systems. In the manual stage, record keeping usually is done in separate files, and staff members working with serials in both technical and public services often need to cross-check several files. Some libraries try to form a master serials records file to improve efficiency, but it is difficult to create a true master file. The file most likely to be the master file is the acquisition Kardex file, which may contain detailed information on receiving, holdings, and payment and brief notes on ordering, claiming, bindery, processing, and routing. Furthermore, a copy of the catalog card may be kept in the file to include complete bibliographic information. However, such a manual master file tends to be untidy and cumbersome to use. In addition, time sharing may become a serious problem when several staff members have to share the same file to perform different functions.

Automation has turned the dream of creating a master file into a workable reality. If a library has a totally integrated automated system, serials acquisition, cataloging, holdings, and circulation information is stored in the same database, which enables checking for all the information related to serials. While the system provides the capability of creating a serials master file, the precondition for having a true master file is that each different function's records must be accurately and comprehensively entered into the database. This is not an easy task. When different functions share the same records database, inputting and updating records for one function may benefit other functions. On the other hand, coordination of records management among different working units is essential so that one function's records manipulation does not produce a negative result for the others.

If a library has different systems for different functions—the serials control uses one system, cataloging uses another, and OPAC and circulation use a third—it still is possible to have a master file, as long as these systems can interface. However, it may take a lot of communication and cooperation among system vendors, the system librarian, and the serials librarian to achieve this goal. It may be more practical to use data manipulation capabilities to create custom files to serve the different needs of technical services and public services. For instance, the serials control system may provide acquisitions with a file that contains cataloging, ordering, receiving, payment, claiming, routing, bindery, and holdings information. Public services can be served by an OPAC that contains cataloging, holdings, and circulation information. The OPAC may download bibliographic records to the serials control system, and the serials system may upload holdings records to the OPAC. With the continuous improvement of system technology and software, system librarians and serials librarians must work closely with system vendors to look for new breakthroughs in serials records control.

Notes

1. Readers may wish to read the latest published textbook on cataloging: Lois Mai Chan, *Cataloging and Classification: An Introduction,* 2d ed. (New York: McGraw-Hill, 1994); and *The Serials Librarian,* v. 22 (1992), which is devoted to the theme "Serials Cataloging: Modern Perspectives and International Developments." For further studies, consult titles listed in *Library Literature* under the subject heading *Serial publications—Cataloging.*
2. Marjorie E. Bloss, "The Two ANSI Standards for Serial Holdings Statements: A Comparison," *Serials Review* 11:4 (1985): 33–42.
3. Lynn S. Smith, *A Practical Approach to Serials Cataloging* (Greenwich, Conn.: JAI Press, 1978), 372–4.

Chapter 9

Public Services Issues

A library's local organization determines whether its serials department provides direct public services. New organizational trends seem to be blurring the defining line between technical and public services. It is not unusual for serials departments to expand their traditional technical services role into public service functions, such as managing the periodical reading room, answering location and status inquiries, and processing document delivery services. Even if their work consists only of technical services, serials departments are heavily involved with services to the public. Because acquisition status is constantly changing, making cataloging and holdings records control more complex, and because the time sensitivity of serials information forces users to search for the most-recent arrival, the public services staff often seeks support from the serials department. Whenever they cannot interpret a record or locate an issue and whenever they need the latest acquisition status information, they turn to the serials department for the information.

This chapter provides basic concepts of the issues involved in serials public service. Cooperation between the serials department and public service department is the key to the success of serials public services. An effective serials librarian has to maintain close links with public services librarians and provide support and services as needed.

Reference Service

The reference desk handles everything from complex research questions that only an experienced reference librarian with knowledge of the subject can answer to simple inquiries about the location of the periodical reading room, answerable by any library staff member. Reference questions come in unlimited varieties. This section does not attempt to list and describe all types of reference tasks that are related to serials; discussion is limited to the major part of serials reference work—assisting users to identify and access serial articles related to a specific topic.

Identifying Articles

The most important reference tools used in identifying serial articles are abstracts and indexes. These tools have defined coverage scope. They usually are limited by the subject, such as *Art Index,* published by the H. W. Wilson Company, and *Chemical Abstracts,* published by the American Chemical Society. Other scope limitations can be defined by the publisher's marketing purpose. For example, *Readers' Guide to Periodical Literature* covers journals of popular interest; *Newspaper Abstracts* covers newspapers only. These tools always specify their scope and provide a list of the titles being indexed. They may add or drop titles from year to year. A serial's usage increases with its coverage in indexes and abstracts, which is a factor to consider in selecting titles for the development of the serials collection. Recognizing the importance of abstracting and indexing, the CONSER (Cooperative ONline SERials) Program started the Abstracting and Indexing Coverage Project in 1983 to add abstracting and indexing information to the cataloging record in MARC field 510. *Ulrich's International Periodical Directory* and some serials catalogs provided by vendors also include this information.

Since the 1970s, the traditional article search of printed abstracts and indexes has been supplemented by online bibliographic searches in databases offered by information vendors such as Dialog and Bibliographic Retrieval Services (BRS). Online searches provide the speed and ease of computer searching, and the information is more current than in the printed format because databases are updated more frequently. However, the high cost involved in such searches has limited their popularity. Searches may be done by trained librarians to minimize search time and maximize results with search costs passed on to users. When abstracts and indexes appeared in CD-ROM in the late 1980s, followed by CD-ROMs with full-text articles, they gained immediate popularity with libraries. In the 1990s, information vendors started offering online searching through site contracts instead of charging by connecting time. This makes it possible for libraries to provide patrons with direct access to vendors' databases. To take the service one step beyond, libraries have made article searches in electronic abstracts, indexes, and current contents available as a menu choice through local online public access catalogs or campus-wide networks.

Assisting users to search and identify articles requires subject expertise and a thorough knowledge of reference tools. Reference librarians or trained reference assistants are needed to analyze a user's inquiry, choose the most suitable reference tool available in the library, and teach the user how to use it. High technology has enabled information to be accessed with faster speed and greater depth. However, new developments in technology mandate that reference librarians learn constantly about new tools and spend more time and effort in user instruction and assistance.

Access to Articles

After articles have been identified, the patron naturally expects to obtain them. Serials cataloging, holdings records, and acquisitions records (if more detailed receiving status information is needed) should tell whether a requested article is in the library's collection. If the patron is using abstracts and indexes in CD-ROM with full-text, then identifying and accessing articles becomes one-stop shopping. With more libraries mounting electronic abstracts and indexes in local OPACs, the new service on the horizon is to match the local serials holdings with citations in abstracts and indexes to inform users whether the library holds desired articles. In other words, as the user identifies wanted articles, he or she is also informed of their availability.

If the library holds the serial issue that contains the article wanted by the user and the issue is found, all is well with this serials reference task. Unfortunately, there are times when users cannot locate serial issues even though the issues are listed as being held by the library. There are many reasons for such disappointment: the issue is being used by another patron, out at the binder, shelved in the wrong place, left in the copy machine by the previous user, or stolen by a selfish patron. Typically, when reference librarians exhaust searching resources and imagination, the serials department gets involved in the investigation of missing issues. The serials staff members' skill in solving such mysteries is acquired from their close contact with serials and their understanding of detailed acquisitions and bindery records that track each item's movements and problems. If the library maintains well-documented records as described in the previous chapter, it will enjoy a high success rate in locating serial articles for patrons.

Compared with other formats, printed serials are more problem prone when it comes to locating articles. Microforms are usually noncirculating and used in a supervised reading area, so their chance of being lost is much smaller. Serial articles in the CD-ROM full-text or electronic journals are safe and secure. The shortcoming of nonprint formats is that they all need equipment to be read, and users need instruction and assistance in using the equipment.

There are several choices in obtaining articles that are unavailable in the library collection. The two most popular methods are interlibrary loan and purchasing articles from commercial document delivery services.

Interlibrary Loans

Interlibrary loan (ILL) is the most traditional document delivery method. For serials ILL, the popular practice is for the lending library to provide a photocopy of the requested article to the borrowing library. There may or may not be a charge for the copy, depending on the resource-sharing agreement between the two libraries. Union lists of serials and shared bibliographic databases provide libraries with information on borrowing sources. They are important tools for processing interlibrary loans.

The popularity of ILL surged during the 1980s for several reasons. With decreasing library budgets and increasing material prices, libraries have to access information from outside to supplement their own collections and meet user needs. Identifying sources for interlibrary loans is easier with shared bibliographic databases and the addition of local holdings to cataloging records. Both the promotion of resource sharing among members of the Research Libraries Group through RLIN and the offering of the ILL system by OCLC have generated more ILL activities. In addition, the advanced technology of fax, telecommunication, scanning, Express Mail, and overnight parcel delivery services have contributed to the improvement of ILL efficiency. ILL no longer has a standard waiting period of two to four weeks or longer; documents can be delivered within two days or less to fill rush requests.

The downside of ILL's success story is that libraries are burdened by an ever-increasing demand on budgets and staffing for ILL. ILL is time-consuming and labor-intensive. It involves verifying the citation of the patron's request, identifying and choosing the borrowing source, transmitting the request, keeping processing records, receiving the material, and notifying the patron. There is follow-up on the patron's loan period if the material has to be returned to the lending institution. Also, the request to borrow can be hit or miss and often requires several attempts. A request may not be filled for various reasons: the lending library's holdings record is wrong, or the material is not available because it is on loan, missing, not in circulation, etc. On the lending side, the work involves locating the requested material, making copies of journal articles or preparing monographs for shipping, keeping loan records, and sending the material. If the material has to be returned, there is follow-up work if it is not returned on time or intact. For both lending and borrowing libraries, there is also work related to statistics, evaluation of procedures, and review of ILL agreements. ILL is an expensive operation, but it may be justifiable as an alternative when the library chooses not to subscribe to journals with very low demand. However, it is more economical to own a much-requested journal than to rely on ILL. Serials collection development may use ILL statistics as a guide when determining whether to subscribe to some borderline journals.

Article Delivery Services

Article delivery services, such as UMI's Article Clearinghouse and the Institute for Scientific Information's The Genuine Article, have been in existence for several decades. In the past they were used only as supplementary sources for document delivery—usually after an attempt for ILL failed, or when speed was a critical factor in filling the patron's request. Most patrons were not aware of such services. However, in the 1990s, the article delivery service has become a booming business. Information brokers, bibliographic utilities, and serials vendors are all in it. Besides the veterans in the businesses, such as UMI, Dialog, and BRS, there is a long list of new players, such as UnCover, offered by the Colorado Alliance of Research Libraries (CARL); CitaDel, offered by the Research Libraries Group (RLG); and FastDoc on FirstSearch, offered by OCLC.

Connecting article delivery services with electronic serials reference tools, available either on CD-ROM mounted on the OPAC or with direct access to the vendor's database through a network, is the attraction of today's public services. Typically, a user may search the abstracts and indexes in the library or from a computer at home or office that is connected to these databases. After articles are identified, the user places an order by using a major credit card or an account with the service. Articles are delivered by fax within twenty-four hours. The charge per article is reasonable, and the cost includes the copyright royalty fee. To library users, this type of service has truly combined article identification and access into one easy step. In addition, suppliers also take care of copyright obligations.

Both libraries and patrons have choices in how to use article delivery services and how to strike a balance between ILL and purchases. Libraries have the choice of processing article purchases and bearing the cost for their patrons, passing the cost on to patrons, or asking patrons to deal directly with delivery services in ordering and paying for their articles. Libraries may also offer the choices of waiting for ILL without cost or paying for the article purchase if speed is an urgent issue. It is not likely that commercial document delivery services can totally replace ILL—some materials, especially older materials, are available only from library collections.

In the 1990s libraries have shifted their focus in serials document delivery service from relying mainly on ILL to relying on article delivery services and ILL for several reasons. One is the flourishing of document delivery services and their efficiency in providing speedy service at reasonable cost. Another reason is the combination of shrinking library budgets and escalating journal prices, which forces libraries to cancel low-demand subscriptions and purchase articles from commercial document suppliers when a request is made. Policies on acquiring low-usage journals have switched from just-in-case subscriptions to just-in-time article purchases. Libraries with such policies often allocate a fund to purchase articles on demand. A third reason is that advanced computer technology has increased the visibility of these services by allowing users to access them directly through connections provided by libraries. In this fast-paced environment users are willing to pay for information in exchange for speedy delivery.

Serials reference work is truly experiencing one breakthrough after another. Reference librarians are busy selecting new tools and users are enjoying new services. The only regret is that the cost of providing reference work is escalating because libraries continuously have to upgrade computer hardware and software for electronic reference services, lease expensive electronic reference tools, and train the reference staff to use them.

Circulation

It is common for libraries to have different circulation policies for monographs and serials because of the differences in usage patterns between them. While users may read the entire monograph, they usually are interested only in one article in a serial. At the same time, more people may be interested in using the same serial title than reading the same monograph because the serial consists of collections of articles. Therefore, general policies tend to keep serials in the library in order to serve more users or, if circulation is permitted, tend to set a much shorter loan period for serials than for monographs. However, it is hard to keep circulation policy simple. There are different treatments for different types of serials.

Periodicals

Libraries tend to limit periodicals to in-the-library use for several reasons. Since users usually want only one article in a periodical issue or a few articles in a bound volume, they can either stay in the library to read these articles or make copies. Copy machines usually are readily available near periodical collections, and the cost is reasonable. Another reason is that serials back files are difficult and expensive to replace. Serials go out of print easily, and the replacement process can be long and costly. In the meantime, gaps in a serial run may greatly reduce the title's value for public service. Keeping the integrity of the serial's run is an important task in preserving the value of the serial and protecting users' interests.

Current periodical issues are in higher demand than back files; thus, they are more likely to be missing or damaged. Missing issues can cause disappointment for users who cannot locate them and extra work for staff members who must search for the issues and order replacements. For some very popular periodicals and newspapers, libraries control use by keeping current issues behind the counter and limiting use to within the library. Users must produce an identification card, such as a library card, student card, or even a driver's license, to borrow issues, and the card will be returned to the user when the issues are returned. Small public libraries that do not bind periodicals may allow current issues to be circulated outside the library for short loan periods and may allow users to reserve current issues that are out. Small special libraries in universities may allow both current issues and bound volumes to be borrowed by professors and graduate students as long as the periodicals are used in their offices. The assumption is that if other users need to use these materials, they can be located and retrieved easily. Some libraries allow bound volumes to circulate just like monographs.

Routing the latest periodical issues to a designated group of users who need current information as soon as possible is a special circulation service. This service is especially popular in specialty libraries. Duplicate subscriptions may be placed for titles that are to be routed. A common problem with routing is that if there is an irresponsible magazine hoarder in the group, he or she can stop the routing flow and make the people following him or her on the list wait forever to see the issue. Some libraries have replaced routing with distributing copies of the table of contents and accepting requests for desired articles.

Continuations

Circulation policies for continuations tend to be less restrictive. Annuals that serve as reference tools and are maintained in the reference collection are for in-the-library use only. Otherwise they may be circulated for short loan periods. Monographic series usually are treated as monographs in the circulation policy.

It is important to remember that the library collection is for patrons' use. The more patrons that can use the collection, the more successful the library's service. Circulation policies should avoid unnecessary restrictions. Limiting circulation to in-the-library use or setting short loan periods should be done only when the privilege of a few borrowers deprives more users of their rights. In addition, unreasonable restrictions can increase the mutilation and theft of library materials.

Nonprint Serials

Serials in microform are usually limited to in-the-library use. Since they require special readers and copies can be made at a reasonable cost, users usually are content with this policy. For electronic serials, both printing and downloading are convenient. In the virtual library setting, users are able to access articles from their home or office; electronic serials are available to them at all hours. With electronically transmitted serials there is no worry about library hours or issues being used by other patrons; thus, there is no circulation problem.

Written Circulation Policy

It is obvious from the previous description that answering questions such as "Do your serials circulate?" or "How long is the loan period?" is not a simple matter. Each library has its own serials circulation policy, and within the policy there are variations for different types of serials. Library staff members can be harassed by annoyed patrons insisting on borrowing a noncirculating periodical issue or demanding to know why periodicals cannot be circulated while monographs can. To avoid such unpleasant scenes, it is important for libraries to have a written circulation policy for serials.

Factors that influence the circulation policy are (1) type of library, (2) type of serials, and (3) type of patrons. Large libraries tend to have more-restrictive rules than small libraries, and periodicals are usually not circulated outside the large library. Such control is necessary to benefit the majority of users. Small special libraries may have more-relaxed rules to serve special client needs. Periodicals have more-restrictive circulation rules than continuations. Professors and graduate students may enjoy more circulation privileges than undergraduate students.

Even with a written policy, occasions will arise when exceptions are required. What if the mayor needs to borrow the latest issue of a periodical from the public library to use in preparing an emergency budget request to the state and has a pressing deadline? What if the sales office is putting on an exhibition for potential customers and needs to borrow some periodical volumes from the company's library as part of the display? What if a library school professor needs to use an annual in the university library's reference collection for a lecture? The circulation policy must address special requests by giving general guidelines and assigning a decision maker to grant them. This person may be the serials librarian, the circulation librarian, the head of reference, or the library director. Special requests often need an immediate answer. To play it safe, it is a good idea to assign a second decision maker in case the primary person is absent.

Collection Arrangement

The serials collection consists of various types and formats, such as newspapers, periodicals, continuations, microforms, and electronic serials. To arrange this complex collection for effective access is not a simple matter. Three main controversies about the serials collection arrangement are whether to classify periodicals, whether to interfile different serial formats, and whether to interfile serials with monographs. Librarians have different ideas about what is best for their patrons; however, the choices often are limited by physical conditions, such as stack capacity or the size and layout of the library building. In addition, traditional arrangements are difficult to change. Unless a library is moving into a new building, planning a new addition, or receiving a special fund for relocating collections, most cannot afford the cost of a major shift to change their collection arrangement. The arrangement of the serials collection is very much influenced by local choices and limitations.

Classification of Periodicals

To classify or not to classify periodicals is an endless controversy closely related to the management of periodical collections. Classified periodicals are shelved according to their subjects in the stacks, and they may or may not be interfiled with the rest of the serials collection and monographs. Unclassified periodicals are shelved alphabetically by title or main entry and cannot be interfiled with other classified collections. Alphabetical arrangement makes it easier for users to locate titles by eliminating the need to find a periodical's call number; however, ambiguity in the choice of main entry or title proper can cause confusion in locating alphabetized titles. In addition, classification enables users to browse periodicals in the same or related subject areas and eliminates the danger of separating periodical issues by title changes.

Generally speaking, the local choice often is influenced by the size of the periodical collection. Smaller collections tend to use the alphabetical arrangement, while larger collections need classification to provide tight systematic control of the collection. According to a survey done in 1989 by the California State University Library at Bakersfield, 82 percent of libraries with fewer than five hundred subscriptions arrange their bound periodicals alphabetically, but only 17 percent of libraries with more than ten thousand subscriptions use alphabetical arrangement.[1]

Shelving Choices

Whether serials should be maintained as a separate collection or interfiled with monographs is another question with no perfect answer. Libraries may prefer to interfile all collections so that users do not have to first determine both the type of materials they are looking for and which stack to look in. However, some libraries choose to separate collections because smaller collections are easier to maintain in good order for public service. Again, the size of the collection may be the factor that influences the shelving arrangement. Small libraries tend to keep one master file for their collections, while large libraries often shelve serials separately.

If serials are shelved separately, a decision about whether to keep periodicals as a separate collection from the rest of serials while shelving continuations with monographs is required. As a general rule, monographic series are shelved with monographs; other continuations may be shelved with monographs or periodicals depending on the local policy. If continuations circulate, they are likely to be interfiled with monographs; otherwise, they may be shelved with periodicals.

Interfiling Different Formats

Periodicals come in loose issues, bound volumes, microforms, and electronic tapes and discs. Popular practice is to keep unbound issues in the periodical reading room, bound volumes in the periodical stacks, microforms in the microforms room, and electronic tapes and discs behind the circulation counter or in the reference area. The general theory behind such a segregated arrangement is that since current periodical issues and newspapers are heavily used, a special room is needed for users to enjoy them and for loose issues to be under better protection and care. Microforms require special readers, and tapes and discs require computers, which have to be stored in areas where suitable machines and staff assistance can be provided. While these considerations are for the users' benefit, such segregated arrangements often frustrate users when they are trying to locate materials in different formats.

Some libraries keep serials all together in one area regardless of the difference in formats. Loose issues, bound volumes, microforms, tapes, and discs of the same title are all shelved together. Users may be happy about being able to find materials stored in one place but will be frustrated trying to find the proper machine or assistance to read the microform and electronic serials unless these are also provided in the same area. Mixing different formats in the same area can create shelf-management problems. Each format requires proper shelving and storage facilities. The bound volume shelf is not suitable for the storage of microforms, and the microfilm cabinet is not suitable for storing microfiches. Newspapers will certainly be a mess if they are not provided with special shelving facilities, such as newspaper holders, slings, or large open shelves.

A survey conducted by librarians at the California State University Library at Bakersfield indicates that 37 percent of libraries with fewer than five hundred subscriptions keep unbound issues with bound volumes, but only 21 percent of libraries with more than ten thousand subscriptions follow this practice. The survey also finds that 91 percent of the libraries keep microforms in a separate collection. Most of the libraries that interfile microforms with bound volumes are small.[2] Again, the size of the collection seems to be a main factor in the collection arrangement.

Collection Locations

For libraries with separate serials collections, there is the controversy over where these should be located in the library. The choice of location often is limited by building layout and tradition. If libraries have a choice about locating the periodical reading room and housing serials collections, major considerations are accessibility, security, and proximity to service points.

Accessibility

Because they are heavily used, serials should be located in an area that is easily accessible by users. If users can see the serials collection area on entering the library or can easily find it by following signs, it will save the staff from repeatedly answering the question "Where are the periodicals?" If serials are separated into different segments, such as current issues, bound volumes, and microforms, these separate collections should be located as close together as possible. It is a poor arrangement to have the current periodical reading room on the first floor, the bound periodical stacks in the basement, and the microforms room on yet another floor. Users must run all over the library with such an arrangement of serials collections, and library staff members continue to be bombarded with questions related to serials locations.

Security

Many libraries do not circulate periodicals outside the library. This policy may tempt users to steal issues or cut pages when they cannot finish their intended reading in the library. Besides security measures, such as inserting magnetic security tapes in issues and providing copy machines near the collection, libraries can avoid locating serials collections in an area where people can easily slip in and out without the staff's notice, or where they may bypass the front entrance with its security check equipment or guard. Unbound current issues seem to have the highest theft rate. Some libraries place a service desk at the entrance to the current periodical reading room. The staff member at the service point may answer inquiries and check materials being brought in and out of the reading room.

Service Points

Inquiries about serials are frequent. Some are reference questions relating to searching and locating resource materials, but most are about locating particular titles and finding specific issues. The former group of questions should be handled by reference librarians; the latter can be handled by serials staff members. Although a few frequent library users may be able to sort their questions and address them to appropriate library staff, the general user behavior pattern is to address questions to the nearest service point, be it the reference desk, the circulation counter, or the service counter in the periodical reading room. The location of the serials collection in relation to public service points usually determines who will receive more serials inquiries. If the periodical reading room has no service counter and is located near the reference desk, reference librarians will receive more serials inquiries. If there is a service counter in the reading room, serials staff members will receive more inquiries. It is economical and efficient to place the serials collection closer to the serials department than to the reference desk. In this setting, serials staff members may help patrons with general inquiries and refer true reference questions to reference librarians.

Periodical Reading Room

The periodical reading room is a popular place in the library. In addition to unbound periodicals, this room also usually houses current newspapers and may include unbound government document periodicals. Library patrons come to this room to gather the latest information for their research and studies, to read newspapers and magazines about current events, or to have a quiet moment and do some leisure reading. Reading rooms are designed to accommodate the services required by patrons.

Stacks

The essential facility in the reading room is the periodicals stacks. There are various types of shelves available to hold periodicals. The most suitable for unbound periodicals is the type that allows the latest received issue to be on display by placing it on a sloping shelf with earlier issues placed flat on a shelf behind it. This design enables patrons to browse titles and identify the latest issue with ease. The concealed shelf for earlier issues gives the stack a neat appearance and provides protection for loose issues. Patrons can easily lift the sloping shelf to obtain earlier issues from the concealed part.

Maintaining order on the newspaper shelving is a time-consuming and tedious job. The large size of many newspapers makes them difficult to handle, and loose pages are easily mixed up by careless readers. Some libraries keep newspapers behind the service counter for better control. If newspapers are kept in open stacks, popular choices for storing them are hanging slings, newspaper holders with two rods securing the inner edge of the paper, and shelves that are wide enough to hold flat, folded newspapers. None of these provides the perfect solution for maintaining a neat and orderly stack. Trying to make newspapers stand up straight in the sling is an endless struggle; holders only hold a limited number of pages and pose difficulty for making copies. Flat shelves provide easy shelving and may hold a high pile of newspapers, but they are easily messed up by users who mix the order of pages and dates while searching for wanted materials. Some libraries use a combination of holders and shelves by keeping the heavily used latest issue in a holder and less-used earlier issues on the shelf.

Libraries rarely bind newspapers unless the paper format has special artifact value. Back files usually are available in microform. However, libraries have to keep the paper version until the microform version arrives. Instead of leaving numerous back issues in the reading room waiting for the arrival of the microform, which would definitely create messy stack areas, older issues usually are removed to a remote storage area where they are available to patrons on request. Since the demand for newspapers declines with time, this arrangement does not pose a public service problem.

Shelving Arrangement

As discussed earlier in this chapter, periodicals may be arranged according to title or call number. Since most patrons come to the reading room to look for specific titles, the title arrangement seems to be more popular among users. Each title has a shelf label to indicate its location. Besides the title, the label may include a brief note about the title's summary holdings and the location of back files. This information is useful for patrons who need to use back files, especially when back files are available in a different format or when the unbound issues use a different shelving arrangement. For example, loose issues are shelved by title, but bound volumes are shelved by call number. Cross-reference labels may link periodicals that have changed title recently or provide directions for locating ambiguous titles. A little more information on labels can save a lot of user inquiries. When stacks are arranged in rows, each row should have a sign indicating the beginning and ending titles or call numbers in that row. This can speed up the patron's search for wanted titles.

To eliminate misshelving, patrons should be discouraged from shelving periodicals after use. Signs asking them to leave used issues on the table, an assigned sorting shelf, or book trucks placed near reading tables should be posted around both the stack and reading areas. The sorting shelf and trucks should be clearly marked with signs asking patrons to use them for periodicals and newspapers.

Seating

There should be adequate seating in the reading room to accommodate all readers. The amount of seating is related to the size of the collection, type of library, and patrons' library-use patterns. For instance, weekends in a public library are usually more crowded than weekdays, and an academic library seems never to have enough seating during the final examination period. Large tables shared by several readers are more space-efficient and suitable for group study, but small desks used by one or two readers provide more privacy while reading. A reading room may include both types to suit different patron needs. If space allows, a few easy lounge chairs are welcomed by newspaper and leisure readers.

Service Counter

A service counter staffed with a serials or public service staff member is part of the essential service in a busy reading room. Users need the service point to address their inquiries and ask for assistance in using the collection. The staff member's presence can discourage mutilation and theft because he or she can check users' bags at the exit and keep an eye on the collection. When the room is not busy, he or she may shelve used periodicals. If the library keeps newspapers and some popular periodicals behind the counter, a staff member must be present to handle their circulation.

New issues of some popular newspapers and magazines constantly seem to be missing from the reading room stacks. Users commonly complain "Where is today's *New York Times*?" or "I have been looking for the new *Time* magazine for days!" A common solution is to keep the newest issue of hot titles behind the service counter where they are available on request. Asking for an identification card from the patron in exchange ensures that issues will be returned to the counter promptly and properly.

If a library cannot spare a staff member for the reading room service, the reading room has to be located near a service point, such as the circulation counter or reference desk or next to the serials department. Leaving the reading room unattended and far away from service points not only results in poor public service but also in a messy reading room and increasing damage and theft to the serials collection.

Other Facilities

Reading rooms should contain serials retrieval tools, such as the OPAC terminal, the library's serials holding list, and the regional union list of serials. The question of whether to keep abstracts and indexes in the reference area or in the periodical reading room often stirs up controversy. Although keeping them near the serials collection gives users the convenience of searching for desired articles, it may be more logical to place these tools near the reference desk. Patrons often need assistance from reference librarians in choosing the most appropriate reference tools and instruction on how to use them. In addition, the scope of some abstracts and indexes is not limited to serials. Modern technology has enabled electronic abstracts and indexes to be available in the OPAC or in a networked CD-ROM, thus eliminating the controversy about where to locate reference tools.

A copying facility is essential for users' convenience and the security of materials. The problem with placing a copy machine in the reading room is that its noise may disturb some sensitive readers. To cut down on noise, machines should be placed in a corner away from reading tables or behind partitions. Placing a table next to the machine provides patrons with the space to place issues, copies, and personal belongings. Otherwise, materials are likely to be put on the floor or on the edge of the machine. Placing a change machine in or near the reading room will relieve the service counter from having to make change for the copy machine. Selling copy cards at the service counter will be a convenience for users.

Notebook computers are becoming popular, and patrons are bringing them to the reading room to write papers or to take notes while using periodicals. Proper electric outlets should be provided for these users.

Microform Room

Since microforms require equipment and users need assistance in using the equipment, libraries usually designate an area or a room to house microforms and a service counter to provide user assistance.

The microform collections may consist of both microfilms and microfiches. The most suitable storage method is cabinets with drawers made of nonreactive materials and specially designed to hold and protect these formats. Cabinet drawers should be labeled with contents for easy retrieval. Within the microfilm cabinet drawers, microfilm reels should be stored in nonacid boxes with each box labeled as to its contents. Dividers within the microfiche cabinet drawers help to store materials neatly. Microfiches need guide cards interfiled with the collection for easier retrieval. Patrons should be strictly discouraged from shelving used materials, especially microfiches, to avoid losing materials. Big boxes may be placed near readers and on top of cabinets for patrons to deposit their used materials.

Microform collections may include both serials and monographs. Serials users usually are looking for specific titles and issues. This poses no service problem, but monographic collection users may have difficulty locating wanted materials due to lack of analytical cataloging for titles within the collection. Helping patrons to use monographic collections usually is done by the microform or reference librarians. If publishers' user guides accompany a collection, libraries may purchase two sets and place one set in the reference area and the other in the microform room. This practice can save users from having to run between the reference desk and microform room to use guides to locate materials in the collection. Publishers may be willing to supply the second copy of guides at a discount or without charge to their regular customers.

A service counter is necessary in the microform room. Besides maintaining collections in good order and helping patrons retrieve materials, the service counter is kept busy with machine-related services. Staff members or trained student assistants spend a lot of time teaching users how to use readers and make copies. In addition, these staff members fix minor machine problems, such as clearing paper jams, adding toner, adding copy paper, and changing bulbs. Microform readers are expensive to purchase and repair. Patrons should be taught how to use them properly, and staff members must learn how to perform basic maintenance work. Machines must be serviced periodically by the manufacturer or its authorized agents.

Some libraries combine the periodical reading room and microform room. This is a logical and economical arrangement if the microform collection consists mainly of serials. To house current issues in paper and back files in microform in the same room is a convenience to users. In the meantime, combining two service counters into one is an economical move for libraries.

Collection Maintenance

Maintaining serials collections in good order so that users may locate wanted material with ease is the last, but not the least, step of serials management. Although maintenance work consists mostly of shelving that can be done by entry-level staff members or part-time student assistants, it can reduce all previous efforts in serials management to zero if it is not carried out effectively. When a user cannot locate the wanted item, all the money and effort that went into acquisition, cataloging, and public service mean nothing because the library has failed its ultimate goal of delivering material to the user.

The main work in collection maintenance is to place serials at their designated shelf locations accurately and promptly. This starts when new receipts are checked in, processed, and shelved in a timely manner. It is continuous, repetitive work to return materials constantly being moved and used by patrons to their proper locations. Shelf reading also is important, i.e., reading the stack from A to Z (either titles or call numbers) to discover and correct misshelvings. This is the only way to recover missing items caused by misshelving. Heavily used collections may need frequent shelf readings. For instance, current periodicals are heavily used, and patrons have a tendency to misplace issues during browsing; thus, periodical reading room stacks have to be read frequently, preferably weekly or at least monthly. It is common for users to pick up materials from one area and leave them in another area. There are also selfish readers who deliberately hide materials. Therefore, making a daily round through the library to find and return materials to their proper shelving areas is an important routine.

Weeding is a regular task in serials collection maintenance. This is different from the weeding projects done by collection development librarians when they review the library collection and make decisions to withdraw materials from the stacks. Serials are constantly being weeded to delete duplicates or obsolete materials, such as when a new annual volume supersedes the previous one. The final cumulative issue of the year makes previous issues published within the year obsolete. Newspaper and periodical issues are discarded on the arrival of their microform versions. Newsletters and other ephemera that are kept for only a limited period need to be weeded accordingly. If weeding is not carried out regularly, stacks begin to overflow with useless materials, causing patrons to miss the most-current information.

Weeding instructions usually are kept in the check-in records. Sample instructions are "Discard paper edition when microfilm is received," "Keep current year only," or "Keep latest volume in reference." The check-in staff may pass the instructions on to the stack maintenance staff by sending a note or inserting an instruction slip in newly received volumes. The stack maintenance staff may batch the instruction notes and carry out weeding periodically or remove older materials immediately when new materials are shelved.

Shelvers also have to pay attention to the physical condition of the material. They must notify the appropriate staff member when they discover volumes in poor condition. Damaged materials need proper attention and care to keep them from further deterioration. When materials are mutilated beyond repair, replacements may have to be ordered.

Library users move materials around the library and put them in wrong places. To control or require users to be responsible by not messing up collections is difficult; however, librarians can create an environment that minimizes maintenance work. For instance, librarians can provide service to assist patrons in locating materials, maintain accurate serials records, keep various serials collections (current and bound periodicals and microforms) close to each other, maintain stacks in good order, make copy machines readily available with reasonable charges, and post signs to discourage patrons from shelving. All of these activities discourage patrons from messing up serials collections. A disorderly collection arrangement with difficult access provokes users, which may cause disruptive actions, thus creating more maintenance work. A well-maintained and easily accessible collection not only makes readers happy, it also reduces maintenance.

Notes

1. Jim Segesta and Gary Hyslop, "The Arrangement of Periodicals in American Academic Libraries," *Serials Review* 17(1) (spring 1991): 21–8.
2. Ibid.

Chapter 10

Serials Automation

The changeable nature and continuous publication pattern of serials contributes to the complexity of designing software for automated serials control. Because vendors need to recover large investments in developing the software, they have to charge high prices for serials control systems. For an integrated system, vendors first tend to develop modules for more pattern-oriented library functions and leave serials control to the last. Libraries also tend to delay automating serials until they have gained some experience because serials control is considered one of the most complicated library functions. Therefore, slower system development, higher prices, and greater complexity of serials control motivate libraries to postpone serials automation until they have completed everything else. During the 1970s and 1980s, libraries were busy with the automation of cataloging, circulation, and monograph acquisitions and the implementation of the online public access catalog. Finally in the 1990s, the time has come for serials automation. Libraries either are about to automate serials control or have just done so. A few may already be on their second system.

Advantages of Automation

During the early 1980s, there was skepticism about the advantages of serials automation. Among librarians there were doubts about whether it was worthwhile to spend the effort and money to convert a well-controlled manual system into an automated system that might not accommodate all requirements of the serials acquisitions process. As computer systems continue to improve and libraries have reaped the benefits of automation, there is no longer any doubt about the advantages of serials automation. Although serials control systems are mainly designed to achieve efficiency in acquisitions, both collection development and public service have benefited immensely. A selection of examples follows.

Two benefits of serials automation for collection development are the abilities to analyze collections and to improve budget control. Selectors can obtain collection profiles easily from system-produced statistical reports, such as a list of serials titles for a specific subject. Such information is valuable in collection evaluation and in selection and deselection decisions. Various system-produced fiscal reports provide data for budget planning, such as the previous year's encumbrance and expenditure report. Price analyses may serve as guidelines for the next year's budget request. Balancing the budget is easier when selectors have immediate access to current fiscal status at any given time to check the balance of encumbrances and expenditures.

Combining various paper files into one database is a major benefit for acquisitions. In an automated system, order, receipt, claim, payment, renewal, routing, and bindery information are combined in one database. This eliminates not only the tedious manual file-maintenance work, but it also cross-checks different files while performing serials control functions. In addition, several users may access the database simultaneously. Therefore, automation also solves the file-sharing problem inherent with the use of manual files.

Improvement in the efficiency of processing acquisitions by eliminating much labor-intensive and time-consuming manual work is another benefit of automation. The savings in time and work are especially obvious with ordering, check-in, claiming, and payment. For ordering, the typing of order slips is eliminated when purchase orders are produced by the system; all the work associated with mailing is eliminated when orders are transmitted electronically. For check-in, presorting titles into alphabetical order is no longer necessary. Furthermore, locating records is easier when there are multiple access points and keyword searching, and recording receipts is faster with keystroking. Claim control is truly a wonder. The system monitors the need to claim and reclaim by producing claim forms or transmitting claims electronically. Improved payment records are obtained when invoice information is loaded in the system electronically to replace manual recording. Entering data electronically not only saves time but also avoids errors that can occur in copying invoice information.

Improved quality control for serials acquisitions is also a major benefit of automation. Keeping up with the maintenance of various files and monitoring them closely in order to take timely action for claims, renewal, and binding are difficult with manual operations. When staff members are overwhelmed by the receiving and processing of continuously arriving new issues, file maintenance and reviewing may be ignored or delayed. Information may be lost in the files, and claims, renewal, and binding are not processed on time. Automated systems not only maintain the order of files but also automatically review files to sort out which actions need to be taken. It is much easier to maintain a high-quality operation with the assistance of automated systems.

Serials acquisitions activities tend to be remote from public service desks in the manual stage. The Kardex file and other acquisitions working files are kept in the serials department. Typically, manual serials control files are unavailable when the serials department is closed after office hours. With automation both the public service staff and users may access serials acquisition status information directly through computers. They can obtain information on titles being ordered, latest issues received, cancellations, and temporary suspensions. Best of all, this information is available at all hours from multiple locations.

Automation solves one problem in the debate over centralization or decentralization of serials acquisitions. One of the main arguments revolves around who has the acquisition files. Both the main library and branches need these files to perform their work, but maintaining duplicate files in both locations is expensive. Automation provides flexibility because all libraries can share the same file. Thus, branches may check the system for their serials acquisitions status in a centralized organization, and the main library may check branch acquisition activities through the system in a decentralized organization.

Types of Systems

Serials automation can be provided by a stand-alone system designed solely for serials control or as part of an integrated system that includes all essential library functions, such as cataloging, monograph acquisitions, circulation, online public access catalog, and serials control. Systems are developed by computer system vendors, subscription agents, and libraries. During the early days of serials automation in the 1970s, when there were scarcely adequate serials control systems available on the market, some libraries developed in-house systems to accommodate their needs. This was a costly and complicated task that required in-house computer and serials expertise and continuous experimentation and improvement. Now a variety of systems are available in the market to match different collection sizes and requirements, and designing a local system "from scratch" is no longer a necessity nor a particularly economical or effective option.

In an integrated system, all functions share a single database. Thus, when a record is created or altered through one function, the information is incorporated when performing other functions. For instance, when a periodical cataloging record is created in the database, this record is used by the serials acquisitions unit for controlling the title's acquisition processing; when a new periodical issue is checked in, this information can be viewed by the public service personnel to answer questions. The shared database provides convenience and economy for coordination among different functions; however, cooperation among librarians and staff members of different departments is vitally important to maintain the harmony and efficiency of the system. To maintain the integrity of the database, there usually are security controls to limit who may input, update, and view records. For instance, only catalogers and trained staff members may be allowed to create or update cataloging records; only serials staff members may be allowed to alter serials receiving records; library users may view titles that have been ordered and received but not other acquisitions processing records. Patrons usually are not permitted to enter or alter data.

The typical development pattern of an integrated system starts with one function, then gradually expands to other functions. The vendor continually improves and upgrades developed functions based on customers' demands and suggestions. Therefore, it is common for an integrated system to be of uneven quality for different functions. The latest function developed often has the lowest quality. The short history of automated serials control explains why it is often a weak link in an integrated system.

Serials subscription agents play an important role in the development of stand-alone serials systems. If a library purchases a system from an agent who is also its major subscription vendor, the initial creation and ongoing maintenance of records is much easier. Since the vendor has to maintain its customers' records in the database to track ordering, claiming, payment, and renewal activities, libraries have the advantage of transferring a lot of acquisitions records from the vendor's database, which saves work in creating records. This is a major selling point of vendor-based systems.

Integrated systems usually are preferred by library administrators because records are shared among functions and both software and hardware cost less when supporting a single system. However, serials librarians are attracted to stand-alone, vendor-based serials control systems because such systems are designed to satisfy serials processing needs and minimize record-keeping work. Serials librarians may also prefer a high-quality serials control module of an integrated system that is not being used by their library. In these cases, available interfaces play an important role, allowing libraries to choose the best system for each function. (To market products flexibly, vendors design systems to interface with one another so data easily may be exchanged among systems, as if multiple systems were sharing the same database.) For instance, bibliographic records from the utility used by the library for cataloging may be loaded into the local OPAC operated on a different system and to acquisitions and serials functions on yet another system; the serials holdings records may be loaded from the serials control system to the OPAC, etc. With the maturity of interfaces, libraries have more freedom in choosing the best system for a particular function and for local requirements based on the quality and value of the system. Although by doing so libraries may have to support multiple systems, the cost can be offset by the savings derived from having the most-effective system for each function.

Computer hardware for the serials control system may vary from minicomputers to microcomputers. Dedicated or shared terminals depend on the size of the collection and the requirements of the system. Hardware capability is constantly improving. The positive side is that the newer models usually are more powerful at a lower price, but libraries must constantly invest in newer generations of computers to keep up the quality of automation.

System Selection

There is a substantial literature on selecting and implementing automated systems. Readers who are given the responsibility of system selection and automation implementation must consult automation literature for step-by-step technical details.[1] As a brief introduction to the topic, the following discussions are limited to general concepts and issues involved in selecting a system.

Functional Requirements

Serials systems are designed to control acquisitions. An adequate system must support each distinct acquisition function: ordering, receiving, claiming, routing, binding, payment, renewal control, cancellations, and fiscal control and the added benefits of supporting union listing and producing management reports. In addition, there are some important basic requirements. First, the system must accommodate all types of serials included within the AACR2 definition. It must accommodate irregularities in publication, such as supplements, accompanying materials, suspensions, and title changes, and it must provide free-text fields when such things can be noted. The system also must accommodate standard records: full MARC-S records, holdings coded according to the MFHD and ANSI standards, and both Dewey and Library of Congress classification numbers. Searching capability should include all the traceable tags in the MARC format. Finally, the system must be able to interface with other systems being used by the library and must keep up with development of electronic data interchange following the Serials Industry Systems Advisory Committee (SISAC) standards.[2]

The Task Force

To select the most suitable system for the library, appointing a task force or forming a working team instead of relying on one person's judgment is a safe practice. Since the system mainly serves serials acquisitions, the librarian responsible for serials acquisitions and the staff member responsible for supervising daily serials operation are two of the most important members of the team. A working team composed of these two members may be sufficient for a library with a small serials collection that is selecting a stand-alone system. However, a library with a large serials collection that needs a comprehensive system to accommodate the complex acquisitions operation may need a task force with more members and various areas of expertise. A serials cataloger or records manager may contribute ideas about the creation and maintenance of bibliographic and holdings records in the system; a system librarian or a member from the supporting computer group can offer advice about selecting appropriate software and hardware. A selector and a reference librarian may serve as consultants to the task force to ensure issues relating to collection development and public service are considered.

The task force is responsible for developing requirements for purchase in accordance with local needs, identifying systems that match the requirements for the purchase and automation budgets, and making a recommendation for acquisition. The final acquisition decision usually is determined by a higher authority, such as the library director or the board of trustees.

Local Requirements

The task force assesses local needs to determine requirements for purchase as a method of identifying systems that are capable of supporting the library's acquisition activities. Local requirements are influenced by existing circumstances and future plans, such as the size of the collection, the types of serials to be controlled by the system, fund code structure and budget allocations, types of suppliers used by the library, single or multiple library locations, and extent of routing requirements. An important factor to consider is the existing computer systems in the library. The requirement may be to investigate a part of an integrated system or to identify a system that can interface with existing systems. Another factor to consider is the local computer technology support. A small library with no computer expertise cannot afford to select a system that needs local technical management.

Identifying Suitable Systems

Potential systems are identified by comparing the vendor's system documents with local requirements. The final selection process should include a system demonstration. Obtaining references from libraries using the system that have comparable serials collections and local needs is essential to confirm the system capabilities and the vendor's service. A word of caution is not to take "rain checks" for future enhancements. It is safer to select a system that already offers capabilities required by the library than a system that is planning to have them because it may take a long time for the vendor to develop new capabilities. In addition, vendors may change their priorities and postpone the implementation of the new enhancement.

Price is always an important issue. In addition to the initial purchase price, attention should be paid to ongoing maintenance charges. Most system vendors maintain continuous customer relations with libraries. They assist libraries in solving system-related problems, provide training sessions and workshops to help libraries use system capacities fully, and upgrade software and hardware periodically to improve the system. Libraries must be sure that they can afford the continuous system maintenance and service costs.

When an integrated system already has been firmly established in the library, some serials librarians face an administrative restriction on the choice of the serials control system; that is, they must adopt the serial module in the integrated system regardless of its quality. A responsible serials librarian should study different systems and recommend the best system to the administration instead of getting stuck with a poor system that will create chaos for serials acquisitions. If the recommended system is the best one to suit local needs, can interface with the current library system already developed by the vendor, and is priced within the allocated automation budget, the library administration may accept the recommendation.

Purchase Agreement

Serious purchase negotiation between the library and the vendor follows the library's identification of the desired system. The negotiation mainly revolves around what is included in the initial purchase, the ongoing maintenance and service, and the price. After the final negotiation is completed, a written purchase agreement should specify all the details agreed on by the two parties. Some agreements may also include a section on the vendor's legal obligation in case the system is discontinued by the vendor in the future. An institution may require its legal service to review the agreement; in the case of public libraries, it may involve the city's legal department.

Implementation

Implementing an automated serials control system includes a number of key steps—all of which are important to success.

Planning

Automating serials control is a complicated task because serials acquisitions are made continually. Converting orders from manual operation to automation without interrupting the daily activities of receipt, claim, payment, and binding requires careful implementation planning. Until the conversion of manual records into an automated system is completed, serials acquisitions will be operated under both systems, with parts of orders in the new system while others are still in the manual file. A thoughtful, well-prepared implementation plan may shorten the conversion period and lessen the hardships of operating under both systems.

The implementation plan may be drafted by the serials librarian in consultation with key serials staff members and other colleagues, such as the cataloger, the system librarian, or a working team. Key elements in the plan include functions to be automated and information to be entered in the database. Ideally an automated serials control system should include all serials acquisitions functions. In reality, some systems still lack certain functional requirements, and some libraries are not ready to automate all functions. For instance, bindery often is not included in the first phase of automation either because the system is not perfected to handle this function or because no effective interface exists with the binder's automated system. Because a manual serials operation often maintains useless information by inheriting the record-keeping practice set many years earlier, this is a good opportunity to review the value of the information in the files for the new system database.

The implementation plan also sets the order and time frame for conversion. Since serials orders must be converted one by one, there are various choices in setting the conversion order. A library may decide to convert periodicals first, to convert titles to alphabetical order, or to convert each order when a new issue is received. During the conversion period, acquisition records constantly are being moved from the manual file to the new system. Once an order's check-in record is created in the new system, new issues are received in the system instead of on the Kardex card. It is important to develop a method that enables staff members to know which record is in which file without double-checking both files.

The implementation schedule is influenced by staff availability. When appropriate funding and staffing are allocated to the conversion project, the progress should be steady and fast. If there is no proper funding or extra staffing, conversion work must be absorbed by the regular staff, and progress will be slow. A realistic approach is to set a slow but steady progress schedule, targeting a reasonable number of records to be converted each week. As long as there are reachable targets, the project will progress steadily to completion.

A written implementation document states the goal, provides conversion procedures, and sets time frames that are essential for the success of the automation. It keeps the implementation on the right course and schedule and maintains the efficiency and quality of the project.

Staff Training

After the implementation plan is completed, procedures are written, terminals are hooked up, and the working area is ready, staff members must be trained to use the new system. Staff training may be divided into three parts. The first part is a general introduction of the system and the implementation plan. This part should be attended by all serials staff members. The second part concentrates on individual functions, and staff members are trained only for the functions related to their work. The third part is for members who will be participating in the records conversion project. Hands-on practice on the system should be a part of the training course. A practice period should follow the training to make sure each member is familiar and comfortable with the system before officially starting the automation implementation.

Building the Database

The main work in serials automation is to enter acquisition records into the system database. There are four basic records needed for the acquisition process: bibliographic, order, invoice/payment, and receipt records, and there are different ways to enter these records into the system database.

Bibliographic Records

Bibliographic records serve as the base records of the data file. Acquisitions information is then added to the bibliographic record. Since cataloging is usually the first function to be automated in libraries, only rarely does a library have to build the bibliographic records in a serials system from scratch by the time it automates serials. If serials control is a part of the integrated system used by the library, bibliographic records are already in the database. Otherwise, records may be downloaded from the library's cataloging utility, the local OPAC system, or a vendor's database. In automation, a library's properly constructed and maintained bibliographic records following national standards become the most long-lasting asset. Software may be upgraded, hardware replaced by newer generations, and systems discontinued, but bibliographic records can be moved among systems and shared by different functions.

If serials control is not part of the integrated system used by the library, a separate database must be built and maintained for the serials system.

Bibliographic records may be brief or full MARC records—this is a local choice. The advantages of full MARC records should not be overlooked because they provide more versatility in searching and producing management reports. Libraries also must decide whether the serials system database should include only active titles or also inactive titles that have ceased publication, have been superseded by new titles, or have been canceled by the library. An inclusive database has the advantage of presenting the library's complete serials collection, but it can be costly. Each title contained in the database takes up precious space, and the larger the database, the more costly it is to maintain. Most system vendors charge maintenance fees according to the number of records in the database. Since the serials control system is used mainly to support acquisitions, keeping inactive titles no longer associated with acquisition activities poses an unnecessary burden on the system's budget.

Order Records

After bibliographic records are in place, order records are attached to the appropriate bibliographic record. Serials vendors may provide assistance in entering the order records by extracting the library's order records from their databases so that they can be electronically downloaded into the library's system. Such downloading demands the proper interface between the serials vendor's system and the library system. Otherwise, libraries have to key in order records.

Invoice and Payment Records

Invoice and payment information often is attached to the order record in automated systems. Again, most serials vendors are able to extract invoice information from their databases and electronically download it into the library's computer system. Libraries usually maintain the latest invoice and payment information in the system. If invoice/payment records have to be manually keyed in, libraries may delay entering them into the system until new invoices are received to avoid the excessive work of transferring payment information from the manual file. In this situation the manual payment file is consulted for the interim period if there is a need to verify invoice/payment information.

Creating Check-in Records

Creating check-in records is the most time-consuming and complicated part of the conversion project because there are no shortcuts to creating these records. In addition to creating the check-in screen, the work also may involve setting the claim cycle, bindery cycle, and routing. Work forms may provide help in the complex process of seeking appropriate information from manual files for the system requirements. One advantage in using work forms is that they ensure that information being input into the system for each order is consistent. The supervisor may review the work forms before the information is input to ensure that it is complete and correct, then data may be input by a lower-level staff member or temporary helper to achieve higher efficiency in using staffing time. Figure 9 shows a sample work form for creating a check-in record. Entering information on this form into the system will create a check-in record, predict the next expected issue, and set the claim and bindery-alert cycle.

Vendors usually provide detailed instructions on how to create check-in records. They explain the relationship between information input into the system and the results it may produce. To make decisions about selecting appropriate information to enter in the system, the planning group has to understand which information is related to which functions. For instance, a periodical's frequency and prediction of receiving dates are related to the claim function. Therefore, without inputting this information, the system cannot perform the claim function. Likewise, if the wrong frequency is entered, the claim alert will not be accurate.

The planning group has to decide how much of the retrospective-receipt records are to be transferred from the manual check-in record to the computerized record. Assuming the summary holdings are already entered (either by being loaded with the bibliographic records or manually entered), the check-in record has to show at least all the issues in the current volume and earlier issues that are not yet bound. If libraries need to keep a receiving-history pattern for claim review, the receiving record may include the previous volume also.

Working with Dual Systems

Although there are quick ways to enter bibliographic, order, and invoice/payment records into the system database, check-in records—the most active acquisition records—have to be manually created one-by-one. If a library has few active orders and sufficient staff to complete the automation within a short time, it may be able to hold all acquisitions activities for one or two weeks until the automation has been completed. Generally speaking, it is difficult for libraries to escape dual systems operation during the implementation period. If libraries plan wisely, it actually is not difficult to operate under two systems.

Converting titles in alphabetical order seems to provide the simplest migration status. The conversion progress is updated each day to indicate which letters have been automated; thus, staff members can easily decide an order's location. When an order's check-in record is created in the new system, it immediately replaces the manual record and becomes the working record. This means that if a new issue arrives for this order, it is checked in using the new system, not the Kardex card. In the meantime, Kardex cards still are used for orders that do not have check-in records in the new system. Using this method, acquisition records are gradually transferred from the Kardex to the system, and staff members know which orders are in the new system from the daily, even hourly, automation progress updates. There is no extra work or confusion in using dual systems to perform daily work.

When a new check-in record is created in the computer system, libraries may record the system-assigned record number on the Kardex card. The number serves as an indication that the record has been converted, and no new issues should be checked in on the Kardex card. It also provides a link

FIGURE 9. Automated Check-In Record Creation Work Form

SEARCH INFORMATION:

Title: t Quarterly review of economics and finance
Author: a
ISSN: i 0038-5797 BCN: f 01695478 CSN: o 692-51388

CHECK-IN RECORD:

Category: P
Copies: 1
Location: Alex
RLOC: S
Vendor: Faxon
Label: Per
Operator ID: KM
Note: RR, Bd each vol., B# 571, Format: vol.
Vendor Note: FT # 091186
Bind Title:
Bind Info: B# 571

CHECK-IN CARD:

Starting cover date of card: Sp, 94
First expected date: 05-28-94
Starting volume #: 34
Starting issue #: 1
Issues per volume: 4
Days between issues: 90
Days before claim: 45
Unit of binding: 4 issues
Binding delay: 1 issue
Number of items on card: 56

Verify input. If necessary, change:

Reset issues: Yes
Default display mode: Card
Default volume mode: Numeric
Default issue mode: Numeric

BACK ISSUES NEEDING CHECK-IN:

Volume	Issue	Check-in date
33	1	05-28-93
33	2	08-30-93
33	3	11-30-93
33	4	02-30-94

Prepared by: KM
Date: 3-15-94

Entered by: MSM
Date: 3-21-94
Check-in record #:
.c 1081585

between the old and new records in case there is a need for verification. Do not be in a hurry to discard old Kardex cards. Although essential information has been transferred to the new system, old cards may be checked occasionally to verify information and solve problems. Their value will diminish with time, and eventually, they can be discarded.

Other acquisition functions, such as claiming, routing, and binding, may follow the check-in and should be performed gradually by the new system. For instance, the system may produce claim-alert lists for orders that have been converted; thus, their claims can be controlled by the computer instead of the manual method.

General Comments

There are some key factors to keep in mind when planning and implementing an automated serials control system. Some of them may seem like simple common sense but are often overlooked, nonetheless.

Records

Converting manual files into the computer system is a time-consuming and labor-intensive undertaking. Serials staff should avoid wasting effort in converting inaccurate manual records, which creates a dirty database, or entering unwanted records, which clutters database space. Therefore, it is important to screen and clean manual records before automation. Two problematic areas in the manual file are holdings records and inactive orders. Serials holdings are elusive and, thus, difficult to maintain accurately. Libraries have to be faithful in updating additions and deletions and performing periodical inventories to maintain the integrity of holdings records. This is easy to say but difficult to achieve because performing inventory is a time-consuming and tedious task. However, the benefits of having an accurate database are worth the effort and time.

Inactive orders are the result of cessations, suspensions, title changes, supplier's errors, delinquencies in payment, etc. They can easily escape the attention of the serials staff unless Kardex reading is performed regularly. If inactive orders are sorted out and taken care of properly before automation is implemented, the conversion process will be smoother.

It is difficult for serials staff to find the time and energy to verify holdings and clean up problems while undertaking an automation project. Problematic orders usually are put aside and dealt with later. It is a good idea for libraries that have no firm commitment for automation to start a manual records cleanup project and to perform holdings inventory whenever time and energy permit. This is solid preparation for possible future automation.

Staff

Well-trained and highly motivated staff members are the key to the success of automation implementation. To be enthusiastic participants during the implementation, they have to be treated as important partners in the automation project from the very beginning. Therefore, they should be informed of the library's intention to automate, the system-selection progress, and the implementation plan. They should be consulted for practical advice on the records-conversion process and the work-area design.

Staff members who have no experience using computers need lessons on basic computer concepts before receiving training on records conversion and system operation. They need time to feel comfortable with the computer before being asked to do records conversion. Listen to staff complaints and suggestions—the procedure may need some revision to improve efficiency. It is reasonable for staff members to need extra encouragement and sympathy when learning to use a new system while still keeping up the manual operation. Proper leadership, training, and communication provide a sound base for maintaining staff morale and improving work efficiency.

Organization

Automation does not change serials functions and acquisition processes but introduces new ways to perform tasks. Therefore, procedures used for manual systems must be revised, staff responsibilities and workload must be adjusted, and some reorganization may be required to use automation to its full advantage. During the implementation period, the serials librarian must observe and evaluate the impact of automation on daily operations and plan appropriate changes to suit the new working method.

A major impact of automation is that staff members are required to spend a large amount of work time in front of a computer screen. This can be unpleasant or unacceptable for some staff members. Although staff members must learn to tolerate this new demand to a certain degree, the librarian may alter their responsibilities by assigning some work performed away from the computer. Serials departments involved with public service have a major advantage because they can break away from computer-related tasks. For instance, the check-in staff can also be responsible for shelving newly received periodical issues in the reading room or answering public inquiries.

The Future

Serials control systems available today are designed for current serial publications and their acquisitions. However, the arrival of electronic serials, full-text CD-ROM, and article delivery services and the emphasis on articles instead of issues will have an impact on managing serials. The promotion of electronic data interchange (EDI) by the Serials Industry Systems Advisory Committee (SISAC) is putting a new demand on computer system vendors. Libraries that have automated their serials control are facing new challenges, such as software and hardware upgrading, internal system changes, external system discontinuation, and the impact of new developments in the serials field.

Notes

1. Readers may wish to consult the following books on library automation as guides to system selection and automation implementation. They may find more material under the subject heading "Automation of library processes—Serial records" in *Library Literature.*

   Marlene Clayton and Chris Batt, *Managing Library Automation,* 2d ed. (Aldershot, England: Ashgate, 1992).

   John M. Cohn, Ann L. Kelsey, and Keith Michael Fiels, *Planning for Automation: A How-to-Do-It Manual for Librarians* (New York: Neal-Schuman Publishers, 1992).

   John Corbin, *Implementing the Automated Library System* (Phoenix, Ariz.: Oryx Press, 1988).

   Edwin M. Cortez and Tom Smorch, *Planning Second Generation Automated Library Systems* (Westport, Conn.: Greenwood Press, 1993).

   Library Systems Evaluation Guide: Volume 1: Serials Control (Powell, Ohio: James E. Rush Associates, 1983).

2. Judy McQueen and Richard Boss published "Serials Control in Libraries: Automated Options" in *Library Technology Reports,* 20(2): 87–282 (Mar.–Apr. 1984), which was later supplemented by Boss's further study on serials control, "Technical Services Functionality in Integrated Library Systems," *Library Technology Reports,* 28(1): 7–56 (Jan.–Feb. 1992). These reports are especially valuable for checking functional requirements.

Chapter 11

Current Topics and Future Challenges

Previous chapters provided basic knowledge about serials management practices used by libraries today. However, these practices have to be modified continuously to accommodate changes occurring in serials publications and library operations. Reasons for changes vary. In recent years, advancing computer technology and the general economic environment have precipitated changes. Computer technology has brought improvement in information retrieval and enabled electronic publishing to flourish. Serials, being essential information sources for scholarly research, are on the cutting edge of new technology applications in information science. Serials management must accommodate new developments. The economic environment also has an impact on serials management in coping with tight budgets, increasing prices, and the devaluation of the dollar. An effective serials librarian must keep a close watch on current topics in the field and assess their impact on the future of serials management. This chapter provides a brief overview of current topics and guides readers to meet future challenges.

Current Topics

Some of the changes currently affecting serials include electronic publishing, the Internet, pricing, copyright, standards, and the role of serials librarians.

The Impact of Electronic Publishing

Electronic publishing and computer technology are affecting the serials scene in three major ways. The first is the availability of reference tools in electronic format. Libraries are providing serial indexes, abstracts, and tables of contents. Some also provide the full text of the articles on CD-ROM or by direct access to publisher's databases. The second is the budding of electronic journals and their impact on scholarly communication. The third is the electronic article delivery service provided by information vendors, which offers libraries and users a new choice for obtaining information in serials. Instead of the traditional focus on subscriptions and journal issues, the purchase of articles on demand is becoming a consideration in acquisition practice.

Discussions about the impact of electronic publishing on serials may be divided into two categories: the impact on serials librarianship and the impact on publishing practices. Topics in the first category include the practical issues of dealing with hardware, software, staff training, contract negotiation with vendors, and budget seeking to support the provision of electronic serials in the library. This category also involves advanced thinking on planning and implementing networks to link users with information sources and realize the virtual library. Topics in the other category focus on more speculative views of how electronic publishing changes the roles of parties in the information chain: authors, publishers, vendors, libraries, and readers. Electronic publishing enables authors to deliver information directly to readers without the intervention of intermediaries and often eliminates publishers as well as editors and peer reviewers. Computer technology has made it possible for readers to access information from home and office. These changes challenge the role of information intermediaries in electronic publishing and information delivery.

The Internet

The Internet is the main information superhighway in the world today. It is a major topic in the library and information science literature and a popular theme at conferences and workshops. The Internet is important to serials management because it delivers both electronic serials and serials reference tools. Popular topics relating to the Internet are the resources available on it, methods of retrieving them, security and copyright issues, commercial use of the Internet, and new developments in Internet use.

Serials Pricing

Serials pricing is a topic that has been around for a long time and never seems to go away. The discussion of serials pricing reached a peak during the late 1980s when libraries started to experience major impacts on acquisitions from the combination of tight budgets, inflation, and fluctuating dollar exchange rates. Discussions have included the investigation of publisher's pricing policies and practices, serials deselection methods and cancellation projects, impact of serials inflation on collection development, the influence of academic promotion practices on the quality and quantity of journal publications, ownership of copyright, etc.

Copyright

Two major concerns have stimulated discussions on copyright in recent years: price increases of scholarly journals and the development of electronic publishing. The first group of discussions centers on whether the author or the publisher should hold the copyright. Scholars and librarians often are frustrated by the high prices of scholarly journals that erode their ability to acquire and access serials information. Although the scholars of academia are the main contributors of journal articles, academic libraries serving these contributors have to pay a high price to purchase the journals in which they are published. Scholars question whether it is fair for publishers to hold the copyright on their writings and, along with librarians, wonder whether it would be beneficial for authors, libraries, and readers if copyrights were retained by authors. Ann Okerson discusses the possibility of establishing university-based publishing to achieve not-for-profit distribution of scholarly information. This may be a workable idea to save universities the expense of buying back their scholarship from commercial publishers.[1] In 1993 the Copyright Policy Task Force of the Triangle Research Libraries Network (TRLN), Durham, Raleigh, and Chapel Hill, North Carolina, drafted a "Model University Policy Regarding Faculty Publication in Scientific and Technical Scholarly Journals" that echoes Okerson's discussion.[2]

The majority of copyright discussions center on how to apply the law to electronic publications and whether it needs revision to control the right to copy electronically published materials. In theory, the current copyright law can apply to publications in any format. The control applies to the contents, not the packaging, so in theory there is no need to revise the law. However, the reality is that it is difficult to control "fair use" of electronic information. As a result, publishers and vendors are using licensing agreements to control the fair use of electronic information. As of this writing, the U.S. Department of Commerce is recommending a rewrite of the copyright law to protect creators of information in digital forms.[3]

Standards

From the introduction of MARC records and library automation to sharing resources and networking, standards have become a vital element in the provision of library services. Libraries use standards to control records, share information, and communicate with other parties in the information chain. Standards also apply to serials operations, such as *ANSI Z39.44-1986, Serial Holdings Statements* and *ANSI Z39.45-1983, Claims for Missing Issues of Serials*. In the fast-paced information-management field, standards should be revised and redeveloped to accommodate new demands as they occur. For instance, the *Claims for Missing Issues of Serials* is already obsolete with the development of the X12 standard for serial claims (a standard that is described later in the chapter).

Two organizations are associated with the development of serials standards: National Information Standards Organization (NISO) and Serials Industry Systems Advisory Committee (SISAC). NISO is accredited by the American National Standards Institute (ANSI) as the developer of standards for libraries, publishers, and information science. ANSI coordinates the voluntary standards system in the United States and is a member of the International Organization for Standardization (ISO) in Geneva. SISAC provides a forum in which members of the serials industry and related groups discuss and resolve mutual concerns and develop standardized formats for the electronic transmittal of serials information. Its members include publishers, librarians, subscription agents, computer system vendors, database producers, and information specialists. It was formed in 1982 as a serials counterpart to the Book Industry Systems Advisory Committee (BISAC), which was formed in 1974. Both committees belong to the Book Industry Study Group (BISG), a nonprofit corporation formed in 1976 to promote and support research and idea exchanges in the publishing industry. Standards developed by SISAC are proposed to NISO for adoption as national standards.[4]

Serial Identifiers

As of this writing, the serials community is promoting the use of the standard *ANSI/NISO Z39.56-1991, Serial Item and Contribution Identifier* (SICI), developed by SISAC after almost ten years of cumulative effort. The goal of this standard is to identify specific issues of a serial title in a unique way to process orders and claims electronically. It also aims to set standards for bar coding at the issue level on journal covers for automatic check-in. The goals have been expanded to allow for article-level identification for document delivery. Figure 10 illustrates the construction of the SICI, and figure 11 shows samples of the SICI and SISAC bar code symbol. Kluwer Academic Publications has been printing the SISAC bar code symbol on its serial publications since 1989. More and more professional, scientific, and technical journal publishers are committing to the use of the symbol. Major library computer system vendors either have developed or have planned scanner capabilities for library check-in systems to use the bar code symbol, which increases the speed and accuracy of the check-in process.[5]

Standard for Electronic Data Interchange

A hot topic in library acquisitions is electronic data interchange (EDI). Wilbert Harri explains: "Electronic data interchange is the telephonic exchange, between trading partners, of routine business transactions in highly structured electronic formats without human intervention."[6] In acquisitions, there are routine business transactions that take place between libraries, vendors, and publishers, such as information exchange for the handling of orders, claims, and invoices. Using EDI in acquisitions would improve productivity because manual keying of data would not be required, which would eliminate human error during manual data inputting and raise the quality of work. However, to implement EDI, business partners have to agree on a standard format for data exchange. In 1979 ANSI chartered the Accredited Standards Committee (ASC) X12 to develop a standard for electronic interchange of business transactions, such as order placement, processing, shipping, receiving, invoicing, and payment. The X12 standard has been adopted by the business community and is widely used.

In 1985 NISO released *ANSI Z39.49-1985, Computerized Book Ordering,* a standard initiated by BISAC. In the meantime, SISAC was drafting a standard for serials business transactions. However, both BISAC and SISAC have abandoned their previous work and diverted attention and efforts to applying X12 formats to book and serials industries because the X12 format

FIGURE 10. Construction of the SICI

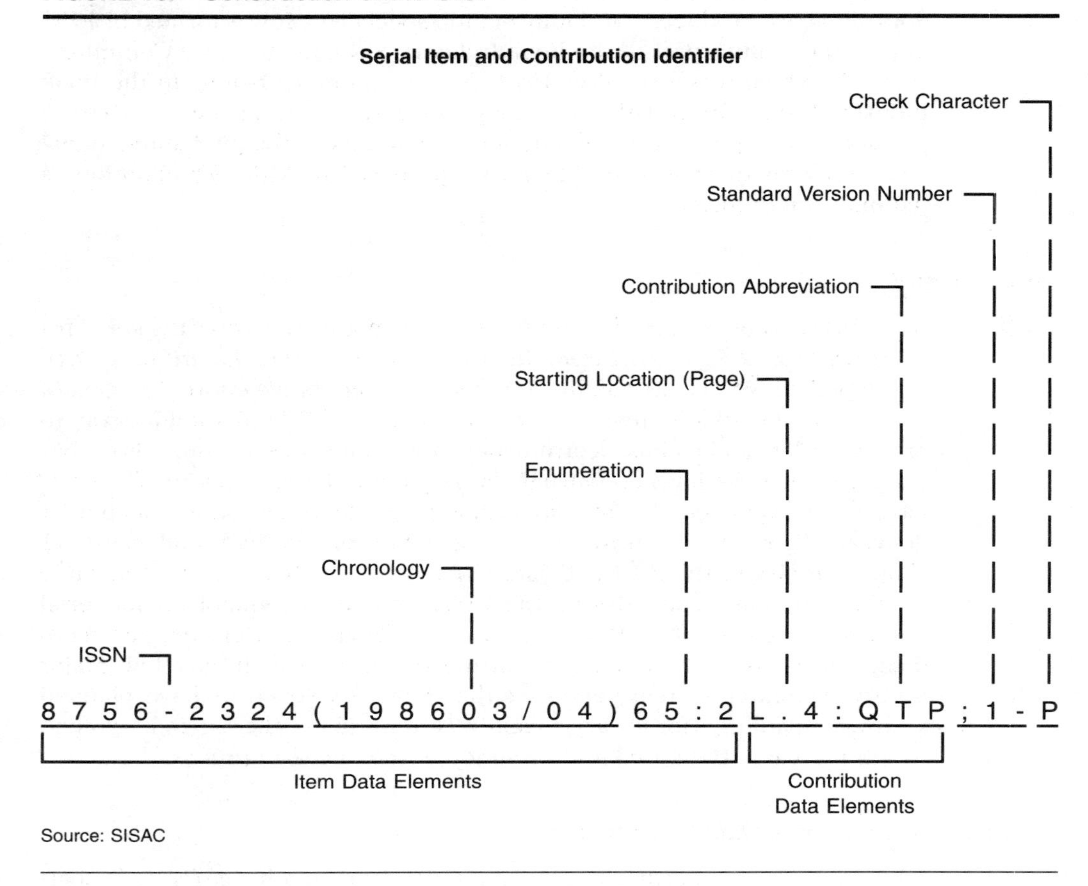

Source: SISAC

FIGURE 11. SICI and SISAC Bar Code Symbol

SICI: 0885-3959(199221/22)7:1L.4:SART;1-U

Citation: "SISAC Announces Release of Time-Saving Diskette."
SISAC News, v.7, no. 1 (spring/summer 1992), p. 4.

SISAC Bar Code Symbol

Source: SISAC

is less expensive to store and transmit than Z39 standards. The trigger to this switch seemed to be the 1989 announcement by Waldenbooks, B. Dalton, Ingram, and Baker & Taylor of a plan to develop a network of telecommunications with trading partners for business transactions using X12.

SISAC is the major force in applying X12 generic standards to the serials industry. It is working closely with the International Committee on EDI for Serials (ICEDIS) and its Canadian counterpart, CSISAC. A close liaison is also maintained with ASC X12. The areas of focus are claims, invoices, and orders. To date, there has been substantial success with claims and invoices. SISAC is the best source for information on the latest in X12 standards development.

Publishers and subscription agents are enthusiastic participants in X12 development and promotion. Computer system vendors are being encouraged to develop X12 capability in their products, and librarians are being educated on adapting X12 to their work to achieve higher efficiency.

The Changing Role of Serials Librarians

Discussions on the changing role of serials librarians emerge with the development of electronic publishing. Practical discussions center on how to manage electronic serials, including adapting to new requirements in cataloging, acquisitions, public services, and computer knowledge. Issues such as negotiating licensing agreements for electronic serial subscriptions, using information resources on the Internet, providing patron access to electronic journals, using article delivery as an acquisition method, and planning and working toward the concept of virtual libraries provoke new challenges and excitement for the serials profession. The more speculative discussions focus on the dominant place of electronic journals in scholarly communication and the potential for the virtual library to eliminate the need for a library building. Positive suggestions include transforming serials librarians into information specialists, who assist users in choosing and collecting information in serials, or into information consultants, who provide custom-made information for individual users. On the other hand, doomsayers predict that there will be no place for librarians when users can obtain information directly from authors via electronic publishing.

Keeping Up with the Future

Some of the issues mentioned in this section may soon lose their value or interest for those working in serials management as new topics may emerge as the center of discussions. Effective ways to keep up with current topics are by joining professional organizations, attending serials-related conferences and workshops, and reading the serials literature.

Professional Organizations and Conferences

Joining professional organizations and attending their conferences and workshops are effective ways to keep up with the newest topics in the serials field. One of the most important organizations in the United States is the North American Serials Interest Group, Inc. (NASIG). It was established in 1985 for the purpose of promoting communication and the sharing of ideas among all members of the serials information chain. Membership is limited to individuals, including librarians, educators, publishers, editors, vendors, binders, bibliographic utilities representatives, and indexers. The group holds an annual conference each June at a North American university or college campus. The cost is reasonable and the atmosphere relaxing. Valuable information is communicated in a series of presentations, workshops, and informal discussions among individuals. Conference proceedings are published in paper and electronic formats and as issues of *The Serials Librarian.* NASIG also sponsors regional seminars and workshops; publishes a newsletter; maintains NASIGNET, the official electronic networking resource for organizational communication and education; and sponsors library school students to attend the annual conference.

The establishment of NASIG was largely inspired by the success of the United Kingdom Serials Group (UK Serials Group). This group holds annual conferences at a university or college campus in the United Kingdom and publishes a journal entitled *Serials: The Journal of the United Kingdom Serials Group* and other serials-related publications. The idea of forming serials groups and holding conferences mushroomed following the successes of the UK Serials Group and NASIG. Regional serials groups have been established in Europe, Asia, Africa, and Australia.

Two other important professional organizations are the Serials Section of the Association for Library Collections and Technical Services (ALCTS), a division of the American Library Association, and the Serials Section of the International Federation of Library Associations and Institutions (IFLA). These sections usually conduct business meetings and present programs and workshops during the conferences of their parent associations. They also sponsor and organize regional workshops.

The Serials Section of the ALCTS distributes information concerning serials literature, encourages specialized training for serials librarians, and coordinates serials-related activities within the American Library Association. Some of its committees are Acquisitions, Education, Serials Cataloging, Serials Standards, and Union Lists of Serials. It also administers awards such as the Bowker/Ulrich's Serials Librarianship Award, the First Step Award—a professional development grant for new serials librarians—and the Worst Serials Title Change of the Year Award. Its Research Libraries Discussion Group provides an informal forum for discussions of current topics and projects in research libraries.[7] Joining the ALCTS Serials Section and participating in its activities are essential for serials librarians who wish to be linked with colleagues and keep up with new developments in serials librarianship.

The College of Charleston Conference, The Feather River Institute on Acquisitions and Collection Development, and the conference on Acquisitions, Budgets, and Material Costs are popular conferences with serials librarians. The Charleston Conference is sponsored by the College of Charleston in South Carolina and concentrates on collection development, management, and acquisitions. It is held annually in November. Katina Strauch, the collection development librarian of the College of Charleston

Library, is the conference convener. The Feather River Institute is sponsored by the University of the Pacific Libraries in California. It is held during May of each year. This conference is attended mostly by acquisitions librarians and is organized in a retreat style at the tranquil Feather River Lodge in Blairsden, California. Sul Lee, dean of libraries at the University of Oklahoma, directs the conference on Acquisitions, Budgets, and Material Costs. It is held during the spring of each year at the University of Oklahoma Libraries.

Serials Literature

Besides joining serials-related organizations and attending their conferences and workshops, reading current serials literature is important in keeping up with events. At the end of this book you will find a selected bibliography that offers suggestions for reading to follow up on current topics.

Conclusion

Serials management has come a long way since it was recognized as a specialty within librarianship by J. Harris Gable in 1935.[8] Its place in the library organizational chart has been changed constantly from being an integrated department to being segregated among different functional departments. Serials working procedures have been continuously altered and updated to accommodate the coming of microforms, automation, and electronic publishing. As Tuttle stated: "Serials management is a library specialty in which some feel that change is the only constant."[9]

The visibility of serials management has been increasing since the late 1980s. This is mainly attributable to the issues of serials pricing and electronic publishing. When serials acquisitions absorb a major portion of materials budgets, they become the focus of collection development and attract the attention of administrators, librarians, scholars, publishers, and vendors. Electronic publishing and computer technology offer new options for the distribution of serials information and are becoming the focus of scholarly communication. Serials librarians, along with serial publishing, become major players on the stage of librarianship and information management in the 1990s. The field of serials management continues to change, providing new challenges. This is indeed an exciting time to be a serials librarian.

Notes

1. Ann Okerson, "With Feathers: Effects of Copyright and Ownership on Scholarly Publishing," *College & Research Libraries* 52 (Sept. 1991): 425–38.
2. The TRLN model copyright document and discussions are published as Numbers 93 and 94 (29 Aug. 1993) of *Newsletter on Serials Pricing Issues.* To request these issues send a message to LISTSERV@GIBBS.OIT.UNC.EDU (Internet) with command GET PRICES.93. Repeat the same message for Number 94.
3. Teresa Riordan, "Writing Copyright Law for an Information Age," *New York Times* 143(49, 750) (July 7, 1994): D1, D5.

4. A free brochure, "NISO Standards," is available on request from NISO, Box 1056, Bethesda, MD 20827 or on the Internet: NISO@ENH.NIST.GOV.

5. Copies of *ANSI/NISO Z39.56 (1991) Serial Item and Contribution Identifier* are available from NISO Press, P.O. Box 338, Oxon Hill, MD 20750-0338; phone: (800) 282-6476. For the most up-to-date information concerning the implementation of SISAC Bar Code Symbol and SICI, contact SISAC at 160 Fifth Avenue, New York, NY 10010; fax: (212) 989-7542, phone (212) 929-1393.

6. Wilbert Harri, "Implementing Electronic Data Interchange in the Library Acquisitions Environment," *Library Acquisitions: Practice & Theory* 18(1) (1994): 115.

7. Detailed information for Serials Section activities is available from the annual *ALA Handbook of Organization and Membership Directory,* published by the American Library Association, 50 East Huron Street, Chicago, IL 60611.

8. J. Harris Gable, "The New Serials Department," *Library Journal* 60 (1935): 867–71.

9. Marcia Tuttle, "Serials Management," in *Guide to Technical Services Resources,* ed. Peggy Johnson (Chicago: American Library Association, 1994), 121.

Bibliography

Alexander, Adrian W. "Preconference on Serials Cancellations: 1993 Charleston Conference, Issues in Book and Serial Acquisitions." *Library Acquisitions: Practice & Theory* 18(3): 327–31 (1994).

Anderson, Jan. "Challenging the 'Good Buddies Factor' in Vendor Selection." *Advances in Serials Management* 3: 153–71 (1989).

Anglo-American Cataloguing Rules. 2d ed. 1988 rev. Chicago: American Library Association, 1988.

Association for Library Collections and Technical Services. Serials Section. Acquisitions Committee. *Guidelines for Handling Library Orders for Serials and Periodicals.* Rev. ed. Chicago: American Library Association, 1992.

———. *Serials Acquisitions Glossary.* Chicago: American Library Association, 1993.

Astle, Deana L. "The Scholarly Journal: Whence or Wither?" *The Journal of Academic Librarianship* 15: 151–6 (July 1989).

Bailey, Charles W., Jr. "The Coalition for Networked Information's Acquisition-on-Demand Model: An Exploration and Critique." *Serials Review* 18(1/2): 78–81 (spring/summer 1992).

Baker, Barry B. "Panacea, Patterns and Problems: Implementation of the USMARC Holdings Format at the University of Georgia Libraries." *Technical Services Quarterly* 9(3): 31–9 (1992).

Barker, Joseph W. "Unbundling Serials Vendors' Service Charges: Are We Ready?" *Serials Review* 16(2): 33–43 (summer 1990).

Barschall, H. "Electronic Version of Printed Journals." *Serials Review* 18(1/2): 49–51 (spring/summer 1992).

Basch, Bernard, and Judy McQueen. *Buying Serials: A How-to-Do-It Manual for Librarians.* New York: Neal-Schuman, 1990.

Bazirjian, Rosann. "Automation and Technical Services Organization." *Library Acquisitions: Practice & Theory* 17: 73–7 (spring 1993).

Bloss, Marjorie E. "The Two ANSI Standards for Serial Holdings Statements: A Comparison." *Serials Review* 11(4): 33–42 (1985).

Bluh, Pamela. "Document Delivery 2000: Will It Change the Nature of Librarianship?" *Wilson Library Bulletin* 67(6): 49–51, 112 (Feb. 1993).

Born, Kathleen. "The Role of the Serials Vendor in the Collection Assessment and Evaluation Process." *Journal of Library Administration* 19(2): 125–38 (1993).

Boss, Richard W. "Developing Requirements for Automated Serials Control Systems." *The Serials Librarian* 11(3/4): 37–70 (Dec. 1986–Jan. 1987).

———. "Technical Services Functionality in Integrated Library Systems." *Library Technology Reports* 28(1): 7–56 (Jan.–Feb. 1992).

Boss, Richard W., and Debora Raikes. *Developing Microform Reading Facilities.* Westport, Conn.: Microform Review Inc., 1981.

Brookfield, Karen, ed. *Scholarly Communication and Serials Prices: Proceedings of a Conference Sponsored by the Standing Conference of National and University Libraries and the British Library Research and Development Department 11–13 June 1990.* London: Bowker, 1991.

Brown, Clara D., and Lynn S. Smith. *Serials: Past, Present and Future.* 2d rev. ed. Birmingham, Ala.: EBSCO, 1980.

Brugger, Judith M. "How the NISO Holdings Standard Works: The Findings of an Investigation at CUNY, 1989." *The Serials Librarian* 20(2/3): 17–30 (1991).

Carlson, Barbara A. "Claiming Periodicals: The 'Trembling Balance' in the 'Feud of Want and Have.'" In *Legal and Ethical Issues in Acquisitions,* 119–27. Edited by Katina Strauch and Bruce Strauch. Binghamton, N.Y.: Haworth Press, 1990.

Carter, Ruth C. "Decentralization of Serials Functions." *Advances in Serials Management* 1: 83–99 (1986).

Chan, Lois Mai. *Cataloging and Classification: An Introduction.* 2d ed. New York: McGraw-Hill, 1994.

Cipolla, Wilma Reid. "Users of the Brave New Catalog: Electronic Access to Periodical Articles." *Advances in Serials Management* 4: 123–47 (1992).

Clapper, Mary Ellen. "Serial Holdings Standards." *The Serials Librarian* 11(3/4): 111–36 (Dec.1986–Jan.1987).

Clayton, Marlene, and Chris Batt. *Managing Library Automation.* 2d ed. Aldershot, England: Ashgate, 1992.

Cohn, John M., Ann L. Kelsey, and Keith Michael Fiels. *Planning for Automation: A How-to-Do-It Manual for Librarians.* New York: Neal-Schuman Publishers, 1992.

Cole, Jim E., and James W. Williams, eds. "Serials Cataloging Modern Perspectives and International Development." *The Serials Librarian* 22 (1992).

Collver, Mitsuko. "Organization of Serials Work for Manual and Automated Systems." *Library Resources & Technical Services* 24: 307–16 (fall 1980).

Cook, Jean G. "Serials' Place in the Organizational Chart: A Historical Perspective." *Advances in Serials Management* 1: 53–66 (1986).

Cortez, Edwin M., and Tom Smorch. *Planning Second Generation Automated Library Systems.* Westport, Conn.: Greenwood Press, 1993.

Cox, John. "Subscription Agents: Why Libraries Love Them and Publishers Take Them for Granted." *Logos* 2: 154–8 (1991).

Davenport, Elisabeth. "The Journal at the Cross-Roads: A One-Day Seminar for Librarians, Publishers, Subscription Agents and the Readers of Serials." *The NASIG Newsletter* 8(5): 22–5 (Dec. 1993).

Davis, Trisha L. "Blurring the Lines in Technical Services." *Library Acquisitions: Practice & Theory* 17: 85–7 (spring 1993).

Dean, John F. "The Preservation of Serials." *Advances in Serials Management* 3: 233–65 (1989).

Desmarais, Norman, ed. *CD-ROM Local Area Networks: A User's Guide.* Westport, Conn.: Meckler, 1991.

———. *The Librarian's CD-ROM Handbook.* Westport, Conn.: Meckler, 1989.

Dow, Ronald F., Karen Hunter, and G. Gregory Lozier. "Commentaries on Serials Publishing." *College & Research Libraries* 52: 521–7 (Nov. 1991).

Drake, Miriam. "Buying Articles in the Future." *Serials Review* 18(1/2): 78–81 (spring /summer 1992).

Ezzell, Joline R. "The Integrated Serials Department." *Advances in Serials Management* 1: 67–82 (1986).

Fisher, Janet. "Electronic Publishing Case Studies: Implications for Periodicals Publishing." *The NASIG Newsletter* 8(5): 30–1 (Dec. 1993).

Fisher, William. "A Brief History of Library-Vendor Relations Since 1950." *Library Acquisitions: Practice & Theory* 17: 61–9 (1993).

Fishwick, F. "The Effects of Unstable Exchange Rates on the Prices of Books and Journals." In *Serials '86: Proceedings of the UK Serials Group Conference, University of Exeter, 24–27 March 1986,* 70–87. Edited by R. M. Burton. UKSG, 1987.

Folcarelli, Ralph J., Arthur C. Tannenbaum, and Ralph C. Ferragamo. *The Microform Connection: A Basic Guide for Libraries.* New York: Bowker, 1982.

Franks, John. *What Is an Electronic Journal?* Available from John Franks, Department of Mathematics, Northwestern University, Evanston, IL 60208-2730, or on the Internet: JOHN@MATH.NWU.EDU.

Gammon, Julia A. "EDI and Acquisitions: The Future Is Now." *Library Acquisitions: Practice & Theory* 18(1): 113–4 (1994).

Gellatly, Peter, ed. *The Good Serials Department.* Binghamton, N.Y.: Haworth Press, 1990. Also published as *The Serials Librarian* 9 (1/2), 1990.

Getz, Malcolm. "Electronic Publishing: An Economic View." *Serials Review* 18(1/2): 25–31 (spring/summer 1992).

Gomez, Joni, and Jeanne Harrell. "Technical Services Reorganization: Realities and Reactions." *Technical Services Quarterly* 10(2): 1–15 (1992).

Graham, Margaret E., and Fiona Buettel, eds. *Serials Management: a Practical Handbook.* London: Aslib, 1990.

Grycz, Czeslaw Jan, ed. "Economic Models for Networked Information." Special issue of *Serials Review* 18(1/2) (spring/summer 1992).

Haley, Jean Walstrom, and James Talaga. "Academic Library Responses to Journal Price Discrimination." *College & Research Libraries* 53: 61–70 (Jan. 1992).

Hanson, Terry, and Joan Day, eds. *CD-ROM in Libraries.* London: Bowker Saur, 1994.

Harri, Wilbert. "Implementing Electronic Data Interchange in the Library Acquisitions Environment." *Library Acquisitions: Practice & Theory* 18(1): 115–7 (1994).

Harris, Patricia. "The Standards Matrix: Developers, Users, Vendors: Introduction." *Wilson Library Bulletion* 67(7): 33–4 (Mar. 1993).

Hawks, Carol Pitts. "Automated Library Systems: What's Next?" *The Serials Librarian* 21(2/3): 87–96 (1991).

Helal, Ahmed H., and Joachim W. Weiss, eds. *Libraries and Electronic Publishing: Promises and Challenges for the 90's; Festschrift in Honour of Richard M. Dougherty/14th International Essen Symposium 14 Oct.–17 Oct. 1991.* Essen: Universitatsbibliothek Essen, 1992.

Ivins, October. "Do Subscription Agents Earn Their Service Charges and How Can We Tell?" *Library Acquisitions: Practice & Theory* 13: 143–7 (1989).

Jackson, Mary E. "Resource Sharing and Document Delivery in the 1990s." *Wilson Library Bulletin* 67(6): 35–6, 110 (Feb. 1993).

Johnson, Peggy. *Automation and Organizational Change in Libraries.* Boston: G. K. Hall, 1991.

Katz, Bill, ed. *Vendors and Library Acquisitions.* New York: Haworth Press, 1991. Also published as *The Acquisitions Librarian* Number 5 (1991).

Katz, Bill, and Peter Gellatly. *Guide to Magazine and Serial Agents.* New York: Bowker, 1975.

Kaufman, Paula, and Angie LeClercq. "Archiving Electronic Journals: Who's Responsible for What." *Library Issues* 11: 1–4 (July 1991).

Kent, Philip G. "How to Evaluate Serials Suppliers." *Library Acquisitions: Practice & Theory* 18(1): 83–7 (1994).

Kinder, Robin, and Bill Katz, eds. *Serials and Reference Services.* Binghamton, N.Y.: Haworth, 1990. Also published as *The Reference Librarian* Numbers 27/28 (1990).

King, Timothy B. "The Impact of Electronic and Networking Technologies on the Delivery of Scholarly Information." *The Serials Librarian* 21(2/3): 5–13 (1991).

Kruger, Betsy. "Serials Acquisitions: Trends and Prospects." In *Technical Services Today and Tomorrow,* 38–49. Edited by Michael Gorman. Littleton, Colo.: Libraries Unlimited, 1990.

Kurosman, Kathleen, and Barbara Ammerman Durniak. "Document Delivery: A Comparison of Commercial Document Suppliers and Interlibrary Loan Services." *College & Research Libraries* 55(2): 129–39 (Mar. 1994).

Landesman, Betty. "EDI Standards for Acquisitions: They're (Just About) He-ere . . ." *Library Acquisitions: Practice & Theory* 18(1): 119–21 (1994).

———. "Standing-Order Series: Serials or Monographs?" In *Projects and Procedures for Serials Administration,* 199–206. Edited by Diane Stine. Ann Arbor, Mich.: Pierian Press, 1985.

Lane, Alfred H. *Gifts and Exchange Manual.* Westport, Conn.: Greenwood Press, 1980.

Langschied, Linda. "The Changing Shape of the Electronic Journal." *Serials Review* 17(3): 7–14 (Fall 1991).

Leach, J. Travis, and Karen Dalziel Tallman. "The Claim Function in Serials Management." *Advances in Serials Management* 4: 149–69 (1992).

Lee, Sul H., ed. *Serials Collection Development: Choices and Strategies.* Ann Arbor, Mich.: Pierian Press, 1981.

———, ed. *Acquisitions, Budgets and Material Cost: Issues and Approaches.* New York: Haworth Press, 1988.

———, ed. *Vendor Evaluation and Acquisition Budgets.* New York: Haworth Press, 1992. Also published as the *Journal of Library Administration* 16(3) (1992).

Leong, Carol L. H. *Serials Cataloging Handbook: an Illustrative Guide to the Use of AACR2 and LC Rule Interpretations.* Chicago: American Library Association, 1989.

Leonhardt, Thomas W., ed. *Technical Services in Libraries: Systems and Applications.* Greenwich, Conn.: JAI Press, 1992.

Lewis, Martha. "Document Delivery Vendors: Benefits and Choices." *The Serials Librarian* 23(3/4): 217–24 (1993).

Library Systems Evaluation Guide: Serials Control. Vol. 1. Powell, Ohio: James E. Rush Associates, 1983.

Litchfield, C. A., and M. L. Norstedt. "Coded Holdings: A Primer for New Users." *Serials Review* 14(1/2): 81–8 (1988).

Lowry, Anita. "Landlords and Tenants: Who Owns Information, Who Pays for It, and How?" *The Serials Librarian* 23(3/4): 61–71 (1993).

Lynch, Clifford A. "Serials Management in the Age of Electronic Access." *Serials Review* 17(1): 7–12 (spring 1991).

Magrill, Rose Mary, and John Corbin. *Acquisitions Management and Collection Development in Libraries.* 2d ed. Chicago: American Library Association, 1989.

Manoff, Marlene, and others. "Report of the Electronic Journals Task Force, MIT Libraries." *Serials Review* 18(1/2): 113–30 (spring/summer 1992).

Marks, Kenneth E., and Steven P. Nielsen. "A Longitudinal Study of Journal Prices in a Research Library." *The Serials Librarian* 19(3/4): 105–35 (1991).

McKay, Sharon Cline, and Betty Landesman. "The SISAC Bar Code Symbol." *Serials Review* 17(2): 47–52 (summer 1991).

McKay, Sharon Cline, and Charles J. Piazza, Jr. "EDI and X12: What, Why, Who?" *Serials Review* 18(4): 7–11 (winter 1992).

McKinley, Margaret. "Vendor Selection: Strategic Choices." *Serials Review* 16(2): 49–53 (summer 1990).

McMillan, Gail, ed. "Electronic Journals: Considerations for the Present and the Future." *Serials Review* 17(4): 77–86 (winter 1991).

McQueen, Judy, and Richard W. Boss. "Serials Control in Libraries: Automated Options." *Library Technology Reports* 20(2): 89–282 (Mar.–Apr. 1984).

Meiseles, Linda, and Sue Feller. "Training Serials Specialists: Internships as an Option." *Library Administration & Management* 8(2): 83–6 (spring 1994).

Melin, Nancy Jean, ed. *The Serials Collection: Organization and Administration.* Ann Arbor, Mich.: Pierian Press, 1982.

Merrill-Oldham, Jan, and Paul A. Parisi. *Guide to the Library Binding Institute Standard for Library Binding.* Chicago: American Library Association, 1990.

Metz, Paul, and Paul M. Gheman. "Serials Pricing and the Role of the Electronic Journal." *College & Research Libraries* 52: 315–27 (July 1991).

Michael, James. "Developing a Standard Vision." *Wilson Library Bulletin* 67(7): 35–7 (Mar. 1993)

Migneault, Robert L. "Serials: an Introductory Perspective." In *Projects and Procedures for Serials Administration,* 1–22. Edited by Diane Stine. Ann Arbor, Mich.: Pierian Press, 1985.

Milkovic, Milan. "The Binding of Periodicals: Basic Concepts and Procedures." *The Serials Librarian* 11(2): 93–118 (Oct. 1986).

Niles, Judith, Pam Burton, Tyler Goldberg, and Melissa Laning. "Management of Serials Records in the Integrated Catalog." *Advances in Serials Management* 4: 15–36 (1992).

Odlyzko, Andrew M. *Tragic Loss or Good Riddance? The Impending Demise of Traditional Scholarly Journals (Preliminary version, Dec. 30, 1993).* Available from Andrew Odlyzko of AT&T Bell Laboratories at Internet address: AMO@COM.ATT.RESEARCH.

Okerson, Ann. "Periodical Prices: A History and Discussion." *Advances in Serials Management* 1: 101–38 (1986).

———. "With Feathers: Effects of Copyright and Ownership on Scholarly Publishing." *College & Research Libraries* 52: 425–38 (Sept. 1991).

Okerson, Ann, ed. *Scholarly Publishing on the Electronic Networks, the New Generation: Visions and Opportunities in Not-for-Profit Publishing: Proceedings of the Second Symposium, December 5–8, 1992.* Washington, D.C.: Association of Research Libraries, 1993.

O'Neil, Rosanna M. "CONSER: Cons . . . and Pros, or, What's in It for Me?" *Serials Review* 17(2): 53–62 (1991).

Osborn, Andrew D. *Serial Publications: Their Place and Treatment in Libraries.* 3d ed. Chicago: American Library Association, 1980.

Osborn, Charles B., and Ross Atkinson, eds. *Collection Management: A New Treatise.* Greenwich, Conn.: JAI Press, 1991.

Padway, Janet. "Serials Automation: Examining of Problems." *The Serials Librarian* 11(3/4): 31–6 (Dec. 1986–Jan. 1987).

Parang, Elizabeth, and Laverna Saunders, comps. *Electronic Journals in ARL Libraries: Issues and Trends.* SPEC Kit 202. Washington, D.C.: Association of Research Libraries, 1994.

———. *Electronic Journals in ARL Libraries: Policies and Procedures.* SPEC Kit 201. Washington, D.C.: Association of Research Libraries, 1994.

Parisi, Paul A., and Jan Merrill-Oldham, eds. *Library Binding Institute Standard for Library Binding.* 8th ed. Rochester, N.Y.: Library Binding Institute, 1986.

Petersen, H. Craig. "The Economics of Economics Journals: A Statistical Analysis of Pricing Practices by Publishers." *College & Research Libraries* 53: 176–81 (Mar. 1992).

Pionessa, Geraldine. "Serials Replacement Orders: A Closer Look." *Serials Review* 16(1): 65–73 (spring 1990).

Rooks, Dana C. "Electronic Serials: Administrative Angst and Answer." *Library Acquisitions: Practice & Theory* 17(4): 449–54 (winter 1993).

Sabosik, Patricia E. "Electronic Subscriptions." *The Serials Librarian* 19(3/4): 59–70 (1991).

Saunders, Laverna M. *The Virtual Library: Visions and Realities.* Westport, Conn.: Meckler, 1993.

Schmidt, Karen A. "Acquisitions." In *Guide to Technical Services Resources,* 27–44. Edited by Peggy Johnson. Chicago: American Library Association, 1994.

Segesta, Jim, and Gary Hyslop. "The Arrangement of Periodicals in American Academic Libraries." *Serials Review* 17(1): 21–8 (spring 1991).

Sellen, Betty-Carol, and Arthur Curley, eds. *The Collection Building Reader.* New York: Neal-Schuman, 1992.

Shoemaker, Sarah, ed. *Collection Management: Current Issues.* New York: Neal-Schuman, 1989.

Smith, Eldred. "Resolving the Acquisitions Dilemma: Into the Electronic Information Environment." *College & Research Libraries* 52: 231–40 (May 1991).

Smith, Lynn S. *A Practical Approach to Serials Cataloging.* Greenwich, Conn.: JAI Press, 1978.

Stern, Barrie. "The New ADONIS." *Serials: The Journal of the United Kingdom Serials Group* 5: 37–43 (Nov. 1992).

Strangelove, Michael, and Diane Kovach. *Directory of Electronic Journals, Newsletters and Academic Discussion Lists.* 1st ed.– . Washington, D.C.: Association of Research Libraries, 1991– .

Striedieck, Suzanne. "CONSER and the National Database." *Advances in Serials Management* 3: 81–109 (1989).

Thorburn, Colleen. "Cataloging Remote Electronic Journals and Databases." *The Serials Librarian* 23(1/2): 11–23 (1992).

Tuttle, Marcia. *Introduction to Serials Management.* Greenwich, Conn.: JAI Press, 1983.

———. "Magazine Fulfillment Centers: What They Are, How They Operate, and What We Can Do About Them." *Library Acquisitions: Practice and Theory* 9: 41–9 (1985).

———. "The Newsletter on Serials Pricing Issues: Teetering on the Cutting Edge." *Advances in Serials Management: A Research Manual* 4: 37–63 (1992).

———. "Serials Control, from an Acquisitions Perspective." *Advances in Serials Management* 2: 63–94 (1988).

———. "Serials Management." In *Guide to Technical Services Resources,* 120–35. Edited by Peggy Johnson. Chicago: American Library Association, 1994.

———. "The Serials Manager's Obligation." *Library Resources & Technical Services* 31: 135–47 (Apr. 1987).

Upham, Lois N., ed. *Newspapers in the Library: New Approaches to Management and Reference Work.* New York: Haworth Press, 1988.

Widdicombe, Richard P. "Eliminating All Journal Subscriptions Has Freed Our Customers to Seek the Information They Really Want and Need: The Result—More Access, Not Less." *Science & Technology Libraries* 14(1): 3–13 (fall 1993).

Wilkas, Lenore Rae, comp. *International Subscription Agents.* 6th ed. Chicago: American Library Association, 1994.

Williams, James W. "Serials Cataloging, 1985–1990: An Overview of a Half-Decade." *The Serials Librarian* 22(1/2): 39–69 (1992).

Appendix

A Selected Bibliography on Serials Management

Literature Search Tools

The best way to keep up with current topics is by using literature-searching tools to capture current publications in those topics. Indexes and abstracts are essential tools for literature search.

Information Science Abstracts. New York: Plenum Publishing. v. 1– , 1966– . Monthly.

Formerly *Documentation Abstracts,* it is published for Documentation Abstracts, Inc., founded by the American Society for Information Science. Its purpose is to promote the science, management, and technology of information. Coverage includes books, journals, conference proceedings, reports, and patents. This tool is also available for online searching via DIALOG as File 202.

LISA: Library & Information Science Abstracts. London: Bowker-Saur. v. 1– , 1969– . Monthly.

This publication supersedes *Library Science Abstracts,* which was published from 1950 to 1968. It is a guide to periodical articles and conference papers in the fields of library science, information science, and subject disciplines of interest to librarians and information workers. Prior to 1991, it was published by Aslib. *LISA* is also available for online searching via DIALOG as File 61 and via BRS as File LISA. Its CD-ROM version is titled *LISA PLUS.*

Library Literature: An Index to Library and Information Science. New York: H. W. Wilson. v. 1– , 1933– . Bimonthly.

This index originally was compiled by the Junior Members Round Table of the American Library Association from 1921 to 1932. It is an author and subject index to library and information science materials. Coverage includes periodical articles, books, pamphlets, and library school theses. There is a separate section for citations to individual book reviews and a separate checklist of monographs cited. Wilson also provides this index with online searching service and on CD-ROM.

Serials

Serials-related articles appear not only in serials management periodicals but also in periodicals devoted to administration, information management, computer technology, and scholarly communications. The following list is not exhaustive but is a selection of titles devoted to serials management or in which serials are a frequent topic.

ACQNET. Boone, N.C.: Appalachian State University Library. no. 1– , 1990– . Irregular. [serial online]

This electronic newsletter provides a forum for discussions of current collection development and acquisitions topics. It is important for serials librarians who are interested in keeping up with the latest information in acquisitions and in sharing news and discussions with fellow librarians. Christian Boissonnas of Cornell University Library created the newsletter and was its editor until 1994. The current editor is Eleanor Cook of Appalachian State University Library. She may be contacted at COOKEI@CONRAD.APPSTATE.EDU. To subscribe, send a message to LISTSERV@APPSTATE.EDU (Internet) with command SUB ACQNET-L <subscriber's name>.

The Acquisitions Librarian. New York: Haworth Press. no. 1– , 1989– . Irregular.

Each issue is devoted to a specific topic relating to library acquisitions. Issues are also published as separate monographs.

Advances in Serials Management. Greenwich, Conn.: JAI Press. v. 1– , 1986– . Biennial.

Covers all aspects of serials management. Articles are of high quality. It appears approximately every two years.

ALCTS Newsletter. Chicago: Association for Library Collections and Technical Services. v. 1– , 1990– . Frequency varies (approximately 6 issues per year).

This newsletter includes reports of ALCTS activities (including Serials Section activities), brief articles of interest to members, and a book review section covering books, serials, and audiovisual titles. It continues the *RTSD Newsletter.*

The online version of this newsletter is ALCTS Network News, also called AN2. It is published irregularly to distribute timely information to ALCTS members. To subscribe, send a message to LISTSERV@UICVM (BITNET) or LISTSERV@UICVM.UIC.EDU (Internet) with the command SUB ALCTS <subscriber's name>.

Australian & New Zealand Journal of Serials Librarianship. Binghamton, N.Y.: Haworth Press. v. 1– , 1990– . Quarterly.

Articles are contributed by regional librarians in Australia and New Zealand and reflect local conditions and practices. Readers in the United States may find that universal issues are covered and may benefit by reading selected articles.

Cataloging & Classification Quarterly. New York: Haworth Press. v. 1– , fall 1980– . Quarterly.

The journal covers theoretical and practical aspects of cataloging and classification, including serials cataloging.

Citations for Serial Literature. Cambridge, Mass.: Massachusetts Institute of Technology. no. 1– , 1992– . Irregular. [serial online]

Also called SERCITES, this online serial lists contents and abstracts of articles related to serials. It delivers fast information on new titles in the serials field. To subscribe, send a message to LISTSERV@MITVMA (BITNET) or LISTSERV@MITVMA.MIT.EDU (Internet) with the command SUBSCRIBE SERCITES <subscriber's name>.

College & Research Libraries. Chicago: Association of College and Research Libraries. v. 1– , Dec. 1939– . Bimonthly.

Serials, a major part of the collection in college and research libraries, often are the focus of attention in this publication. It has offered informative and provocative articles on serials pricing, scholarly communications, copyright, and more.

Journal of Library Administration. New York: Haworth Press. v. 1– , spring 1980– . Quarterly.

Each issue is devoted to a specific theme. Serials are discussed in this journal because they are a major concern of library administrators, especially in budget planning.

Library Acquisitions: Practice & Theory. New York: Pergamon Press. v. 1– , 1977– . Quarterly.

Devoted exclusively to acquisitions, this journal regularly features articles relating to serials acquisitions. Its reports on acquisitions-related conferences are valuable to librarians who wish to be informed of current topics in acquisitions librarianship but are unable to attend the conference.

Library Administration & Management. Chicago: Library Administration and Management Association. v. 1– , 1987– . Quarterly.

This is the official magazine of the Library Administration and Management Association of the American Library Association. It covers serial topics that are of concern to library administrators and managers, such as serials budget, recruiting, and training of serials librarians.

Library Journal. Newton, Mass.: Cahners. v. 1– , 1876– . Monthly.

A journal for the library profession in general, its News section covers current events. The Infotech section reports on new technology applications and developments in library and publishing, and the Review section coverage is extensive, including newly published serial titles. A large number of advertisements are informative about new publications, products, and systems. With serials being a hot topic in librarianship and the publishing business, there are occasional discussions and articles on this topic as well.

Library Resources & Technical Services. Chicago: Association for Library Collections and Technical Services. v. 1– , winter 1957– . Quarterly.

This scholarly journal devoted to library collection and technical services topics contains articles related to serials cover acquisitions, cataloging, collection development, and preservation. It has an annual review of the literature of serials librarianship.

Library Software Review: SR. Westport, Conn.: Meckler. v. 3– , 1984– . Bimonthly.

Besides reviewing software packages, this periodical also includes articles dealing with library automation, networking, and systems. Occasionally, there are articles relating to serials automation and reviews of serial systems. It continues *Software Review.*

Newsletter on Serials Pricing Issues. Chapel Hill, N.C.: Marcia Tuttle. no. 1– , Feb. 1989– . Irregular. [serial online]

This newsletter includes articles, news, and conference reports relating to serials pricing. It provides a forum for librarians, publishers, agents, and scholars to exchange news and discuss issues relating to pricing. Articles are not only informative but often provocative. To subscribe, send a message to LISTSERV@GIBBS.OIT.UNC.EDU (Internet) with the command SUBSCRIBE PRICE <subscriber's name>.

Publishers Weekly. New Providence, N.J.: R. R. Bowker. v. 1– , Jan. 18, 1872– . Weekly.

The focus of this weekly is the publishing industry. News and articles about new publications, publishing formats, marketing trends, and current events provide useful information for serials acquisitions librarians. There occasionally are articles about serials.

Science & Technology Libraries. New York: Haworth Press. v. 1– , fall 1980– . Quarterly.

The major concern in science and technology libraries is serials, which often are discussed in this journal.

Serials: The Journal of the United Kingdom Serials Group. Bradford, Eng.: United Kingdom Serials Group. v. 1– , 1988– . Three times a year.

This periodical continues and merges *UKSG Newsletter* and the publication of proceedings for the United Kingdom Serials Group conferences. It also contains articles that reflect the European view on serials management.

The Serials Librarian: The International Quarterly of Serials Management. Binghamton, N.Y.: Haworth Press. v. 1– , 1976– . Quarterly.

Devoted exclusively to serials management, this journal is a must on the serials librarian's reading list. Its articles include all aspects of serials librarianship in both theoretical and practical presentations. A regular feature is the published proceedings of North American Serials Interest Group (NASIG) conferences.

Serials Review. Ann Arbor, Mich.: Pierian Press. v. 1– , 1975– . Quarterly.
This journal not only reviews serials and serials management resources but also contains articles relating to serials management, columns on special topics, and reports of conferences. It is an important title to be included on the serials librarian's reading list.

Serialst. Burlington, Vt.: University of Vermont Library, 1991– . [electronic discussion group]
This discussion group covers all aspects of serials management. The owner and moderator is Birdie MacLennan. To subscribe, send a message to LISTSERV@UVMVM (BITNET) or LISTSERV@UVMVM.UVM.EDU (Internet) with the command SUBSCRIBE SERIALST <subscriber's name>.

Technical Services Quarterly. Binghamton, N.Y.: Haworth Press. v. 1– , fall/winter 1983– . Quarterly.
Articles on all aspects of technical services, including serials control, appear in this quarterly. Reviews of recent publications, news of conferences, and announcements are useful in alerting librarians to current happenings.

Technicalities. Lincoln, Nebr.: Media Periodicals, a division of Westport Publishers. v. 1– , Dec. 1980– . Monthly.
This monthly includes articles, news, reviews of new products and publications, and columns on general issues and specific topics by well-known librarians and library educators. Cataloging has a strong presence, and serials cataloging is often discussed.

Books about Serials

In this fast-paced information age, books often are viewed as lagging behind in providing current information, and their contents soon become outdated. However, books have the advantage of projecting a comprehensive and cohesive view of a topic. Books listed here are textbooks that offer basic concepts of serials management and solid foundations to the understanding of principles in serials management. They have long-lasting value on the serials librarian's reading list.

Brown, Clara D., and Lynn S. Smith. *Serials: Past, Present and Future*. 2d ed., rev. Birmingham, Ala.: EBSCO Industries, Inc., 1980.
Brown and Smith, practicing serials librarians, have written from a practical operational point of view. Although many of the procedures and forms are obsolete due to automation, the book provides sound advice relating to basic principles and rules in serials management. It furnishes easy reading of interesting tales.

Graham, Margaret E., and Fiona Buettel, eds. *Serials Management: A Practical Handbook*. London: Aslib, 1990.
Serials Management is a collection of essays written by British serials specialists. Contents include topics on collection development, collection

management, automation, and standards. Although not all British practices and perspectives apply to American librarianship, the book is valuable reading because of the high quality of contents and relatively current information.

Osborn, Andrew D. *Serial Publications: Their Place and Treatment in Libraries.* 3d ed. Chicago: American Library Association, 1980.

This book is considered a classic in serials management because of the author's in-depth scholarly approach to the subject. Its comprehensive coverage, historical background analysis, and theoretical discussions encourage the reader to look beyond "how to do it" into "why we do it" in serials management.

Tuttle, Marcia. *Introduction to Serials Management.* Greenwich, Conn.: JAI Press, 1983.

This is a well-organized and well-written textbook for serials librarians and students. It provides both principles of and practical guidance in serials management. The contents include collection development, acquisitions, cataloging, preservation, public service, resource sharing, standards, and an annotated bibliography. Although coverage on automation is scant due to its publication date, it remains essential reading for novice serials librarians.

Bibliographies

Ginneken, Jos van. *770 Articles and Books on Serials: An Annotated Bibliography 1983–1989.* Wageningen, The Netherlands: Library Agricultural, 1991.

This bibliography includes five subject categories: general, acquisitions and collection development, technical services, finance, and automation. It is international in scope, but the annotations are in English.

Robison, David F. W. "Bibliography of Articles Related to Electronic Journal Publications & Publishing." In *Directory of Electronic Journals, Newsletters and Academic Discussion Lists.* Edited by Michael Strangelove and Diane Kovacs. Washington, D.C.: Association of Research Libraries, 1991– .

This bibliography has been a regular feature of the directory since its publication. It is based on citations appearing in the electronic journal *Current Cites,* published by Information Systems Instruction & Support of the University of California Berkeley Library.

Tuttle, Marcia. "Annotated Bibliography." In her *Introduction to Serials Management,* 213–306. Greenwich, Conn.: JAI Press, 1983.

The annotated bibliography covers books and articles published prior to 1982. It contains 649 entries and is a substantial feature of the book.

———. "Annotated Bibliography of 1982–85 Books and Articles on Serials." *Advances in Serials Management,* 1: 135–230, 1986.

This 625-entry bibliography continues the one in Tuttle's book cited previously.

———. "Serials Management." In *Guide to Technical Services Resources,* 120–35. Edited by Peggy Johnson. Chicago: American Library Association, 1994.

This chapter contains resource materials on all aspects of serials management. Categories include general works, management of serials units, serials publishing, serials processing, automation of serials processing, serials pricing, resource sharing, union listing, and serials holdings. Most titles were published between 1985 and 1992, with a few important older works included. Entries are annotated.

"Year's Work in Serials." In *Library Resources & Technical Services.* Chicago: Association for Library Collections and Technical Services. v. 1– , winter 1957– .

This bibliographic essay usually is published annually in *Library Resources & Technical Services.* Each year it is written by a different serials specialist. The essay title may vary slightly from year to year, but the contents remain informative about the events and publications during the past year.

Index